6-24-88

To Larry on 41st - once you get by 40 its all up hill -
"Happy Birthday"

The Murray's
Jerry, Carolyn,
Leslie, Jodi.

Trial by Terror

Trial by Terror

The
Child-hostage Crisis
in Cokeville, Wyoming

Hartt & Judene Wixom

Cover painting by Wade C. Wixom, adapted from a television news photo taken minutes after the bomb exploded. Depicted are his mother, Judene Wixom, and his brother Kamron, a hostage.

ISBN: 0-88290-298-X
Library of Congress No.: 87-080151
Horizon Publishers Catalog & Order No.: 2011
First Printing, April 1987

Printed and distributed
in the United States of America by

Horizon Publishers
& Distributors, Incorporated
50 South 500 West P.O. Box 490
Bountiful, Utah 84010-0490

Contents

Dedication **8**

Prologue **9**

1. A Town of Trust **13**

David Young's Philosophy **29**

2. The Dark Side **33**

3. The Incredible Plot **51**

4. A Town Without Children? **64**

List of Hostages **91**

5. The Bomb is Real **94**

6. The Children Were Screaming **122**

7. The Miracle **141**

8. The Spiritual Message **149**

9. A Time of Coping **166**

10. A Massive Investigation **191**

11. The Press Arrives **215**

12. A Personal Connection **229**

Kamron's Press Release **248**

13. Love Pours In **250**

Dedication

On the afternoon of May 16, 1986 news media from across the nation gathered at a small community in western Wyoming to unravel a bizarre story. Two people with an arsenal of guns and a highly explosive bomb had declared a "revolutionary takeover" of an entire elementary school.

What was the purpose of David and Doris Young in holding these children hostage? The answer is chilling. For as the events unfolded, it became apparent David Young wanted much more than money. He wanted control of the youngsters' minds in another world.

But the full story of his diabolical scheme, within the mind of a man holding only contempt for the trusting and God-believing, is told in detail within the following pages. In many ways the simple facts outline an unusual confrontation of the Godly vs. the ungodly.

It did not happen in far-off countries, nor merely on television where violence is watched daily and shrugged off. This time it was real. And it happened in America, one of the only (if not the only) times so many school children's lives have been threatened in such a hostage crisis.

The courage of school officials and teachers entrusted with the lives of these children—and the unusual grit and moral fortitude of the traumatized youngsters themselves in reacting to this trial by terror—is a most unusual, gripping, and unique success story.

The authors express a sincere hope that this book speaks for all those who experienced the event, and that by sharing it, many more might also be encouraged in overcoming future adversity.

Prologue

NEWS BULLETIN: COKEVILLE, Wyoming—"A man and a woman with guns and a bomb took over a grade school here, threatening to kill all the students in it if they did not comply with the pair's demands." May 16, 1986

This book tells the inside story of the school-bombing crisis in a small western community that stunned the nation on that quiet May afternoon. After being a news-business colleague and friend of Hartt and Judene Wixom for many years, I can think of no one more qualified to research and write this unusual account. As a newspaperman and magazine writer for three decades, Hartt has won many awards for objective and in-depth reporting. The five books he has authored are in the same vein. At the same time, he loses nothing in intrigue and meaningful interpretation of those facts he has uncovered.

But in this case the Wixoms were not watching only as casual observers—their twelve-year-old son Kam was one of those frightened hostages. Most of us can only imagine the thoughts in the minds of families who received the word that their children were being held for millions of dollars in ransom.

As a mother who was involved herself, Judene Wixom probes the heights and depths of heroism, of emotions, of dread, and of decisive actions that rise to the surface when the world of a family seems tottering on the brink.

Here is a profile of that disturbed bomber. But more importantly, how the hostage children coped with imminent death, how families rose to the occasion, how they found faith and inner strength in the ordeal, and how they were able to think and act courageously—that is the story of this book. The conclusion may well make all of us pause to ponder what is truly most powerful and meaningful in our lives.

Dr. Jack Nelson
Department of Communication
Brigham Young University

Pine Creek Canyon, east of Cokeville, is a beautiful place. Pools and waterfalls are treasured places for wild flowers, deer and birds, trout...and family picnics. Trouble anywhere seems incongruous. (Photo by Hartt Wixom)

A Town of Trust

> *"We picked Cokeville to take hostages because it is a close-knit town where they love their children . . . and will do anything to get them back. . . ."*
>
> *—David Young*

Friday, May 16th, 1986, seems like any other spring day in the quiet western Wyoming community of Cokeville. The sky is clear, the sun warming. But anything can happen with the weather in this part of the country.

Today there is enough of a nip in the air to keep a jacket handy. By late afternoon hail is falling.

Children laughingly skip their way down dirt roads to bus stops along U.S. 30. Some tarry to play in the haystacks along the way; others call to the slow-pokes to hurry up. "Here comes Art's bus!"

It is a call heard frequently along the south route. In this little community school buses are personalized. Drivers are close friends to the children all week long. They take a personal interest in the welfare of the community's number one resource. As in many small towns, trust and warm friendship are not only counted on, they are taken for granted.

Fathers pause to wave routinely to their offspring, then return to the challenge of planting hay in ground finally frost-free. Some folks say western Wyoming has only two seasons, winter and July. That's not true, of course, but it is vital to take advantage of every growing day possible.

The natural elements have a major effect on life and attitudes here. Ranchers work outside with livestock, regardless of cold, rain or blizzard.

Others must travel 90 miles each day to work in the nearest town of Kemmerer. Many are employed at the power company or the coal or phosphate mines near there. Though the highway is kept plowed by efficient crews, battling icy roads and commuting long distances is a way of life. But it seems worth it because Cokeville is such "a nice place to raise a family."

Children think of it mostly as a nice place to explore and roam free. There is always something to do. In the winter, dirt roadways are just right for sledding. Now that the snow is gone, there are mud puddles to jump among the tire ruts. A hike to the reservoir in the summer provides a refreshing swim. There are squirrels to chase and badger holes to find.

Sitting on a hillside after dusk, one can try to count the uncountable stars in the forever sky.

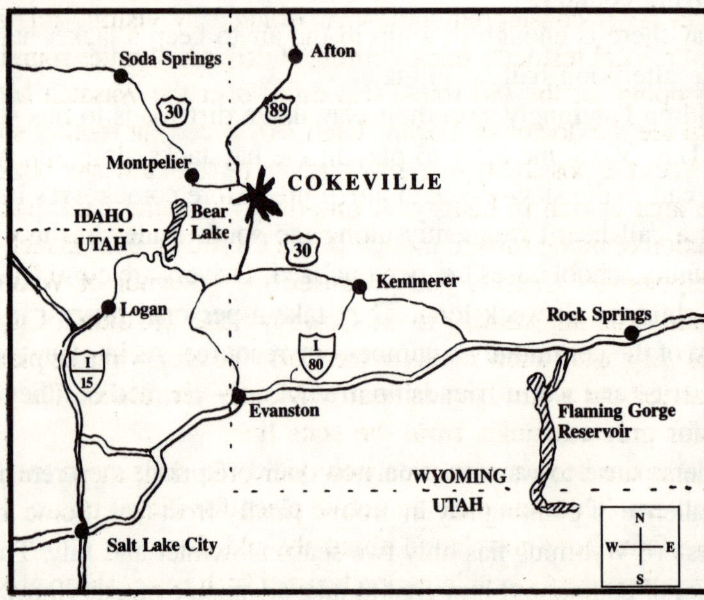

Map showing location of Cokeville in relation to neighboring communities.

The town's welcome sign posted some time ago still reads: "Pop. 515, Elev. 6192 feet." Numbering those living outside the city, the population is about 900. It is located some 70 miles north of Evanston, Wyoming, and 120 miles south of Jackson Hole. It is about fifteen air-miles east of Bear Lake, which straddles the Utah-Idaho border.

Most media stories written about the community say little more than this. One publication somewhat poetically suggests Cokeville is a green oasis on the high plains, against the Sublette and Raymond Mountains.

It is also a scenic setting at the confluence of Smiths Fork (named after Western explorer Jedediah Smith) and the Bear River. Emerald meadows, conifer forests, and waterfall-studded trout streams crowd the town's eastern perimeter.

The Pine Creek ski resort there, operated by community and county, couldn't have a more picturesque background, all just five minutes from town.

Cokeville is considered somewhat isolated by visiting relatives. However, local residents think nothing of driving 74 miles round trip for shopping, or the 180 round-trip miles over the Wasatch Mountains to see the doctor in Logan, Utah. An expectant mother sometimes faces the possibility of giving birth en route in a winter blizzard.

The area is rich in history. A one-time Cokeville bank had the distinction of being robbed though Butch Cassidy's Wild Bunch was not responsible. Cassidy had promised the governor of Wyoming he wouldn't do any stealing in the Cowboy State. He didn't. Cassidy and his gang spent a few weeks in the Cokeville area while he planned and carried out a bank job in nearby Montpelier, Idaho. The location was only ten miles from the state line.

Hills in the border area even now yield old stills from the Prohibition era. This was once an active place for illegal booze. Law-abiding folks here now laugh about the old days.

At one time the Cokeville region boasted such heavy sheep production that the Union Pacific Railroad stopped almost daily to pick up another shipment of the woolies. "The Sheep Capitol of the West," old newspapers used to say.

Activity was such that there were once five busy dance halls in town. One old-timer reflected that "when one of those halls burned down, a third of the population was left homeless. . . ."

The original Stockman's Hotel, circa 1897, was the last remaining facility of this type. Silent movies were shown in the basement of the old hotel. "As a young girl, I used to play the piano for those old silent films," Lois Dayton smiles.

Heavy snows from the 1985 winter caved the roof in, and the old building was torn down.

Times have changed. Now the trains stop for nothing, save to occasionally sidetrack one freight train for another's passage.

Where there were once a number of swinging saloons and dance halls, now the two grocery stores, the barber shop, a bar, and an auto repair shop are the only commercial facilities to drive past along Main Street off Highway 30. The Town Hall, post office, and library make up the other side of the street.

The library is open afternoons and two Saturdays a month. Among other things, it boasts a very active children's reading program. Nothing is too good for the children's education, and it shows in this little library, as well as in the schools.

Things are a little busier out on the highway. Two motels, a saloon, a cafe, and a couple of truck stop service stations comprise the remainder of private enterprise. Tourists who pass through may never even see the town's Main Street to the west.

One visitor to the high school's annual musical production was overheard to say, "You drive past here on the highway and think this is just a little hole-in-the wall town. They would never believe such things as this could go on here."

There are no movie theaters nor even any video game parlors, except for a few machines at one truck stop.

Youngsters don't have much time for such idleness anyway. There is too much to be done in this active community.

Children sometimes drive tractors before they are big enough to see over the dashboard of the family car. Even youngsters help with hay balers and irrigation pipes.

Many know what it is like to get up before dawn to feed the calves. They rescue newborn lambs from frosty winds, bringing them into the warmth of the family home, feeding them with a bottle until they are strong enough to be turned out to their mothers.

However, it would be a mistake to say recreation is lacking. An innovative citizenry has learned how to turn such chores as wood-gathering in the hills into a hot dog roast. With January temperatures dipping to 40 or 50 degrees below zero, firewood can mean more than just a cheery glow; it can mean survival itself. Yet there seems nothing particularly grim about that woodgathering process. Families doing it together often make the whole thing fun.

A Dutch oven cookout is the finishing touch for a day spent rounding up wandering cattle. Folks talk about "character-building opportunities," but they don't have to be contrived here. Opportunities for "character-building" abound.

Summer evenings often see town teenagers "dragging Main," a pastime that takes all of one-and-a-half minutes. Youngsters may head for the high school field to play tag while teens gather to talk at the bridge over Spring Creek. Occasionally a couple or two will negotiate the rough road up "Big Hill," location of the traditional block "C."

Veteran Police Chief Cal Fredrickson says problems are rare. Fredrickson is not a native of Cokeville, but says of the community's youth: "They're some of the best kids in the world. They usually stay out of trouble."

Trust is big here. A man's word is binding. When agreements are struck, the matter may not be written down at all. Youngsters grow up knowing they can turn to many other members of the community with confidence.

Small towns are known for their propensity toward everyone knowing everyone else's business. The advantage here in a close-knit atmosphere is that no one needs to be alone; there is always someone to care and assist where needed.

Most citizens are related in some way. Some families trace their roots back to original settlers. Many marry into local families, while others bring college sweethearts back to make a home in Cokeville.

In many ways, the town itself is like one big family. One rancher spent much of the harvest season visiting his seriously ill child in a distant hospital. He returned home to find his crops in for the winter. Every field had been cut, baled, and stacked, but no one will tell who did the work.

It's probably the last place anyone would think of trying to hurt someone else.

Cokeville is sometimes called a "Mormon" town. Statistically, the valley's residents are about 80 percent members of The Church of Jesus Christ of Latterday Saints, known as Mormons. Yet in a larger sense, Cokeville is not so much a Mormon town as a family town. Families are traditionally large, and involved in church activities held among Catholic, Episcopalian, and other religious persuasions as well.

The different religions work relatively well together. If there is a problem such as a drought or flood (both could happen here a short time apart, with instant impact on local ranchers), a fast and prayer might be called by leaders of any local church. Concern for the welfare of the community overcomes any religious differences.

Local citizens may recommend their religious preferences to self-described agnostics like sixth grade teacher Jack Mitchell. But differences are respected. To counter a blue "BYU" shirt worn by a Mormon Brigham Young University fan, Jack will good naturedly display a brightly-colored competitor's shirt such as Oklahoma University. It is not even his alma mater, but the mild rebellion is understood.

Jack long ago announced he had no intentions of changing his personal convictions. He will remain a nonbeliever. He sees no reason not to.

Rocky Moore, the red-bearded fifth grade teacher, is a mountain man type, complete with musket come each hunting season. He also calls himself "agnostic." Moore states flatly, "I'll believe in God when I see the burning bush."

John Teichert, bishop of a local Mormon congregation may simply pat Moore on the back and turn the subject to the next Boy Scout project where Moore is enthusiastically involved in outdoor activities.

Over at the school, Moore enjoys teaching a science or a history class, or coaching the wrestling team with equal gusto. Under his tutelage, a student preparing a geology display finally labels it "Strange Rock."

Moore not only leaves it that way, but praises the fifth grader for her enthusiasm. Another student's display is labeled "half-insect, half-spider."

In the hallway, if a boy gets boisterous, Moore locks an arm around his neck. "Remember how to break this one?"

"No," the lad confesses.

With a loud guffaw, Rocky leads his forgetful protege by the neck back to class before releasing him. "That's how," he says. Both teacher and student laugh again. Moore is not your stereotyped tough-guy. He loves the kids. The kids love him.

There are some anomalies. An Episcopalian mother has a son on a mission for the Mormon church. A Catholic teacher attends LDS meetings when one of her students is honored.

Music teacher John Miller is of Methodist stock, but since there is no Methodist congregation in town, he attends the "closest thing to it" at the Episcopalian services.

At no time is the community more involved than during the Mormons' annual Pioneer Day Celebration in July. School children and alumni march together in the band. Floats made by groups ranging from small children to senior citizens, from political candidates to marathon runners, come in. The entourage will tour Main Street once, circle the community park dedicated to early western settlers,

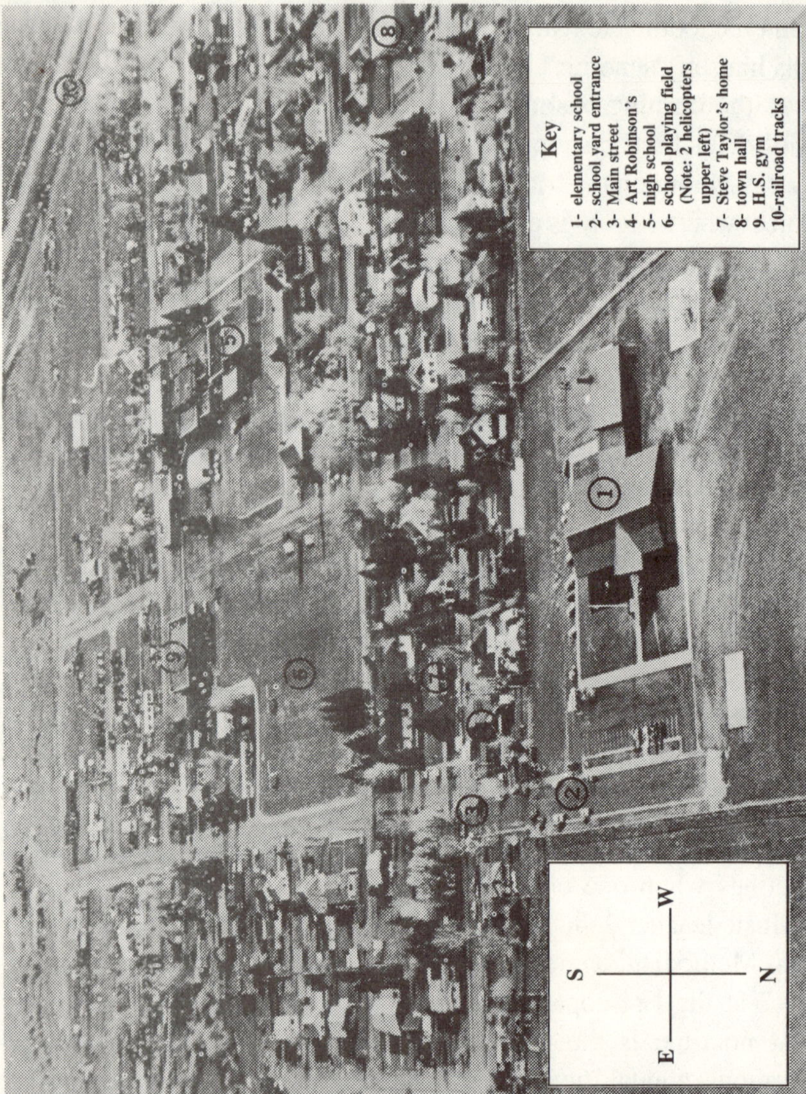

Aerial view of Cokeville Main Street. Library, post office, and stores are to the west (right) along the street. (East across U.S. Highway 30 is Smiths Fork road, Pine Creek, and the town cemetery on the bluff of Big Hill.) (Gerald Silver photo courtesy of Deseret News.)

and then move back down Main Street for another look. Bystanders may include family and friends from several states.

A worship service is held next, where a speaker typically reminds the congregation of the strength and valor of their ancestors who settled the area. Prayer in overcoming adversity is emphasized for all listeners and all faiths.

While this partisan part of the day's activities might be skipped by the community's non-Mormons, they too are soon mingling with celebrants for the feast to follow. In fact, the barbecue, featuring the best of local beef, generally feeds as many as a thousand.

Shortly thereafter, most will head for the rodeo grounds. Here the spiritual comraderie may be shared by a self-described agnostic who helps a Catholic youngster onto a calf provided by a Mormon bishop and encouraged by a Protestant cowboy.

Some have described it as "a slice of western Americana, where apple pie and the American flag are more than a saying." People try to make it real here. It isn't easy, but these are not people looking for the easiest way out. It's considered a matter of pride in attempting to live up to one's potential.

"Here comes Art's bus!" the children call again.

As they climb into the yellow-orange school buses, they are temporarily forgotten. Mother has bread dough to mix before the men descend upon the kitchen for a hot lunch.

This afternoon some of the neighbors are gathering to help on the patchwork quilt being prepared for a wedding gift. It would be nice to serve some fresh cinnamon rolls.

"Bye, Mom," seven-year-old Shiloh Pope calls out. He is gone before mother can answer. She opens the door to call quickly after him: "Don't forget to hurry home. We'll need your help with the lambs and calves today right after school."

Though only a first grader, Shiloh has responsibilities on the family ranch. He loves working alongside his dad and three older brothers and can handle a horse well enough to help with stray cows on the range.

Back down the highway, Pat Bennion has watched her two daughters climb onto the bus and rushes to answer the telephone. "Can you substitute for Mr. Teichert today? He has a track meet out of town." The call to Mrs. Bennion is not an unusual one. She had taken the third grade class on other occasions.

"Sure, I'll be right there," she responds. She has plenty to do, but she can arrange for her son to stay with someone till his afternoon kindergarten begins.

Some projects can be left until she brings the children home. There should be nothing preventing her from being back by at least 4 p.m. But she knows nothing about the day's events which will change those plans—just as they will for nearly everyone in the valley.

It is easy for everyone to learn first names at school. Total enrollment in elementary school numbers under 165. With growing young families in town increasing, a fine new facility was constructed in 1984.

Before then, the grade school youngsters had occupied one crowded wing of the forty-plus year old high school still housing the approximately 135 students making up grades seven through twelve.

Youngsters are proud of this "school of their own." It is complete with a spacious media center, and brightly colored classrooms equipped with the latest technology, including a computer in each room. They are going to be ready to go out into the world when the time comes.

The children feel particularly comfortable and secure here. Most of them even admit they love coming to school each day. Apparently teachers do too. There is almost never any turnover among the faculty.

Generally the students in Cokeville have a record of high academic achievement. Small class size and supportive parents help dedicated teachers.

A large majority of the high school graduates continue their schooling. Last year ninety-six percent went to college, most on scholarship. Four of the twenty-two seniors were members of the National

Honor Society. This year's class will send all but one to further their education.

Cokeville has a reputation for cultural achievement. The school has a strong music program. John Miller, a thirty-year-old band teacher, splits his duties between high school and elementary school every day. A large number of young musicians receive training and an abundance of opportunities to perform.

The high school has its own jazz band and swing choir in addition to regular bands and chorus. Several of these groups have won top awards in district and state contests in competition with schools many times larger.

Many a concert is held here where Miller and his students receive a standing ovation from an overflow audience. There is rarely room to get everyone in. The two local school board representatives have been vigorously petitioning school district headquarters in Afton for funds to build a larger auditorium.

Another occasion which puts demands on the old facility is the annual musical production directed by Miller and fellow teacher Glen Birch. Every year a major portion of the high school studentbody and many of the townspeople are pressed into service to bring to life such plays as "Oklahoma," or "Music Man."

With "Sound of Music," Mormon mothers descended on Catholic home economics teacher Clara Dayton to learn how to make a nun's habit.

The "community family" thinking takes precedence for the cause of the show, and the show is usually a roaring success. Visitors from outside the area often express amazement at the enthusiasm and quality of production from such a small town.

School provides considerable community activity, but it also requires practice time. An eleven-hour day is not unusual for students involved in drama, music, or sports. Most of it is with the full support of the families, even though they may not see the student on a school day until well after nine p.m.

During football season, for example, one can drive past idle swathers in the field when the team plays at home. In fact, it is not at all unusual to see a convoy of family vehicles heading out of town to cheer at an "away" game. People are accustomed to traveling many miles for shopping or medical care. It seems only natural to do the same for sporting events as well. Everyone wants to see what the kids can do—wherever they're doing it.

Anyone living in Bear River Valley for long understands the need for an acquired pragmatic approach. Since you cannot walk down the street to a repair shop, you rely on your own ingenuity when the furnace or hot water heater go out. People just learn to do whatever they can for themselves.

In the absence of any physicians, dozens of citizens have taken Emergency Medical Training (EMT). That training includes preparation for fires and any problem or disaster which could possibly occur. "We can't wait around for someone else to do it for us," a housewife explains.

Two of those new EMTs are Travis Walker's mother and father, who have just completed their training. Now they wonder what their first on-call major challenge might be.

With no paid fire fighters nearby, the community has built up a large volunteer force. They check equipment in weekly meetings.

Then too, the Cokeville Elementary School holds frequent fire drills. When the buzzer sounds, no child stops for a hat or coat even though temperatures may dip below zero for weeks. Children are trained to not stop until reaching the edge of the lawn. Many reach it within a dozen or so seconds.

The school had, in fact, held just such a drill last week. For the first time, the mass exodus was from a single room, the cafeteria, which also serves as auditorium and gymnasium.

The old Boy Scout motto of "Be Prepared" seems to prevail here, although not because anyone anticipates a problem. "It's something to do, a way to improve and grow," one Town Hall employee with extensive EMT background puts it. "Of course, you just never know when someone might someday need the help."

Long distances to the doctor tend to make one willing to "tough it out." With few people on hand, everyone has extra responsibilities to get things done. A local boy limping toward the bench at a football game could very well be told: "Rub some dirt where it hurts and get back in. We haven't got anyone to replace you."

Such grit seems to pay off. With only 20 to 24 boys available for a football squad, the quarterback and the ace field goal kicker must also play defense. Still, the team is expected to win, and they usually do. The school trophy case is filled with considerable evidence that this little town can make things happen when determined.

During Homecoming Week the same people who organize the festivities and parade will have to help light the block "C" on the mountain, then rush back to give a pep rally speech. Next day they'll be in the parade and participate in the "Big Game."

When morning buses converge at the school, children are frequently heard to say a cheerful "thank you" to their drivers: to Ted Brooks, father of a grade school student; to Bob Ferguson, retired game warden, and to Ed Dayton, the town barber. The fourth driver, grandfatherly Art Robinson, retired, lives next door to the elementary school.

For the afternoon session of kindergarten, just one driver makes the rounds throughout the valley driving north past acres of fields spotted with black Angus or white-faced Herefords or sheep. To the south it's much the same.

Those inside the bus longest often enjoy a wildlife tour. Driving along this highway it is not unusual to see deer browsing near the road. The elk sometimes come down to feed in the fields with cattle. This winter a young bull moose took up residence in town. Throughout the summer, antelope are seen regularly in fields south of town. Canada geese and the awkward-but-graceful sandhill cranes are frequent visitors. Golden eagles are often sighted, even by children with a short ride to school.

The route west crosses the Bear River and the railroad tracks to the hills overlooking a pastoral landscape. Every spring the run-off from melting snow muddies the water, and now the high water is beginning to spill its banks onto farm land.

Eastward, up Smiths Fork, the driver must go ten miles to get one of Clark's eight children. The family is building a lovely new log home nestled in pine trees just behind a bend in the Smiths Fork River. It's as peaceful a place as exists anywhere. The Clarks moved here to enjoy the closeness of nature, the rewards of hard work and the tranquility away from city traffic, noises, and newspaper headlines about crime.

Quiet and efficient, Eva and Lowell Clark are typical of the pioneering spirit so abundant here. As with other valley homes, their door is opened warmly to visitors.

No matter how much there is to do, there always seems time to visit. Things are casual. There are no pretenses.

Two of the Clark children attend high school. Kathy is still too young, but the others are at the elementary school. Paul is in afternoon kindergarten, but today he will be a little late. Eva has already called the school. "I'll drive him in shortly," she promises. "You don't need to make a trip up for him."

Elsewhere, a mother tells her youngster to be sure and take the money on the hall table. Mrs. Petersen has loaned lunch tickets for two days in a row now. It's time to catch up again. The girl flips her hair, a signal she has at least heard on her way to the bus stop.

Pretty little kindergartener Jody Pope has her blonde hair combed and curled and eagerly awaits her ride to school. Last year she envied her brother Shiloh when he brought his beginning readers home. She learned much just looking over his shoulder. Now she has developed the skill herself and can hardly wait to learn more.

Jody is bright and friendly. Little brown freckles dot her turned-up nose. Because their families are so close, her face especially lights up when she sees sixth grader Kamron Wixom in the halls. These two have spent many hours together playing in the fields or jumping on the trampoline.

Kam recently had a lead role in "Tom Sawyer," this year's production by the elementary school. He is rather serious-minded, yet loves to clown around mimicking voices of well-known characters.

He waves in response to Jody's greeting, then heads toward class with freckle-faced Travis Walker. Blond and full of fun, he had the role of "Huck Finn." The more you know him, the more he looks the part. His blue eyes sparkle with his mischievous grin. He even seems to carry Huck's casual, airy confidence.

Noon break is over. The afternoon school bus pulls in. Two minutes later, the l p.m. bell rings. Full-day students flock from the cafeteria and playgrounds for another afternoon of school.

As they do so they walk past a bulletin board displaying photos from the January twenty-eighth Challenger shuttle disaster.

Earlier this year, the students demonstrated their deep concern felt for the seven people who died in this national tragedy. When the craft blew up, children watched in horror on their classroom television sets. Later they posted newspaper clippings in the main hallway. They couldn't get over feeling a deep empathy for the astronauts' families.

However, that wasn't enough; the children wanted to personally help out. In the spirit of "when the going gets tough . . . " they began bringing their dimes and quarters to a fund for the space program. It was meant as a tribute to the courageous space pioneers who perished—in particular to school teacher Christa McAuliffe and her family.

Some of the children cared so much they gave up part of their daily lunch money.

While the students hadn't met the seven who died, they felt a deep kinship with people who tried so hard to reach their goals but then, through no fault of their own, were denied. The space pioneers were people trying to reach worthwhile, although difficult goals. The school kids cared about them and anyone trying to make the world a better place to live.

The kids—there are many of them gathered here this Friday. If school work is difficult, "Well, remember," says Travis, "that summer vacation and little league baseball are not far away." Tomorrow will be the first little league practice game of the season. It will be an opportunity to show the coach that he has recovered from the broken arm suffered last summer in a fall at the rodeo. Travis is anxious to work out the frustrations of playing one-handed. Before that, he had talked about being a big-leaguer.

Gina Taylor, winding up her first year in grade school, isn't that eager for the year to end. She is the only girl in a family with four older brothers, and she's the serious type who likes what serious girls like, even if boys don't. But she is adored by her brothers who play the piano and several other musical instruments—just so long as she will belt out another magnificent number.

Her repertoire is versatile. It includes everything from a humorous routine for the Senior Citizens' Benefit, where she "stubbornly" refuses to be pushed by brothers off her piano stool, to "I am a Child of God" sung for the terminally ill at Montpelier's Bear Lake Memorial Hospital.

Most children here are uncomplicated, obedient, giggling. Towheaded fourth grader Rusty Birch likes to talk about his many lofty ambitions. One is in drama, since he played "Winthrop," the stuttering little brother in "Music Man."

There is Jeremiah Moore, looking forward to a special day, because today he is seven years old.

A fourth grader, Kimberly Thornock is shy but energetic, and intent on succeeding in everything she does. Second grader Tina Morfeld and first grader Billie Jo Hutchinson are plucky, effervescent, determined. They will need to be on this day. It is one they will never forget. They have no way of knowing about the crisis looming directly ahead, nor the evil plot behind it. But it is already at work.

David Young's Philosophy

The following statement is David Young's philosphy distributed to Cokeville students and teachers the afternoon of May 16th. Similar copies were mailed to the press and to President Ronald Reagan. It is reproduced here exactly as written by Young himself although his paper allowed only a 3/8 inch left margin and ran off the page on the right side. His infinity symbols were hand drawn.

Zero equals Infinity

Seemingly, some thousands of years ago, several individuals combined, or perceived their combination and therein created Man.

This creation was, and is, a concept; a thought or idea, neither right or wrong (left) but a way among ways.

For the better part of the interim then, men played with Man making love, fire, food, mores, children, Gods, language, tools, wastes, etc: combinations of divers sorts, in almost as many directions (purposes). Now people come and people go, but always as people, no longer as individuals from which people had risen (or succumb). Almost as frequently as people come and go, additional, more distant concepts (from whatever reality is the individual/that precedes them); families, clans, tribes, villages, towns, cities, states, and civilizations make their brief passages and then leave the scene.

These various combinations of Man with their various concepts of themselves invented war in order that any singular combination might achieve dominance over other combinations. This came to pass as Man attempts to preempt those rights of the individual. The individual remembers reality only in learned (rather than the original and innate, therefore false) responses to right (his combinations values) and wrong (other combinations values differing from his own.)

History is the study of these combinations.

As a matter of record, therefore, some 2400+ years ago, Socrates, an individual, addressed himself to an evolving concept called knowledge. Knowledge is again a way to conceive, but conception is enlarged through rules less combination specific. Philosophy, remote as ever, is slowly displaced by science (mathematics, medicine, astronomy, etc.), a disciplines observing the singular rule that a fact becomes knowledge when it can be proved.

Proof is a concept, it suggests something that "is" on account of itself—it "is" proven. At best a probability, at worse nonsense, proof in any event is very distant from reality. Nevertheless it has been the predominant concept these 2000+ years and any combination that has competed with other combinations using it has eventually either adopted it or ceased to exist.

Be this as it may, knowledge and its attendant proofs remain but a way among ways. Socrates, reputed to be the wisest man of his time, investigated the basis of knowledge in a manner still available (Plato wrote it down and it survives), still as viable, and still as conclusive as it was 2400+ years ago. Socrates concluded, just as we must, "As for me, all I know is that I know nothing."

Nothing? This knowledge of 'nothing' then is all we have for all the lessons of history, these 2400+ years, Christ, revolutions, insurance, relativity, moon and space probes, crusades and inquisitions, Shakespeare, Newton, medical science, hydrogen, fusion, metalurgy, Hitler, electricity, government and law, etc.?

The answer to this concern regarding the nothingness of knowledge is rather yes and no. The Knowledge of Nothing is all there is (to know), but 99.9% of us don't even know that. Mostly, as in all these several thousands of years, we believe (another concept!) we know that 2 plus 2 equals 4 or that a line perpendicular from the ground is up, or that Christ is good (bad or indifferent), or that our names or ages are such and such.

All these beliefs we accustom to call knowledge (and knowledge ordained to have been proven, yet!) we wont to impress on all combinations (peoples) for their (and our) collective salvation (moral integrity).

That our belief that the moon is something we can put men on, or that a certain creed offers a unique conclusion, or that E=MC2 is not one whit more true than a New Guinean tribes concepts and rationales that have preserved its stone age culture into our world, leave the majority of us feeling wronged. Therefore, rather than learn the reality and limitations of knowledge, we refute truth with some age old axiom (bullets conquer stone axes), note the bobbing heads of surrounding bigots (99.9% of eve-ryone) and retunr without doubt or question to selfish, self-centered, egotistical sub systems and social specific cultures from which we otherwise might free ourselves.

Were we to continue, however, the investigation of knowledge, we'd need to interna-lize Socrates'; All I know is that I know nothing. O = [infinity symbol], Zero (or Nothing) Equals the Infinite. TRUTH!

How is this to be? Believing 2pplus 2 equals 4 hardly invalidates Knowing O = [infinity symbol]. The diabolical trick we've otherwise learned (internalized) is realativity; when in Rome do as the Romans, when doing math do as the mathematicians, when fighting a thermonuclear war, discard spears and arrows for the thermonuclear devises, etc.

While 2 plus 2 equals 4 (and there would have been no men put on the moon if it hadn't) it might just as well equal 22 or many ('primitive' tribes frequently respond thus to any mathematical concept above 3) or various other concepts that are easier to ignore than to realize, know, and internalize. But would we internalize these various concepts, we realize the relativeness of these various formulas, that knowledge is indeed relative, therefore untrue, therefore unknowledge, certainly nothing unless falsehood.

That O = [symbol for infinity] is TRUE, REALITY, and a symbolic manner of rephrasing Socrates' conclusion regarding the limits of knowledge is another matter. Here we confront what we thought we pursued all these years, what we should have remembered from 2400 years ago. The imortal Greek told us, showed us, and taught us the limitations of knowledge and we killed him for it, not merely one individual once, but in all this nonsense we've engaged in since. Still, 2400 years, 24,000 years, or 240,000 eons, there is truth-relativity and TRUTH. Let's cease to be beasts and begin to be Gods!

As was suggested at the beginning of this writting, Man is an invention, he is lots of individuals. Rather or not individuals ultimately exist (and what we mean by asking that question) is matter for another writting, it will presently suffice to remember that we still singularly (individually) conceive and perceive in the ever-present. Aware of the relativity of the games we play in our various existances, we will allow our individual trajectories (precepts and concepts) their original and innate freedom to achieve their own accords (determine their own natures) without the hindrances of Man, families, clans, villages, towns, cities, states, or civilizations.

Responsible, as ever (we die our own death, remember?) for our own actions (no Man, family, clan, village, town, city, state, government, or religion condoning withholding the above noted original and innate freedoms) we will collectively evolve into the next step of wherever it is we're going (Nowhere in the REALITY of O = [symbol for infinity] but still a long way from achieving it.).

"We are all ONE and 'we' came apart to do 'this' for something 'to do' in Nothing and Infinity."

David G. Young
4/th Oct. 1978
Tucson, Arizona

The Dark Side

"There is no doubt in my mind that David Young planned to kill the children to gain control of their minds."
—Sheriff's Investigator

David Young had long grappled with the purpose of his existence, yet he seemed little intrigued during his forty-two years with learning any personal relationship to mankind or deity. Rather, he sought to get along without such encumbrances.

Young often referred to his years at Nebraska's Chadron State College, where he graduated in police science with an "A" average. Apparently, a philosophy class there helped shape his thinking. In fact, prior to leaving his mobile home in Tucson, Arizona, for his planned takeover of the Cokeville school, he sent a copy of his theories to officials at Chadron with a handwritten notation on the bottom:

"This equasion [sic] true and therefore what I do now as I play with it, came to me in the Fall of '73 in a 231 philosophy class there. I thought you might find this coincidence interesting (altho hardly note worthy)"

DGY

Young seemed proud and eager to share his profound thoughts with his alma mater. As shown, however, he sometimes questioned whether his thinking would be considered as profound or "noteworthy" to others.

It indicated a certain self-consciousness. At least it did in this footnote instance. In spite of the addendum, he never seemed to question the validity of the philosophical conclusions reached in attempting to fathom the purpose of his existence. He was so certain he had found the "secrets of the universe," it would appear, that he committed completely to them.

As it turned out, he was even willing to die for them. If he did wonder how others accepted the thoughts in the back reaches of his mind, the answer to that question was easy: poorly—very poorly, indeed.

His declarations of belief were often rambling, confused, and almost always critical of the human race. A growing bitterness against society and government seemed to intensify, according to his diaries. A total of forty-one volumes were found. In them he brooded over the tyranny, as he saw it, in adhering to laws and rules, whether the author of the law was listed as man or God. His writings almost always indicated a struggle to comprehend reality.

One early statement read: "Seemingly, some thousands of years ago, several individuals combined or perceived their combination and therein created man . . . proof is a concept, it suggests something 'is' on account of itself—it 'is' proven. At best a probability, at worse [sic] nonsense, proof in any event is very different from reality . . . "

Young began entering such statements in his journals in the early 1970's. From then on, his desire to take action on his emerging philosophies intensified. They had increased to a feverish pitch by the time he threatened to blow up the Cokeville Elementary School with 136 children and 18 adults inside. If he would reason with mankind earlier, he would not by this point.

A compulsive thought recorder, particularly of his own minute-by-minute impressions, Young wrote this on the back of an envelope:

"If nothing but individual entities, what is the state, the Army, the church, the university, but conspiracies of privileged individuals to frighten and control, to form and deform, to rule and tax, to herd, to slaughter the indoctrinated rest?" Then, still uncertain about the validity of anything, he added, "I deny nothing, but doubt everything."

In its deepest sense, it seemed more than a mere wrestling match with logic. His life grew daily more bitter with the ugly realization his profound conclusions did not bring any meaningful satisfactions. Life was still empty. He seemed to have all the intellectual answers, but where were life's rewards for finding them?

One problem was that his thought processes often operated in a vacuum of positive emotions. Negative emotions such as fear and hate were there—but he distrusted most emotions anyway.

His solution for that dilemma was not so much an attempt to reconcile those emotions as to renounce them altogether. They were often cumbersome; they seemed like a waste of time.

From his writings it would appear the process of day-to-day emotional giving and receiving between close friends—the recharging of the human spirit so much a part of people everywhere—had all but became a lost art.

As for things like faith and love, trust and reverence to any higher power, they were more than a lost art. Somehow along the way, he never developed them.

The little decisions of shutting other people out finally took its expected toll. After a while, the so-called "milk of human kindness" was only for "inferior creatures." He would no longer partake of such pap.

Wesley Meyers, David's uncle from Grinnell, Iowa, said Young was born in California. He moved to Grinnell at an early age and grew up a loner. After high school, Young moved from Grinnell to the Nebraska panhandle where he attended college.

Time magazine (May 27, 1986) stated, without any attribution, that David was an "orphan." Such a designation might infer he was shuttled about, not wanted, and experienced the usual things suffered by parentless children.

However, relatives simply said Young just didn't associate with others, and grew up alone like an orphan. Lawmen later confirmed there was no known record of David having been an orphan.

"He was different," David's sister Janet Arduser said. "David had wanderlust." He left Iowa in 1971 and lived in at least seven other states before finally settling in Arizona.

He married and had two daughters, but the marriage ended in divorce. His ex-wife said of him, "He was always fascinated with firearms, physical force, and violence. He was for real. I was always frightened of him. One didn't get in his way, and I certainly didn't." She also described him as one who pored over sociology books and white supremacist doctrines, "although he never joined any of those right wing organizations."

Following his divorce, he drifted about until he answered an ad in 1979 for a marshal's job in Cokeville. But as elsewhere, David seemed to care far more about parading weapons than protecting townspeople.

"He always wore a gun in a holster tied down to his leg," one long-time citizen recalled. "He loved to wear big hats and straddle a chair backwards like the old barroom cowboys in movies. He often sat there like that on the porch of Cokeville's Stockman's Hotel. Some thought he "looked like Wyatt Earp." Or at least he tried to.

Mayor John Dayton said Young gathered firearms around him, and "gave out tickets for trivial things." He seemed to enjoy the power his title gave him, without particularly worrying about the responsibility.

Once David made up his mind, it seemed no one interfered with him. Town Council members said Young was his own authority. "He didn't like to take orders." Added Mayor Dayton, "He wouldn't."

Since he proved either unable or uninterested in taking advice from even those who hired him, Young was dismissed after a six-month probationary period.

Yet Young came highly recommended. "Maybe someone was just trying to get rid of him and avoid a lawsuit," Mayor Dayton was to say later.

While he was in Cokeville David ran a retail gun shop, although no one can remember ever buying anything from him, or seeing anyone else do so.

However, someone in town did share his enthusiasm for guns. This proved to be one of several common interests he had with the woman who would eventually become his next wife. When Young left Cokeville, Doris Waters, six years his senior, left with him. She left her family in Cokeville, and rode off with David on his motorcycle, black coats and all—if not into the sunset, at least out of town to be seemingly forgotten. But it was only for a time.

Doris originally came to Cokeville in 1976. She and her first husband had divorced; they had each remarried and divorced again.

"I don't think my mom and dad ever quit loving each other," her daughter Bernie explained. "It was just that they couldn't live together and make it work. They decided to try a trial reconciliation.

"We moved to Cokeville where he had a job, to see if they could make a success of marriage, but it was doomed from the start. It wasn't going to work and we all knew it."

While some people had blamed David for taking Doris away from reuniting with her ex-husband, Bernie's testimony doesn't hold David responsible. Doris just felt her reconciliation was failing. "She shared some interests with David and left Cokeville with him." It was as simple as that.

Perhaps the most important thing Young and Doris both believed in together was reincarnation, Bernie said. "They had no particular fear of death."

Doris arrived at this theory independently, prior to meeting David. "Mother's belief in reincarnation developed after my seventeen-year-old brother was killed in a very senseless accident. He was replacing a large truck tire. As he rolled it toward the truck to put it on, it exploded. The rim flew up and hit him in the head. He was in a coma for six months before he died. It was terrible. She couldn't reconcile this awful thing with a just God, so she decided there was no God."

In their atheistic-naturalistic belief, David and Doris shared what was to them a deeply rooted philosophy. Not all believers in reincarnation necessarily believe in the absence of God, but this description fit the Youngs. They focused on the naturalistic, in particular, rejecting the idea of supernatural significance, of revelation from a Supreme Being, or of miracles. Reincarnation, according to their writings, was more of a Godless destiny imposed on man, whether he willed it or not.

Perhaps it was a reason David so much confided in Doris and vice versa. They were not able to talk about their style of godless belief with just anyone. For a time, it made them cleave more closely to one another.

They enjoyed some good times together—one of them a well-documented honeymoon trip via motorcycle covering 2,437 miles using sixty-eight gallons of gas which totalled $129.83. Other trips went "BB and CC,"—border to border and coast to coast. Adventure on a budget was a forte of David's that Doris seemed to admire in him. He could certainly have fun when he wanted to.

Young's step-daughter, now Bernie Petersen, married a Cokeville native and still lives there with her own family. In a personal interview on October 12, 1986, she said of David: "He was in his own universe—he WAS the universe."

Throughout the next interval of his life, David lived even more within the walls of his self-constructed world. He trusted few, and talked little, associates said of him.

Bernie tried hard to keep the peace and would often listen to David ramble on because she said, "it made my mother happy. But I never did care for him personally," Bernie added. "We got along with the man mother married only for her sake."

"Mother was always an unstable person. We really had some problems between us for a long time."

Bernie characterized David as a highly self-centered man. "He was self-oriented to the point of making diary entries on his own most mundane thoughts and actions. Entries such as 'I am now sitting at the kitchen table. It is 0737. I just took a sip of coffee. . . .'

"His mind would often jump quickly from one subject to another, leaving the person he was talking to trying to fathom what he had just said.

"David considered himself on a level completely above the rest of the world. He would tolerate other people around him; that was all right. But he would sometimes use them."

Bernie stopped to emphasize something else: "David sometimes wasn't in this world. Mother told me that more than once.

"He was completely caught up with his own thinking," Bernie explained. "He wasn't a reasoner, but a thinker. For example, a reasoner would see a hole in something, and try to analyze how it got there. But David would try to analyze the hole itself, what was inside it, **deep** inside it, and why it was there. He would want to explore its deepest parts.

"His philosophy was that we 'perceive' ourselves to be here, and so we are here. Man exists in his own mind. Then we had to 'perceive' a master, and so we made up a god. 'God is just in our minds,' David would emphasize. Infinity was just in our heads."

Young wasn't afraid of confronting any god in a post-earth life because he considered himself equal to, if not superior to any god. This feeling came through in his writings.

When asked if he was lonely, Bernie said, "Yes, he was lonely . . . he *seemed* lonely. But maybe he just didn't need people. He just didn't seem to want friends."

There were people who tried to cultivate David's friendship over the years. One acquaintance summed up his perception of David with the observation that "he just didn't like emotional entanglements."

During the years David was away from Cokeville, associates characterized him as a person "seemingly like anyone else most of the time." For several years, he worked for Beker Industries in the phosphate mining hills north of Soda Springs, Idaho, apparently getting into no obvious trouble.

He had spent a six-month probationary period as town marshal in Mountain Home, Idaho, but was not taken on permanently because "fellow officers felt he was unable to fulfill his duties," according to Elmore County Sheriff Larry Olsen.

He was arrested once, according to Olsen, when he later visited the department carrying a concealed weapon beneath his coat. Toting a firearm was not unusual for Young, since he loved guns and apparently was rarely without one. It mattered little whether he happened to be a town marshal at the time or not.

"He didn't always tell the truth," Bernie said. "He manipulated people to his own purposes. He could be a skillful liar."

Young didn't work, she said, because "it would interfere with his thinking." He stayed inside his Tucson mobile home and read or wrote.

This meant that Doris had to provide money for them to live on most of the time. She brought in some of that money as a country singer. The singing talent was developed as a youngster, then taken to bars under her previous married name of Dorsie Waters. She had, Bernie explained, established her own group, "Country Cream," to entertain at Cokeville's Red Dog Saloon years earlier.

When that didn't work out, she did odd jobs scrubbing homes for others. About the only money David ever brought in was from an occasional sale of one of his guns.

Yet ironically, while economizing by buying clothes at garage sales, the Youngs owned a new truck and motorcycle, and relatives talked of property the couple owned in Arizona and Idaho.

"In the last few years Mom and I had gotten very close—more like best friends than mother and daughter," Bernie said of her relationship with Doris. "I would call her in the middle of the night, and she would say 'I was just thinking about you.' We even gave each other the same thing for Christmas last year."

Bernie was highly irritated on the morning of May thirteenth after David arrived in Cokeville. Driving up in her Subaru separately from David, Doris spent a day with her daughter. They planned on one more day together.

But David declared flatly that Doris "couldn't remain any longer" with Bernie. "She must come along and be with the group." Young used that term, "the group," to vaguely identify an entourage of six persons later thrust into the spotlight in various ways.

"I was annoyed that she was letting David do that to her again," Bernie explained. "He used to make her do crazy things when they were first married, but she had learned to stand up for herself and tell him she 'wasn't going to do that.' Yet here she was going along with him again."

Doris thus went dutifully with David to stay for two days in a motel about two miles across town. She told her daughter it was to be her last activity with him.

"Mother promised me we would get together and go shopping after they were finished with the 'biggie' David talked about. I had no idea what it was, nor do I believe she knew completely what he had in mind when she walked into the school building with him. But I know this, she planned on coming back and visiting with me next time whether David approved of it or not. She would never have promised the way she did if she had thought otherwise.

"She had come a long way, a LONG way," Bernie emphasized. "She had learned that you don't make promises you can't keep. She had learned that the hard way. That's why when she told me 'when all this is over, we'll spend a whole day together and go shopping,' I knew she fully intended to keep that promise."

Only later did Bernie learn why her mother was not allowed to remain with her. David was finalizing his secret hostage plans, and Doris was an integral part of his entire school takeover scheme.

"Mom was one who could remain very calm during a crisis. Then, when the crisis was over, she would fall completely apart. I don't think she had any idea what was going down. Oh, she knew there was something big. We all knew that, but figured it was a scientific thing of some kind."

Doris also found that despite Young's often iconoclastic philosophy, he was a man she could live with—for a time. Although David preferred to pass himself off to others as a macho type "needing no one," Doris may have remained with him as long as she did because of his health.

David was diabetic. By the spring of 1986, he had the disease under control, requiring a routine two injections of insulin a day. On the surface, he made certain he ate regularly, took his shots, and suffered no particular problem or discomfort.

Many diabetics live alone, inject themselves, and seem to live as normal a life as anyone else, according to medical experts.

However, Young may have felt some emotional dependency, that is, counting on his wife to have the insulin ready for him, preparing the right diet without excessive sugar intake, supplying needed vitamins and minerals etc.

It is known that while Young took an occasional drink, often imbibing a few beers, there is little evidence if any that he drank heavily, or frequently got drunk.

It would appear neither of the Youngs dabbled much in drugs, even marijuana, although newspapers would later say the pair must have been on drugs "to do what they did." Quite possibly, David was disciplined enough that he didn't want to foul his mind with such things.

In any event, David apparently didn't think he needed a "high," proceeding with his hostage plot minus drugs. Rather, he relied upon his emotionally bereft but gifted intellect to decide on such a course of action.

David had a "pornography problem." A grandfather of David's two daughters stated that Young took nude photos of the girls, peddling them for whatever money they might bring in. At the time the girls were of junior high school age.

Said one furious relative who couldn't verbally coerce Young out of the reprehensible act, "I had a .45 sitting on the table one day while David was in the house and I should have used it on him right then." When Young would not refrain from his perverted habits, it made for increasingly strained relations between him and most of his kin.

There is little mention over the years about Doris becoming disturbed about these corruptions. It would appear that after a time David's intellect, if it was almost all he had going for him, wasn't enough for Doris. David also saw nothing to longer bind him to her. They agreed in early May of 1986 to live their lives separately, although Doris did agree to "do this one more thing with him."

Statements in Doris Young's diaries about "making love for the last time" were generally translated to mean "before dying together," or before their "biggie" attack on the Cokeville school.

In reality, according to Bernie, it was not that cryptic. They were only declaring a separation and David had, in fact, moved most of his things out.

"Friends from now on. Changes . . . D. is packing," Doris's May 9th journal entry reads. "Both of us excited. Thinking we should be saying things profound and dramatic, but it just didn't come out that way. Instead it was 'do you have' and 'don't forget,' We kissed goodbye at 1745 and both of us were teary-eyed."

From then on, it was to be strictly business. Just this one more time.

From a disposition point of view, Doris and David never did seem to have much in common. Others said David rarely showed much sense of humor. Doris, however, seemed more like an oft-smiling grandmotherly type. It depended on the mood she was in, friends said. Neighbors in Soda Springs remembered her as the nice lady who use to bring over home-made bread.

One woman who worked with Doris for awhile at a cafe described her as a "fantastic lady." She quickly added, "This David, I didn't care for him at all."

Some people called Doris "brainwashed" for following her husband. That is probably too simplistic—at least to begin with. She found herself "believing in him" at first. As David's philosophy of "being a god himself" developed, Doris may not have fully agreed, yet she rarely openly disputed him. Instead, she tried to be tactful, if not sometimes placating.

Young was not only intrigued with guns but with bombs as well, and was considered by many who worked with him to be a devoted student on many types of weapons. In one diary entry he boasted of successfully exploding a bomb, a prototype of one he later took to Cokeville, in the Arizona desert. "It worked perfectly," he noted with unconcealed pride. He knew how to make a bomb right. He paid attention to little details other human beings overlooked.

Many dismissed Young's peculiarities as due to his being a mountain man with a leave-me-alone attitude. Few ever thought of Young as a survivalist, however. He didn't live off the land, even though he did wear a gun wherever he went.

To his Tucson landlord, Jim Billingslea, Young passed himself off as a gun dealer from California. If he was, he made little money at it, even though in a journal entry he once valued his fifty-five weapons at $27,785. The weapons he took with him to Cokeville were only a portion of the arsenal he owned.

David may have been aware of his remarkably high 180 intelligence quotient (I.Q.). It was mentioned later by investigating lawmen. Chadron State College probably had records of it. Apparently, David developed little tempering discipline to harness its use in behalf of anyone else.

It would later seem that Young viewed all attempts to change his mind with somewhat the same "superior" contempt Hitler held for minority races in Nazi Germany.

In short, his self-styled thinking was on a collision course with the democratic country he lived in. It was one which protected his right to complain about almost everything to do with the government and its officials, although he never expressed any particular appreciation for it. Young let the rancor grow inside until he felt fully justified in acting on his hostilities. There was nothing in his writings to indicate any remorse whatsoever for the malice he felt.

People reading David's writings later labeled him as "growing crazier and crazier" in his philosophies.

This was hindsight after he had already demonstrated his violent behavior at Cokeville. The truth is, Young was considered a promising intellectual by many who knew him. An egghead perhaps, but not particularly off the deep end. True, after reading his diaries, lawmen concluded that within the last decade of his life, he showed signs of increasingly irrational behavior; but it isn't surprising that many not scrutinizing his writings considered him little more than an eccentric.

Nor did Young's writings suggest even an inclination toward joining some of the extremist groups he had read about. That made several newspaper headlines all the more ludicrous later as they soared into fantasy. After a mere mention by lawmen that David's journals ofttimes coincided with philosophies of Posse Comitatus, a group asserting that "local laws supercede all others," the *Las Vegas Sun* tied it into a neat package: Young was a "member of Posse Comitatus."

That was printed in a headline size so large several publications often jokingly talk about saving it "for the announcement of the Millennium."

There were other attempts to fit Young into a convenient niche. None of them worked. According to the Lincoln County Sheriff's office, even the white supremacist Aryan Nation leaders wouldn't admit to having any ties with David Young.

While Young did have a reputation for belittling government organizations, including federal taxation, anyone who simply tabbed the man as a tax protestor didn't peer beyond the veneer. It would be like saying Hitler didn't care for Jews.

More importantly, anyone who took the trouble to research anything at all in his life knew he wasn't a joiner; he acted aloofly on his own. He wasn't one who ever liked doing things with others, or letting someone else call the shots. And he didn't, not even with the hand-picked few he cajoled into accompanying him to Cokeville.

The takeover idea had David's adrenaline flowing so freely that for several nights before his "big day" he couldn't sleep. For a time, he also had others excited with him. He often seemed enthused about his own decisions, less so for anyone else's.

Young sometimes wrote of his "awesome responsibility" as one who had all the terrible burdens of the world upon his shoulders. But it was such a terrible "burden" because he allowed no one to fully share his ego-burgeoning responsibilities. He considered others incapable of solving the world's problems. If they were to be resolved, he, David Young, would have to accomplish this task. To this end he wanted respect, someday even an audience, for his vastly elevated intellect. Yet it seemed only Doris truly understood him, and sometimes he couldn't even count on her.

With a reputation for innovative thinking, Young seemed to have no initial difficulties in recruiting colleagues for his "biggie."

True, he had never made anyone a lot of money, but the potential for it always seemed to be there.

Gerald Deppe, David's cousin from Iowa, thought enough of David to meet him in Des Moines, riding all the way to Wyoming to help Young in his "deal." It loomed as a certain success for both of them. Idaho co-worker Doyle Mendenhall felt the same way about his old friend.

Between them all, they seemed to enjoy a close relationship. David's May thirteenth journal entry says: "And the plot thickens. Slept decently for as excited as I was. Up at 0700 and into day. . . .My mind is going from thought to thought, trying to keep everything in order. Nice weather. Dorsie and I into Cokeville. Got Gerry and Doyle. Still full of fun and lots of laughs. To cafe for breakfast. It's been quite a while. . . .Entered at airport and got letters of 'zero equals infinity' ready to go off to newspapers, president of U.S. and etc."

This almost light-hearted diary entry indicates the calloused state he had reached by this point. Within the next 36 hours he was going to head for the Cokeville school with a plan to kill over a hundred innocent children, and anyone else who got in his way. If anyone was to think this incongruous—even that would not do the Young conspiracy justice.

There had scarcely been such a large scale and bizarre plan in all non-military history of the western world. However, Young had just such a colossal plan of that precise magnitude in mind. In the self-esteemed mind of David Young it was a plan that only he could orchestrate and carry out.

Young was often characterized as a salesman, one who could persuade you with the intensity of his ideas if he could just get you to listen long enough. One reason was his supreme confidence. It was also a shallow confidence—ballooned over the years by avoiding anyone who might try to change his point of view or shoot holes in his argument, as well as his ego. Still, at times it loomed like the real thing.

"Sometimes he would change his stories," Bernie said. "For instance, he told members of the 'group' that they could back out if they wanted to. He actually let one go. I drove him to the airport myself so he could fly back to Atlanta," Bernie added. "But David wouldn't let the others leave the next day."

Many considered Young "very bright" and "quite capable of someday making a scientific breakthrough" in his research. Young sometimes talked about this breakthrough as "finding a flaw" in the government system for personal gain.

When David invited Arthur Hoyt from Tucson, who also knew Young in junior high school in Iowa, to participate in his "get-rich-quick scheme," Hoyt refused. "I never did know what the plan was," Hoyt said. "He just told me we could purchase 747's and fly forever. I didn't buy it. I knew something was up, and then all of a sudden he was gone. . . ."

Hoyt apparently was not aware that while in Tucson, Young was gathering components for several bombs. He must have kept it a well-guarded secret, mentioning it only in his diary.

Young's obsession with firearms and explosives appears to have reached a zenith when he returned to Cokeville. He was to brag later, "I've got enough explosives with me to blow up the entire school." At another point Young said, "I may be in infinity when this is finished. If I go up, a lot of people will go with me."

If David had waited just one more year to put his take-over plan into effect at the Cokeville school, one of the hostages would have been Bernie's boy, David's own step-grandson. "I think that is why he did it this year," she said, feeling painfully aware of the favored discrimination. "I think he loved—no, he 'respected'—me enough not to do it when my son was in school," she confided.

After wearying of this world and his earthly existence, David wrote of his intense determination to find a place of refuge. In such a sphere he would personally rule as the god of a new race. In later years he seemed even more obsessed with the idea. Unfortunately, this reincarnated world could be reached only through death.

Yet as investigative lawmen later concluded, Young was prepared to end both his own life and the lives of others in his well-planned plot. In this case, it would even require killing a school full of children to make certain he got what he wanted.

There were strong indications in his diary that Young chose the Cokeville school for a particular reason. He not only knew they had many close family ties, but learned when living in the town the school program produced children scoring high on nationally compared achievement tests. If he was going to take children with him to people a new world, he might as well take smart ones with him—like himself.

Young often referred in writing to entering a "Brave New World" of reincarnated spirits, a thing which Doris contemplated with increasing anxiety. In one journal entry, she mused with some growing anticipation, "I wonder what we'll be called in the Brave New World?"

References to it appeared frequently enough that he later abbreviated it "BNW."

"There is no doubt in my mind that David Young planned to kill the children in order to gain afterlife control of their minds," sheriff's investigator Ron Hartley stated after studying Young's diaries.

Young himself intimated the same idea when taking over the school building.

So enchanted was he with his own wisdom, he considered teachers the enemy of intelligence. His resentment of them was apparent with the emphasis he placed on an underlined passage in *Zen and the Art of Motorcycle Maintenance* which alluded to "self-satisfied and truly ignorant teachers."

This philosophy book by Robert M. Pirsig seemed to have held almost Biblical importance to Young. He mailed copies of the book to close friends and quoted from it in his journals. His own copy was heavily underlined. He later noted that it was "My kind of stuff. Scary almost."

Elsewhere, he wrote concerning the entire educational process: "Why intelligence? To protect the system from knowledge."

In some entries he treated death as if it were a conspiracy of mankind. After stating that man needlessly worries about death, he concluded: "Death makes this existence seem important."

If death weren't in God's plan, according to Young, God mattered little to him anyway. In one place he wrote, "Let us cease to be beasts, and begin to become Gods!" But there is little likelihood he viewed this in the conventional or ecclesiastical mode of repentance and self-improvement, humility and rendering service to one's fellow man. On a greeting card he also wrote in large octagonal letters, "ME, GOD."

One of his most constant passions was trying to mathematically disprove the existence of God. It was a theme throughout all his diaries and journals. One of the harshest entries he ever penned seemed to hold utter contempt for all who believe in deity: "God is infinite.

Therefore God is nothing. Mathematically. God plus a pissant equals a pissant."

It seemed to be the summation of his beliefs.

This philosophy was to run head-on into the trusting, spiritually oriented environment at Cokeville where an industrious self-sufficiency was inseparably connected with a deep family belief in the power of love and prayer.

The community's genuine brotherhood and interwoven family ties were viewed by Young as a sign of vulnerability—traits seemingly tailormade for him to take advantage of by holding hostages.

Here then, was the same David Young whose sometimes charismatic and probative intellect originally attracted people who thought him bright. But in his ultimate decision, Young's years of loneliness, his brooding grudges, pre-occupation with self-godhood, and even his distrust of outside thought, led his dark side to an inevitable destiny that quite possibly even he hadn't fully contemplated.

David Young. A police file photo.

The Incredible Plot

"David had his mind made up. There was nothing any of us could do now to stop him."
—Gerald Deppe, locked in the van

During the morning of Friday, May 16, 1986, David Young found a rebellion on his hands. David had hinted at "finding a new source of cheap energy." He had talked of something "which is legal now, but when the government finds out, they'll pass a law against it."

That wasn't enough explanation of David's "biggie" for potential business partner Robert Harrison. Pressed for details, David would not elaborate. Harrison was weary of asking. Finally, Bernie was asked to drive him back to the Jackson Hole Airport, where he had been picked up, for a return flight to his home in Atlanta. Since Harrison knew nothing he could alert police about, Young let him go.

He still had helpers Deppe and Mendenhall. After departing a Montpelier motel, eating breakfast and quaffing a few beers, the two pushed Young again for details of the day's work. As they neared Cokeville, David apparently felt it safe to divulge his hostage-taking plans. After all, they would soon be at the school building.

However, the two disappointed Young. "No way!" Deppe protested. Mendenhall was equally aghast. Both wanted out immediately.

Some lawmen may have questioned how the two men could fail to suspect something illegal. It would be impossible not to notice the arsenal of guns Young carried in his van, but both men had known Young long enough to savvy that he liked to parade weapons.

Besides, he had never before attempted anything like taking young children hostage.

With the two now in rebellion, Young saw no recourse but to finally pull a gun on his old friends and handcuff them to the back of the van. Lawmen believe that Young stopped the van somewhere along Smiths Fork, east of Cokeville, to lock up his reluctant confederates.

Then he turned his attention to his nineteen-year-old daughter, Princess. Young had particularly counted on her help, but she told her father that she, too, wanted no part in the cowardly act of taking small children hostage.

Apparently, deciding he had enough control over Princess to prevent her from running away and upsetting his plans, Young did not bother to chain her as he had the two men. So long as they all remained inside the van and didn't shout for help, Young needn't worry about them.

While in Montpelier, Doris had painted over the van windows so no one could peer inside. "This is my flower van," Doris answered anyone at all who asked. "I'm going to paint flowers on the window." At the time it was probably meant to prevent people from looking upon the weaponry inside. Now it served an even more significant purpose to effectively make the van an unwindowed prison for Deppe and Mendenhall.

As for any struggling or yelling to attract attention, the two men decided it would do no good. They could get themselves shot. Besides, Deppe said later, "It was clear David had his mind made up. I hadn't seen him act like this before. There was nothing we could do now to stop him!"

Seeing that all reasoning simply fell on deaf ears, the two resigned themselves to fate. They would have to wait now to see how it all ended.

By now, Princess must have wished she had left home years before like her younger sister, Angela. Angela announced one day she couldn't live with her father's irrational edicts. She departed with little fanfare, and didn't return.

Princess realized she was trapped. Glancing occasionally at Doris, she saw no sign on her stepmother's face of backing out. Princess had also watched with trepidation as David shackled two of his closest friends. What could she do to stop this whole crazy thing?

Shortly afterward, David drove into the school yard. It was recess. Children were playing games, scattered actively almost all the way to the far fence. Young could see it was not yet time for him to strike.

The picture that lawmen put together was of Young driving toward the Bear River on the west side of town "to kill time."

Bernie says she learned David came to her house, but she wasn't home. She had decided, with some frustration at Doris's going away with David, to walk a mile and a half to town and join her husband, Brent, at work. Seeing her frustration, he offered to take her to a movie that night. Then, looking at the disappointment again on her face, he suggested they go for a drive now. He would also buy some supplies out of town that he needed. In so doing, neither she nor her husband knew anything at all about David's or Doris's actions that day.

Returning to the school ground a second time, Young found the children again outside, this time apparently for lunch hour. All right, he could wait. Why not, he had waited seven years as it was.

Young drove up toward the block "C" on the mountain. Then, satisfied with the view of the school yard from the hill by the cemetery, David stopped. Uncasing his field glasses, he began to visually stalk the school area, not unlike a predator surveying helpless prey.

Anticipating that lunch would soon be over, Young likely reanalyzed his long-laid plans. There were some hitches. With Mendenhall and Deppe secured in the van, he had only his obedient wife and Princess to help carry in all the firearms and wheel in the bomb. The latter, in a portable two-wheel shopping cart, was meticulously wired together according to written specifications.

David's bomb was designed to detonate five blasting caps from an electric charge via a battery. The caps, each in a can filled with gunpowder, aluminum dust, and flour, were designed to blow the component particles into the air. A gallon of gasoline was then to explode on a delayed fuse and ignite the particles.

According to bomb experts, the theory of such air-oxidized particles is explained in many military manuals. "The device works on the principle of a dust explosion, the type which has leveled many large grain elevators," they explained.

It is divulging no deep secrets in bomb making to say that sprinkling flour granules over an open flame readily demonstrates highly combustible little explosions. Taken all together, in a simultaneous and larger conflagration, the results could "blow up an entire room of medium size, cave in the walls, and kill everyone in it," experts emphasize.

Young's particular device was labeled a "deadman's bomb" because of its lethal properties to anyone near it.

There are other details which bomb authorities are understandably reluctant to make public. But essentially anyone demented enough to build a bomb for human destruction can conceivably learn how to do so.

Inside the Cokeville dump yard, Young selected a plastic jug to contain the gasoline incendiary. Several people there at the time observed the bearded stranger doing so, but they thought little of it. Why Young left this detail until later, rather than bringing a gasoline container with him, is left to conjecture.

There are, however, some most plausible reasons. He also assembled the wiring later, apparently in the Wyoming-Idaho motels, bomb experts stated. That would make more sense than attempting to transport the bomb ready-made from Tucson, with the possibility of having anyone see it, or most importantly, risking the long ride loosening the wiring—or even setting it off.

From the large arsenal carried in his van, Young set the following weapons aside to transport into the school: five rifles, including two AR-15 semi-automatics, five pistols, ample ammunition for all the above, additional ammo to be placed inside the bomb, and 30 blasting caps, as well as the bomb with its aforementioned five blasting caps.

However, Princess posed a flaw in Young's feeling of physical power. If he were to hold the children under threat of death long enough to attain center stage—long enough to vent his political vendettas with other diabolical plans—he would need help he could count on. Already, Princess seemed to be buckling under the strain. At one point during the morning, she was ordered to move part of the arsenal. She dropped something.

David looked at his daughter coldly. "Screw up one more time," he told her with a scowl, "and I'll shoot you."

Princess determined to be more conscientious in what she was doing.

"My knees were shaking. I concentrated only on getting his errands accomplished without getting shot. But I didn't know if I was going to make it out of the ordeal alive," she later confessed to her stepsister Bernie.

From what is known about Young, and more particularly what Princess had already learned about her father, he was not a man to cross.

Sometime the day before, Princess had risked harm from her father by sneaking away from his vigilant eye to make a cryptic telephone call. A clerk at the Lazy T's Motel heard her say to someone, "Tomorrow is the big day . . . I miss you. I'll be home soon."

When this conversation, including the reference to "tomorrow," was shared with investigators, Princess temporarily became tied in with the hostage conspiracy. However, she hurriedly explained she was only aware her father's project would be completed "tomorrow," and that she could, at last, return home to discuss wedding plans with her fiance.

Someone thought they heard Princess saying something about "not letting them in without a warrant." This was an apparent reference to lawmen later searching the Youngs' Tucson home, but it was never tied in with Princess knowing about the act David was to perpetrate on the Cokeville school children.

Fortunately for Princess, she extricated herself from her father's scheme just in time to avoid being charged as an accomplice.

As Young's van circled from the cemetery area toward town, Princess again looked at Doris. Was she determined to continue with this ugly business? Princess had no way of knowing about her stepmother's full commitment to David's plot. Back in the Young's mobile home, lawmen later found a note from Doris to Princess inviting her to select out of her assorted jewelry whatever she wanted. "To remember me by," the note concluded.

Since Doris had also promised to visit her daughter Bernie later, there is a seeming contradiction here. Some said Doris didn't know what she was getting into, and Bernie was certainly given every reason to conclude just that. Whether Doris later changed her mind, or perhaps referred (in the "unstable" state sometimes ascribed to her) to return in some form of reincarnation, or was just confused, is not fully known. In any event, Doris gave little moral support to stepdaughter Princess in her terror. She seemed, to the last, to side with David.

Suddenly, David put down the binoculars. His waiting was over.

Down the hill, past the junction with the Smiths Fork road and across U.S. 30, drove David. Then, over the Spring Creek Bridge—it was just a few blocks to the school yard. Sure enough, the kids were nowhere to be seen.

The only movement in sight was the slightly rippling American flag on the tall pole by the front entrance.

David decided to use the south entrance, probably because it was less conspicuous. Princess may have stalled, but then it came time to carry in the nefarious supplies. The three must have posed quite a sight, if anyone had noticed, struggling up the walk with all those guns and wheeling a cart full of bombs. In addition, they had some of their journals, philosophy pamphlets, and of course, David's syringes and insulin supplies for his diabetes.

Up the long concrete walk they trudged, then into the school entrance itself, down the long hallway looking for a receptionist or front office.

If Doris had harbored any inner thoughts about getting out, it was probably too late now. David apparently gave it no further consideration. Before leaving Arizona he had talked to others about missing the desert and "leaving all this behind." Then, he didn't discuss it much more after that.

As for Princess, a look at her terrified face probably convinced David she could never summon up anything like his own fanatical zeal. Realizing this, he hesitated no longer. He must get Princess out of the way.

"Take these then," David snarled, tossing her the keys, "and get the hell out of here!"

Princess ran down the hallway with the precious keys, but she couldn't resist a parting shot: "My God! My God! I can't believe you would do this to innocent children!" As she sprinted for the white van, Princess thought it strange that David and Doris left themselves no getaway car. She wasted no time at all in heading two blocks west to Cokeville's town hall. There she burst hysterically into the first door she located, confronting a startled clerk. "Is there a police officer here?" she wanted to know. Nadine Dana informed her there was not. "What is it?" she said. "Maybe I can help you." But Princess wanted a policeman. Nadine told her she thought she could handle it.

Frustrated, Princess poured out an incredible tale. Not all of it was decipherable. If Clerk Dana had difficulty understanding the urgent and violent nature of the message, it was only logical. The two jail cells in Town Hall hadn't had an occupant for years. Both Mrs. Dana and city employee Kevin Walker, now approaching the commotion, heard several rarely heard four-letter words in the vocabulary of the strange woman with the dark hair.

Walker took the stranger aside."We don't talk like that around here," he told her.

"Don't you folks care about your children?" Princess took the practical position that this was no time for proper protocol.

Finally, deciding the two community employees still did not comprehend what she was saying, Princess slowed down sufficiently, using the appropriate words, to make herself understood.

"My father has a bomb, and he is going to blow up the grade school!"

Mrs. Dana had twin daughters in the third grade of that school. She knew all the other children in there.

Across the hall, an emergency strategy meeting was just breaking up. Wyoming regional watermaster John Teichert, Civil Defense, and U.S. Army Corp of Engineers representatives were discussing a flood threatening northside residents along Smiths Fork. Having decided about emergency measures to be taken, the corpsmen had already left for homes in various parts of the state.

Teichert lived in Cokeville, but the three Civil Defense workers were eager to be on the road. It was just after one p.m.

The story was repeated to them. Suddenly the urgency of the potential flooding paled in comparison.

As a lifelong resident of the area and a Mormon bishop, Teichert knew most of the kids at the grade school on a hello-by-first-name basis. If what Princess was saying now proved true, their families could suffer monumental tragedy. He realized most did not even yet know about this impending disaster at the school.

"I sought out a private room downstairs," Teichert later said. "On my knees I pleaded with the Lord to please intervene in some way for the sake of the children."

Fortuitously, the three civil defense workers knew precisely how to obtain the immediate emergency assistance needed from throughout the entire state. They were Kathy Davison, Bob Looney, and Grant Sorensen.

Davison had been a sheriff's dispatcher. She joined Mrs. Dana in contacting community and Lincoln County ambulances in the county seat of Kemmerer and also in Afton, both about fifty miles away. Ms. Davison was able to summon sheriff's deputy Earl Carroll in Kemmerer, who headed quickly for Cokeville. Carroll lived in Cokeville, but was working in Kemmerer when he was called. He was the first lawman on the scene at Town Hall.

Either by coincidence or perhaps because Young had done some homework on the small community, all four local lawmen were out of town. Wyoming Highway Patrolman Brad Anderson was located via radio near Kemmerer; Sheriff's deputy Ron Hartley was on a day off in Utah, and local police chief Cal Fredrickson also was out of town. All turned their vehicles without delay toward Cokeville.

One of the first things Carroll learned was that lawmen had better not let themselves be seen near the school building. Young warned through school principal Max Excell that if he did, "I'll start shooting." Princess affirmed to lawmen that her father was fully capable of doing just that. The warning was disseminated to each new law authority as he arrived.

Unfortunately, there was no elaborate landscaping around the newly constructed school, just lawn all the way to Art Robinson's backyard fence. Anyone looking out the besieged classroom window could easily see them.

Lawmen arriving on the scene could only attempt to see what was going on inside the south wing classroom by crouching down from Robinson's backyard. It was a little over 100 yards to the two small classroom windows.

The town hall officials had to decide, in the absence of any lawmen, what to do with the two men chained like escaped convicts inside the van. With Princess exonerating them and acting as a corroborating witness, the two men were released from their temporary prison even before Carroll arrived. The key to their handcuffs was located in the vehicle, but just in case their part of a hostage plot had gone awry, they were detained for a time.

Teichert volunteered to keep an eye on them until Carroll and more deputies arrived. Deppe and Mendenhall were then questioned for every known detail of Young's scheme.

Princess told authorities more about her father, including the fact that she considered him most dangerous, indeed. She added other details about the weaponry and everything she, Doris, and David had transported inside the school building.

Lawmen realized now, if they hadn't before, that they were dealing with genuine terrorists, the kind you can rarely reason with. In this realistic appraisal, the authorities were only beginning to gain a handle on the problem they were dealing with.

Carroll remained in the town hall to direct emergency operations. Between Kathy Davison and the local officials, authorities alerted the Sweetwater County sheriff's office, including bomb expert Rich Haskell; Teton County's SWAT team; Bear Lake County, Idaho's sheriff Brent Bunn and deputies, plus men from the sheriff's office in Rich County, Utah. Other neighboring counties also promised help if needed.

Later, U.S. agencies, including the Federal Bureau of Investigation and the Federal Bureau of Alcohol, Tobacco, and Firearms entered the case. Four hospitals in Kemmerer, Afton, Montpelier, and Logan notified personnel to be ready for emergency assistance. Every local EMT and firefighter contacted rushed to the school area to be ready immediately for any service required.

Considering all this, it is somewhat ironical Young selected Cokeville because he "didn't want lawmen or others swooping down on him to thwart his plans!"

This crisis at the schoolhouse was the first call to be answered by new EMT Glenna Walker, Travis's mother and one of the first for her husband, Kevin. They had three children inside the threatened building.

Radio broadcasts, via Ken Rand of Kemmerer's KMER and Robin Spurling of Afton's KRSV, began reaching local homes. Several valley ranchers pondered by their gun cabinets trying to decide whether to take a big game rifle to town. Many mothers rushed to the scene. Others held back. Things like that didn't happen here. It took time for the incredible news to filter into the brain and into the soul.

In one of several major ironies this day, not one single weapon among the many trained on the school building would do anyone any good. No one dared lift a trigger finger so long as a single child inside could be harmed by premature physical force. But in the end, Young's mighty arsenal was not to do him much good either.

Some parents throughout the valley learned of the drama from their high school students returning home early. Many students thoroughly understood the grave situation and were unable to hold back the tears. Neither could the bus drivers who were delivering only half their usual cargo that afternoon.

High school principal Dale Lamborn had the unpleasant task of notifying students of the intense situation nearby. He suggested that the students remain away from the hostage scene two blocks away—even though many had younger brothers and sisters in the grade school. All had little friends, neighbors, or children they had baby-sat in the school. Older high school students were especially close to these grade schoolers. A number of the seniors were teacher's aides at the elementary school, offering the youngsters help several hours each weekday morning. If these aides had been serving in the afternoon, they would have been included with the hostages. It is quite conceivable that if they had included husky football and wrestling team members who often served as aides, they would have been tempted to jump the terrorists. One ex-aide suggested as much.

A hostage later replied: "then it's best you weren't there. You would have just been shot."

Nevertheless, it indicated the concern these teenagers had for the younger children. They expressed their feelings, in particular, to schoolmates like Danny and Billy Mitchell. They not only had a younger brother, Chad, in the besieged school, but both parents, Jack and Jean, were in the grade school too.

Teacher's aide Cindy Wixom said her class first learned of the dilemma when their teacher, Richard Pieper, one of the town's volunteer firemen, was called from the room; custodian Bob Dayton came in to be with the class. He explained the matter to the high-schoolers bluntly, "He's got the kids and he's got a bomb."

Before school dismissal, these students gathered together in the high school auditorium and joined together for prayer. Principal Dale Lamborn pleaded for divine guidance. "Students and teachers were spiritually united as we had never been before," many seniors said. Male or female, many wept openly during and following the prayer.

"All this and no one even consulted the American Civil Liberties Union," a high school sophomore said.

"Well, the ACLU can go hang its head," another student said. "Those are my friends in there, and I want to do everything possible, and I mean everything possible, to get them out alive."

As word spread around the valley, more and more parents gathered outside the school. Some initially planned to wait out the long siege at a place near the schoolyard entrance. This could be a dangerous situation if the perpetrators attempted to escape with hostages. Some were having difficulty facing the cruel fact that they were talking about the death of their children as if it might be just around the corner.

Lawmen faced the ugly possibility of a shootout if the people with guns attempted to flee. Young children would unwittingly be caught up in such a melee.

As rumors circulated, friends and relatives of the school youngsters tried to brace for the outcome, whatever it was. National newscasts concerning other events of the day were steeling them for brutal realities. On Mt. Hood, Oregon, nine teenagers had just perished in a blizzard, and only slim hope was held for two others; a grand jury in Salt Lake City was hearing evidence in a fraud and bombing case where two people were killed; a gunman in Colorado Springs walked into a bar, and shot five strangers to death.

With taut emotions swirling about them, many wondered if the whole world had gone mad. What could they expect of this sudden local turn of events?

Lawmen had learned long ago in seminars and symposiums not to expect too much from a madman-hostage encounter, whether in the Middle East or anywhere else. Lives were often "wasted" without reasons. Could there be much hope here for loved ones to escape, especially little children?

It didn't bode well at all. A pall of despair settled heavily over the little community of Cokeville.

A Town Without Children?

"He said one jerk from his wrist and the bomb would blow . . . and I kept watching to see that he kept his wrist down."

—a twelve-year-old hostage

"One wrong move and a child would be shot."
—Jean Mitchell, first grade teacher

It would be impossible to know precisely what flitted through the minds of David or Doris Young a few minutes after one p.m. as they entered the school building. It is known that David, in particular, had long vacillated between the shadowy lines of reality and imagination. As he became more obsessed with his Godless Weltschmerz, it is even possible Young's weary bitterness led him to believe all children would be better off in the reincarnated state he had in mind for them.

He also desperately wanted an audience to discuss his festering grievances with. In his rambling writings he had offered some solutions, but no one paid him the homage he felt he deserved. Society had ignored him, but he would show them; he would "grab" that same society by the throat.

To be sure, his outrageous act gained immediate attention around the globe. People everywhere found it difficult to believe anyone would be so deranged as to attack defenseless six-year-old children with guns and a bomb. Lawmen even conjectured at first that David carefully contrived his writings for a future court defense, so he could be found innocent by reason of insanity. After further study, those same lawmen concluded the man was what he purported to be—deadly serious.

To Young it must have been a duty, however twisted in the eyes of others, to act on his ideas, much like a fanatical terrorist in the Mid-East stops at nothing to complete his mission. Like tunnel-visioned extremists, the act of terror becomes easier if rationalized somehow as serving an outside purpose.

Young had seemed possessed in threatening violence to prevent old acquaintances Deppe, Mendenhall, and his own daughter from halting his perverted purpose. In dismissing Princess, he also gave up his escape vehicle. He could never just walk away. If he changed his mind, or for any reason decided to attempt a physical escape from the building, he could always try to comandeer a car. But it appeared, just as he wrote in his journals, that he planned to remain and die with the children. Obviously, his commitment was not a shallow one.

His superior intellect must prevail over all else. Was it revenge? No, a trivial reason for returning to Cokeville. Besides, if he was to seek vengeance upon every community which fired him, he would have several others to visit as well. Revenge did not carry philosophical roots. If Young was to put his energy into action, it must be for a deeper purpose than revenge alone.

The primary reason for Young's visit was in his hands, the same mimeographed statement of philosophy he mailed earlier to Chadron State College, and then to President Ronald Reagan. Neither returned even so much as a polite response to Young. But Young would force those inside the school to look at his higher sphere of intelligence. David Young would be ignored no longer.

The leaflets, however, were difficult for anyone else to follow. One summation read: "Zero equals infinity." Then two questions: "Nothing? This knowledge of 'nothing' is all we have for all the lessons of history. . . .Christ, revolutions, insurance, relativity, moon and space probes, crusades and inquisitions, Shakespeare, Newton, medical science, hydrogen fusion, metallurgy, Hitler, electricity, government and law?"

Elsewhere he wrote, "Knowledge is indeed relative, therefore untrue, therefore unknowledge, certainly nothing unless falsehood."

He talked about the "pollution" perpetrated by government and teachers upon students. And, of course, he believed God existed "only in man's mind."

As a thinker, Young often compared himself to Socrates and Hitler. Right now, his only thought was to inaugurate his plan. This was "the day of the biggie."

Just as David expected, no one recognized him behind his straggly beard as he headed for the school entrance. Nor did anyone pay him or his bomb-laden entourage a second glance even as a stranger. Tourists paused here during the summer as they headed for Yellowstone and Jackson Hole. In the autumn, big game hunters swelled the town's population. Before the price of oil plummeted, petroleum energy, fuel-seeking seismographers descended on this sector of western Wyoming. Bearded strangers roamed motels, cafes, The Red Dog Saloon, and Goldie's Bar. They were not asked their off-hours business. No one saw any reason to distrust strangers.

David Young would change that.

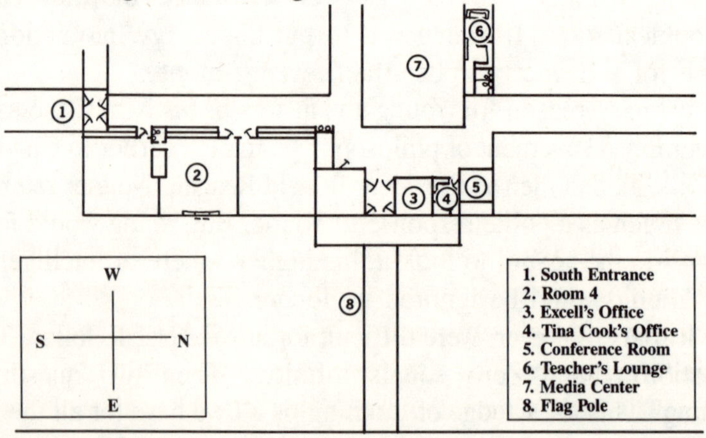

Floor plan of Cokeville Elementary School shows south wing of classroom including besieged room four and Mrs. Cook's receptionist desk.

As he stepped inside the hallway, he hesitated. He had not been here before. His years of planning this moment began well before the modern red brick building was constructed. Young had no floor plan of the school rooms.

After pushing the bomb down a hallway, he turned to the right. Near the front entranceway, he saw a receptionist's desk by the principal's office. The Youngs moved closer.

Meeting them there with her usual tall smile on a short frame was secretary-receptionist Christine "Tina" Cook. Having moved to town from her native Canada after the Youngs left Cokeville, she had no reason to connect either David or Doris with anything at all unusual. Still, she had a foreboding feeling as she pondered the pair before her.

It wasn't the man's faded jeans or the dirty, unbuttoned yellow sweater and dark blue nylon windbreaker over the navy blue T-shirt. It scarcely seemed like appropriate attire for business hours, but few people here judged others by outside appearance. It was not uncommon for ranchers to pop in directly after working with livestock to talk with a teacher about a child's grade or pick up something left behind.

Doris wore black slacks and contrasting red terry-cloth shirt. But it wasn't the clothing. It was the grim countenances. Tina wasn't accustomed to this. Even strangers usually exchanged some kind of pleasantry about the weather or a bulletin on the wall.

David felt time was wasting. He did not bother returning her friendly "hello."

Tina saw another woman she had never seen before move up to the counter. She assumed Cynthia "Cindy" Cowden was with the strange pair standing in front of her. Cindy had arrived for an appointment with school principal Max Excell to interview for the new kindergarten teaching job. Since Mr. Excell wasn't here at the receptionist's desk, Cindy decided to step into the nearby restroom.

"Can I help you?" Tina asked the pair who remained. "You sure can!" the man stated. Then, he was silent. Tina thought she had never seen eyes as cold as those staring back at her. She had never looked at anything as depressing and cheerless—chilling.

The woman spoke up. "Your name over the door. Are you Mrs. Cook?

"Yes, I am."

The man took over. "Well, Mrs. Cook, don't step on any alarms." He said it with a resolute efficiency, as if it had been well rehearsed. "Step back from the counter. Now! And I'm warning you not to use any telephones. Do not try to scream. . . ."

There was a look of disbelief on her face. "Mrs. Cook, look down here at this clothespin. See here where I have pulled out the plug between the two ends of the pin. I have only to let them touch, and this entire building, with everyone in it, blows sky high. Mrs. Cook, we are only one-half inch from death."

He stared at her with those eyes again. "Try to hit me on the head, jump me from behind, or anything at all, and I will pull on this bomb trigger before I go down. Do I make myself clear, Mrs. Cook?"

Bewildered, Tina looked for a sign of human warmth in those eyes. There was none, no personal insight, no light at all. She suspected there hadn't been in years. They were like no eyes she had ever seen before. Gray, intense, barren, utterly without compassion. They looked right through her. She had never imagined such a feeling of terrible coldness.

She didn't know what they expected her to say or do.

He spoke again. "How many telephones do you have here in the school, Mrs. Cook?"

"Five," she managed to say.

"Well, unplug them. All five." Again it seemed he had premeditated the mathematical precision of the command. She did not dare look at his eyes. Numbly she stepped toward the principal's office to comply.

"Stop!" she heard him scream at her. Doris walked around to join her. The woman acted as if Tina would have the audacity to try making a premature phone call.

"May I impress upon your mind, Mrs. Cook"—the way they said it, she momentarily hated her own name. Why did it have to be so personal the way they said it—"that the lives of everyone in this building depends on what you do in the next several minutes?"

By then, teaching candidate Cowden reappeared from the restroom. She saw the pair motioning everyone into the office area. That included her. "No, I'm fine," she told the pair. "I'll just wait for Mr. Excell right here." The man motioned at her.

"Lady, you better get here with the others."

"No, I'll just wait right here," she said a trifle irritated. By now, Ms. Cowden was growing impatient with the delays. She had a long drive later in the day to her home in Nevada.

An angry David Young lifted his pistol barrel at the woman's head.

She laughed. "What's this, a new interviewing technique?"

She asked it with what she felt was a justified mixture of levity and sarcasm. But instead of anyone laughing, she saw an anxious Mrs. Cook motioning her to join them.

Janel Dayton had been a first grade teacher here for several years. Her husband ran the family ranch north of town, and she had a boy in the morning kindergarten.

Quiet and responsible as a no-nonsense mother of six, Janel had approached the office to get her mail. Her first glimpse of the unkempt Young told her he "was up to no good." Being one who chooses to avoid ugly confrontation, she wanted to disappear back into her room, but she realized he had noticed her.

"This is a revolution!" he announced.

"Who do you represent?" she asked the man.

"Ourselves!"

He said nothing more. Janel turned to walk away, but she too was told to join the small crowd gathering behind Mrs. Cook's door.

About this time, fifth grade teacher Rocky Moore looked at the entourage. He thought it strange, but headed for the papers he wanted to look at again on his desk.

"Get over here with the others behind this counter!"

Not the quiet type, nor one to be bullied, Moore moved his stocky frame on down the hall.

Rocky didn't like the man's tone. "That'll be the day." He hardly missed a stride.

"I know you, Rocky!" that same voice boomed again. Moore stopped now, to see who would be talking to him like that. He stepped toward the voice. Suddenly, he found himself looking down the barrel of a pistol. It was less than a foot away. As he watched, Young cocked the gun. It was so close Moore could see the slug in firing position.

The teacher did not realize it, but the taller man standing before him was an old acquaintance. Moore had been David's landlord some seven years earlier.

There had been the usual disagreements between renter and owner about repairs and rent paid on time. David wanted more than repairs; he wanted remodeling. Rocky indicated Young was free to leave. He thought little more of it when Young moved away.

David Young, however, hadn't forgotten he'd failed to get his way. He didn't like that. He wasn't accustomed to it.

"You don't remember me," Young grimaced. "But I'd just as soon kill you right now as later." His eyes narrowed. "Get over here and keep quiet!"

Rocky shrugged his shoulders. "Okay. Hey, I'm coming, if that's the way you feel about it." His body language, among those who knew him, showed he did so under protest. Then he looked at the faces of the other teachers pleading with him to join them quietly. The infectious smile he usually wore faded. Sizing up this strange encounter, he remained as quiet and inconspicuous as possible. For the time being, he would shut up to prevent anyone from being hurt.

Tina could think of no way to probe any deeper into the man's "revolution." Then the stranger pointed ominously to the shoelace on his wrist. "Do what we tell you," he warned the teachers, "Or I'll pull this and trigger that bomb on the cart!"

The look on his face indicated he meant what he said. Yet the words just didn't compute. Not in their lifetimes had any of the people here ever encountered a bizarre threat like this. At the same time, no one wanted to upset the man. The bomb may be a fake, but the guns he carried looked real enough.

Looking toward the conference room next door, the Youngs asked, "Is that a large room?"

"No, it isn't," Tina answered. By now, some of the teachers, including Mrs. Dayton and Ms. Cowden, had been motioned inside. Could the whole thing be just a strange joke, or was this pair crazy?

Everything seemed all too real to not take it seriously. Cowden noted an open window. She suggested to Janel that they climb out and run.

However, Dayton had just turned her firstgraders over to teacher Jean Mitchell for some afternoon activities. It was the first day of this trade arrangement. Both teachers hoped the children would like the approach.

"Why am I concerned about that?" Dayton asked herself. The real problem would be if the intruders noticed her missing and took it out on Mrs. Mitchell or the children. Unpleasant or not, she knew she must remain to see this whole thing through.

Already, the "loving force" David Young had counted on was at work. For the remainder of the day, every person in the schoolhouse would be so concerned about the welfare of the others they wouldn't try to effect their own personal escape. Not if it left the children behind with this apparent madman.

Because of their deep concern for each other, all of the school's occupants were soon at the mercy of the man with the cold eyes and his guns and bomb. It was just as Young's pragmatic and opportunistic mind projected it would be.

Since the receptionist's area was the central focus of the school's business activities, it was only a matter of minutes until others were drawn into the nefarious net.

White-haired Verlene Bennion, sixty-six-year-old teacher's aide, usually had a smiling face. She wasn't wearing it now as she was ushered toward the conference room. There were only deeply sober faces.

With a glance inside, the pair now decided the room was too small for their giant scheme. Soon, Cowden, Dayton, Bennion, Moore, and the others were herded down the south hallway, escorted by the Youngs and their persuasive hardware.

Why Young selected the middle door on the left is not immediately clear. It is likely he sought a classroom with no outside entrance which would be accessible to any lawmen wanting in—or hostages wanting out. He opened the door with such a deliberate precision, Tina thought they must have checked it out as they came down that same hall earlier.

Through this door on May 16, 1986 passed nearly every grade-school child in town. For over two hours, they doubted they would ever see beyond that door again. (Dan Dockstader photo courtesy Star Valley Independent.)

Young found the double class of first graders conveniently assembled. His plan was quickly taking shape. Here were little children in place and ready to learn. Young figured he was just the one to tell them what to do. This was where everyone would assemble.

He wheeled his bomb-laden cart inside the room. Doris was sent to make certain everyone else in the building gathered there.

When Young burst inside, he disrupted a flannelboard story Mrs. Mitchell was just completing. It was a classic often enjoyed by children across America, "Goldilocks and the Three Bears."

After the story Jean, who termed herself "something of a disciplinarian," wanted to move smoothly into an afternoon of discussion on magnets and dinosaurs, something which always held the young ones' attention. From there they would get into basic arithmetic and spelling.

It appeared her seven-year-olds were ready for work. So was she. It was a little after 1:15 p.m., and a full afternoon was planned. It struck Jean as singularly "insensitive" that this shaggy-looking interloper would barge in this way.

Although his wrist was attached to the trigger of a lethal bomb, David Young chose to further impress hostages with these weapons leaning against the wall of the first grade classroom. (Dan Dockstader photo courtesy of Star Valley Independednt.)

The man then began stacking weapons against the wall. People in Cokeville were not unfamiliar with hunting firearms. The large rifles were not as shocking as the lethal-looking pistols. He carried several on his person, tucked into his belt. They could only represent an evil intent, Jean realized, although she tried never to pass negative judgment on anyone. She would try to force herself to maintain an open mind.

Within minutes, more children began swarming into the room, and the woman leading them stopped to hand out papers. Jean's room, designed for approximately 30 students, was rapidly filling up. Many youngsters were lured in by Doris' Pied Piper enticement: "Follow me . . . I have a surprise for you!"

Never treated with such duplicity in the past, the children flocked behind Doris eagerly. Ten-year-old Jerry Dayton, enthusiastic as usual, thought it might be an assembly to learn more about "defending against terrorists like we'd been reading about in Libya."

Delbert Rentfro, school custodian, saw Max Excell return from his mail-gathering errand. "The fifth graders are gathered in the music room," he said, "but Mr. Miller isn't there. The kids are starting to get a bit noisy."

Noting that it was most unusual for Mr. Miller to not be in the classroom, Excell looked for him elsewhere in the school. Down the south hallway he observed considerable confusion and was surprised to see teachers and students crowding into one room.

An administrator with a penchant for details, he expected to know everything planned for his school. "I try not to have someone else know more about what's going on at my school than I do," he had said.

Excell was a physically active man, younger in appearance than his forty-seven years would suggest. His previous experience as a Utah high school athletic coach had taught him an appreciation for discipline and respect for authority. What he saw now in the hallway caused that appreciation to rise to the surface. What was this, an unauthorized assembly—in a classroom? He saw teachers motioning him to keep out. Still, he questioned the propriety of the whole thing. He opened the door to room four more widely now.

"What's all this?" Excell demanded.

Young asked him if he was the principal.

"Yes, I'm the principal. What's going on here?"

David repeated his earlier pronouncement: "This is a revolution!"

Excell sat down.

Small but spunky, Jean refused to be intimidated by this wierdo's untimely "uprising."

"You've got to be kidding!" she fired back at him.

The man's deepening scowl told her he was not.

"This is my room . . . " Jean said with rising consternation. "What is going on here?"

Ready at any moment to grab a pistol, David had the upper hand. "Sit down and shut up!" he declared loudly.

A deep chill surged through Jean's consciousness. There was no reasoning with this man.

Jean's young ones had never been subjected to blatant physical threats like this. She could see the fear in their eyes, feel the mounting bewilderment in their hearts. The guns and the look of anger on the man's face—here was terror, not in some foreign land nor on television's make-believe. It was right here before her eyes at this very moment.

Several unexpected events were bringing in additional prisoners. Gloria Mower, special education teacher in an adjoining room, wondered what the commotion was all about. Not wanting the student with her to be left out, she peeked into the besieged classroom. When she did, tutor and tutored were trapped. Young now waved them in.

Mrs. Mower saw the look of concern in each of the teachers' eyes. She had better not do anything out of line. Looking around at the grim faces, she and the student became part of the plot. Moments later she became aware of the guns and the bomb. Only then could she begin to realize how grim it really was.

Grandmotherly fourth grade teacher Kliss Sparks, deciding there was too much confusion in the hallways, took her children outside to finish reading "Tom Sawyer."

She was just beginning to enjoy the warming sunshine on the lawn when she thought there might be a program inside which was supposed to include her class. When she brought her class inside, she discovered a gun and treachery. She was told to stay put. Why had she been so eager to join the others? All these children who could have walked away were now prisoners, and she had been the one to bring them here.

Petite and shy Sandy Gonzales left her United Parcel delivery truck to "run in some packages." She drove this route every day from Rock Springs, 135 miles away. Familiar with the area but only casually acquainted with a few of the people, she was escorted in among strangers. She was not allowed to leave.

It was a peculiar situation she found herself in. While not normally counted among these people, yet she felt an immediate kinship with them. Now a hostage, she might watch for a chance to hurry out the door or window. But she resolved to make no false move for the sake of everyone assembled.

Eva Clark left four-year-old Kathy in the car while she escorted Paul to kindergarten. The class wasn't in the usual room, so they headed for the library. Maybe the youngsters were in there today. It was empty.

She found teacher Jack Mitchell hurrying toward the hall. "They might be down in my wife's room," Jack told her. "It looks like they've got something going on there. Jean is always cooking up something," he laughed.

Eva and Paul followed. As they looked inside room four, she found Paul's classmates.

Leading him in, Eva turned to leave. She had many things to do that afternoon. Included was shopping in Montpelier before returning home to help her husband Lowell get the cattle in. The next day they would begin a major task, traditional springtime branding. It would be Saturday and many relatives were invited from out of state. To host them properly, she would have to hurry for groceries and get everything ready.

Now, a woman at the classroom door beckoned her to come in.

"I've got to go," Eva smiled.

"No, come in. You'll want to see this."

"I just haven't got the time," Eva repeated.

Again the woman insisted. Eva saw the smile change to irritation. Then Janel Dayton sidled over to the mother. "You may want to stay," she said quietly. "We have a problem here."

Eva had begun to sense a sinister atmosphere; "something reeked of evil here as I had never felt it before." She didn't want to stay, yet she had five children in the room. There was something here which threatened them.

Soon Eva saw Young's guns. Then she saw the shoelace attached to the man's wrist and connected to something in a shopping cart.

Several teachers examining the device from a healthy distance "saw that it seemed to be just what Young said it was, a highly explosive bomb." Jack Mitchell had a logical, scientific mind, with a passion for computer programming and ham radio. He noted that the bomb's wiring looked "deadly real."

Young said little about it after his initial pronouncement. He just held up his wrist or reached for a belted gun if someone moved too close. If the bomb was a fake, Young was a most confident and consummate actor. Mrs. Cook suggested that the bomb could be easily detonated. They would have to take the pair at their word. They did not dare do anything else.

Children made efforts to play or read, but every few minutes they looked up. It was as if they hoped the pair and their terror might have somehow vanished. They had not. This wasn't the world of fantasy in movie or television.

During the afternoon, Young held his hand down near the cart, never raising it more than a few inches.

"I didn't get the feeling he was acting," said one wide-eyed child. "He was too careful to keep his hand down all the time."

His friend explained: "A teacher told me that we needed to be quiet and not upset the man. One jerk from his wrist and the bomb would blow. I kept watching to see that he kept his wrist down."

There were many questions in the hostages' minds by now. How would such intense anxiety affect these youngsters? Was he simply holding them for money, or was he a schizophrenic prepared to kill for perverted political purposes? Was he also volatile enough to give in to a sudden and uncontrollable rage? Then he was all the more dangerous.

To those like Rocky who now recognized Young, the matter of revenge had to be considered. The message filtered down in whispers to the children. "He used to be a policeman here." They wondered if he had returned to get even with the entire town.

While the hostages pondered such questions, some realized not everyone in the school building had been forced into the room with them. Custodian Delbert Rentfro was still outside somewhere.

Rentfro had noticed the extraordinary bustle going on in room four. He opened the door and started in. Doris, apparently concerned about Rentfro's six-foot 3-inch frame, well over 225 pounds, quickly decided this was one hostage they didn't want. He was much larger than any of the other men.

"Forget it," she told him. He thought it rude, but apparently he was just not needed in the room. There was work to be done in the kitchen. He soon busied himself there.

No one really yet knew what purpose the man and woman had in mind. They were soon to find out. Excell was allowed a few minutes to gather Kleenexes and aspirin and things children might need to keep them settled in the next few hours. Then he was summoned for special duties.

"You're my spokesman," Young stated. "You'll notify authorities. Tell them I want two million dollars apiece for each of these kids. And I want no part of the negotiations. They have a way of trying to break you down. I don't want to waste my time with that. You do the talking."

"Who do you want me to call first?" Excell asked evenly. He attempted to sound as businesslike and calm as possible. The children were looking to their adult leaders for some sign of normalcy, even if there was none.

It seemed every time Excell looked down at the children he found them looking up at him for their own cue on how to feel. He must not display the fear he felt for the children, or for any of the other hostages. "Shall I call the sheriff?" Excell asked.

"That's fine," David answered almost benignly.

He did not swear or curse. That seemed odd, considering his other actions and his arrogant takeover. Was it carefully contrived to keep them calm and patient for something even worse ahead? Was it because he would exercise more control over them in a long ordeal in this manner? Would it be easier to subjugate the children's feelings if they didn't see their teachers constantly badgered?

Some also wondered if they might infer that the man who held them hostage might relent later. If so, they had no clear idea at this time that David Young meant to kill as many of them as possible even if he did sometimes seem quiet and polite in the process.

"Tell them I'm prepared to be here for ten days or more, if necessary. It may take that long for Congress to raise all the money," Young told Excell.

Keeping his voice down to avoid unduly exciting the children, Excell asked, "Why this school . . . why here?"

"Because this is a family town where people love their children, and they'll do anything to get them back," Young stated matter-of-factly. Excell thought he made it sound like a routine business deal such as those daily conducted in office buildings everywhere.

Before sending Excell to his telephone bargaining, Young fairly bristled with a sharp warning: "Be back here every ten minutes to report—or I'll start shooting these kids one by one!" Later, ostensibly to be more practical if not more compassionate, Young lengthened it to every fifteen minutes.

"Because we love our children. . . ." These words swirled in Excell's head as he hurried toward his office. "He makes it all sound like no big deal—but doesn't everyone love their children? Why did he come all the way here to announce a platitude like that? Why should we be punished for loving our children?"

Up to this time, those in the school were not certain anyone outside the building knew of the extraordinary circumstances inside. However, when contacting the sheriff's office, Excell discovered it had just received "a strange report." Something about a "hostage crisis" at the elementary school. He quickly confirmed what Princess had told officials at the town hall.

"It's happening to us. Right now!" he assured the sheriff's secretary.

Had Excell been allowed to look outside in the next half hour, he would have witnessed local emergency vehicles assembling near Robinson's back yard. A town fire truck was placed as a barricade to keep vehicles on Main Street from entering the school yard.

Town citizens were beginning to respond methodically to the implausible happenings inside the elementary school. Though they could not comprehend, they were responding with habitual intensity. Still, would someone now step forward and declare the whole thing a mock drill or a cruel joke?

No one did. And the preparations outside continued—for whatever might happen.

Did the pair in the school truly have a bomb, a real one, in there with innocent school children? With little, loving children? By now they had been assured this was the case. Still, it had to sink in.

A child nudged Mrs. Dayton. "Will we be all right?"

Mrs. Dayton saw the youngster's anxious face. There was no way she could evade the question. "We are right now. We're . . . okay right now," she managed to say with measured honesty.

With the lives of everyone in the school resting on his shoulders, Excell felt compelled to say a prayer. He had always programmed it carefully into his daily family life. His family included sixth grade daughter, Tess, who was also a hostage, and his wife, Glenda. This prayer he offered on the move, enroute from office telephone to room four. That statement of Young's kept ringing in his ears. "I'll start shooting the children one by one. . . ."

He was to hear that solemn threat of death again during the afternoon. So were many of the other teachers who left to get crayons, papers, and toys from other rooms to keep the children busy.

"You can leave, but you better return quickly," Young emphasized to teachers. For everyone who doesn't, one of these kids will be dead." He said it with an assumed superiority that pierced Jean's soul.

Second grade teacher Carol Petersen passed along story books for the children to read. As she began handing some to older students, she realized the books were geared only to small children.

"Wouldn't you like to read about these dinosaurs?" she asked brightly. Things were gloomy enough. Maybe someone could get the children to smile. But, she noted, it didn't always work with such desperately frightened children.

Young had a way of looking that seemed to say he would "remember you." You better not try to get away if you cared about the others in the room. Every threat, even if said with a weary casualness, seemed deeply personal.

Mrs. Petersen remembered those eyes. They seemed to be watching her, looking at her directly every time she looked at him. "How can I escape his eyes?" she asked herself. She knew he was probably making everyone in the room feel that same way, but why did he always seem to be looking at her?

Then something happened to convince her she would be the first teacher shot. The man was motioning with his finger for her to leave her seat by the door. He wanted her to walk up right next to him! Why else would he want her to be directly in front of him except to shoot her?

She walked with measured dread, one step, two, closer. . . .

She looked into his face, carefully. She did not want to stare—just try to see what that face was saying. Then, she felt utter relief.

He did not look back at her. Was it just that he didn't want her by the door, she wondered. She would never find out. His mind was now on something else.

Inconsistently, he let other teachers later sit by the door. It contributed all the more to her feeling that the man was an incoherent crackpot, possibly more dangerous than she had at first feared.

As Eva's mind cleared from the initial shock of being a hostage, she remembered little Kathy in the car. "Mamma will be right back," she recalled telling her. By now many minutes had gone by. Eva turned to the woman. "I've got to get out to that car and get my young daughter!" she explained.

"You aren't going anywhere!" the woman said.

In another ten minutes, Eva was growing desperate. "Please let me go out and get my baby. I'll bring her right in here with me," she pleaded.

But Doris wouldn't trust her adult hostage. "You'll stay right here," she repeated with more irritation. She did not look to David for advice. Apparently, he was content with Doris' decision and said nothing.

Finally, Eva tried a new approach. "I'll stay here," she agreed. "But can someone else go out and get her?" She suggested Christy or Elisabeth, two of her older children in the room.

Still, no positive response.

"How about you getting her then?" Eva tried as a last measure.

Doris surprised her. "Sure, I'll get her," she said somewhat pleasantly. When she returned, Kathy seemed little ruffled by her mother's long absence. "The lady was nice to me," the preschooler offered cheerfully.

After a time the intruder talked about the aberration he had introduced here. He said, almost with a sympathetic tone, "Children are precious. We don't want to hurt them. I'll only shoot the kids with a .22."

Mrs. Petersen wondered about the hypocrisy. "How could he so selfishly place the children under such terrible tension? They feared they might be shot in the next instant or see their closest friend killed or their teacher. For several students even their parents could be killed before their eyes."

Young didn't bring the "precious" talk up again. Hostages never knew whether it was said to gain more sympathy for his own political platform than for the children. By not knowing what the man would do next, the hostages were on even shakier ground. No one knew what was going through his mind.

When the threatening terms of his takeover were fully understood by all present, David made his only long speech of the entire hostage crisis. "I'm the most wanted man in this culture. . . ." He did not hesitate to explain the word "culture."

He turned to the kids. "The government and your teachers are polluting your minds. We're going to get some money . . . " It was difficult to hear what he said next, even by those closest to him. "I've got these papers here I've handed to the teachers. They tell you about my philosophy. You will learn later what we have in mind for you."

Some children thought he said something about sending a letter to President Reagan, but no one dared ask. Everyone had questions, but no one dared ask him anything.

Afterward, David pulled the bomb cart about, not certain exactly where he wanted to place it for maximum surveillance of the thirty by thirty-foot room. Finally, he pulled up a child's desk and leaned on it. Seemingly satisfied with the arrangement, he sat there, sullen, sometimes expressionless, watching every human activity out of the corner of his eye. It was with the tiresome scrutiny of one obliged to duty.

"He looked mean," one child explained, "as if to keep us frightened." The child added, "And he did."

Doris did most of the talking as the afternoon droned on. She mentioned "several stages" to the day's surprises. "We'll get to the others later."

For the next hour, she also became an advocate for the children under siege, realizing as a mother herself the strain the youngsters were under. At one point, she said, "Think of this as an adventure movie. You can tell everyone how much fun you had."

She smiled to lend encouragement as if she believed it would have no more effect on these young minds than that.

If the events of the afternoon appeared disjointed, leading nowhere, something else puzzled many of the adult hostages. David looked extremely relaxed.

Was he growing more confident that his plan would bring the result he sought, whatever it was? Frequently, he agreed to anything which kept the children from moving around too much. He waited calmly for reports from Excell on how negotiations were going.

"Perhaps," Jean thought, "it is just that he is preparing for a long wait—but a long wait for what—the money?" She thought about it. "I knew that no one, not even Congress, was going to raise that much in a week, if ever. I could only ask myself: how long will the children wait? How long before they dart off to the restroom without asking or out the door to their mothers? And if they do, will David start shooting them for just doing what small children naturally do?"

"Above all else," Jack Mitchell thought, "we've got to not let this overwhelm our thinking process."

Finally, he decided, "We've got to minimize the danger in our own minds so we can outlast this guy. But how does he intend on getting out of here? By taking some of the smaller kids hostage—past all the lawmen who'll be after him? This guy doesn't make any sense. We'll just have to take things one minute at a time and try to pretend it's no big deal. Will these little ones have the stamina?"

By now it was after two o'clock. The minutes dragged by, yet what difference did it make anyway? Was time in their favor or against them?

Jean thought of all the children entrusted to her and the other teachers. What would happen if someone said or did something which irritated Young? She didn't want to think about it.

It wouldn't be possible to bear life with the children gone, their little voices stilled. She feared that somehow she might inadvertently cause David to do something resulting in a child being maimed or blinded. The future of this entire community was sitting right here next to her—next to a bomb.

If something went wrong, the children would feel betrayed in following what their teachers told them to do. They would lose their trust in the teachers. These kids were enthusiastic huggers. She had never known children who loved hugging so much. She couldn't bear for them to ever lose trust in their teachers.

To be sure, only a few children fortunate enough to be home that day would escape the long-term psychological damage Jean surmised was already being wrought upon her children. Lucky were those too sick to be at school today. . . .

Why did all these people have to concern themselves with this demented man's irritation threshold anyway? Suddenly, she felt a rage within herself, a rage that this one man held the fate of an entire community in one small flick of his wrist.

What could she do? The stench of the gasoline in the plastic jug reeked across the room. It must be leaking. Jean observed some children looking ill. Was it the odor of gas, or was it the tension that was getting to them? Even now, a girl was vomiting. Not daring to walk to the restroom, she threw up in the sink. Later, another girl threw up in a waste basket rather than risk upsetting her captors. Several others were sobbing softly.

Holding Kathy and Paul close to her, Eva thought of the times she had experienced personal narrow escapes and witnessed them in the lives of others. The fear she felt then was nothing compared to this.

The smell of gasoline was growing worse. Jean asked permission to "air out the room." She received clearance with David's nod of the head to open the two windows. Then she asked about opening the two hallway doors.

Young agreed to these requests, but only on the condition the one door he could not see as well, near the restroom, have tables and chairs barricaded against it. The obstacles allowed easy access into the restroom, but not beyond them into the hallway.

Janel Dayton was ordered to sit by the door and prevent any child from leaving through it. However, David ruled that children could not use the water fountain, even though there was one in the room. "If you drink too much you'll have to go to the bathroom."

Doris pointed out how to avoid getting thirsty. "Wet some tissue paper and place it on your face." Several of the children did so and reported that it seemed to help.

Mrs. Dayton kept careful control of those waiting for the restroom. It helped keep her mind off the feelings that this day was not real.

At one point she noticed that a small boy was eyeing the barricade at close range. Was he going to climb through to the other side?

"You'll have to come back," she commanded the youngster. As she did so, the question struck her, "What am I doing?" All her natural instincts were to escape and take children with her to safety. Yet here she was helping keep them prisoner.

She looked at David. He was still sitting where he could watch her every action and that of every child who neared the restroom side exit. There seemed little she could do now but to comply.

It was clear that David feared, as if it detracted from his power, that one single child would slip away from him.

How could he be so cocksure about his bomb? His was a supreme confidence because he had exploded a prototype of his device earlier in the Arizona desert. The hostages didn't know that, but they could see the look of assurance on his face.

David did not need to talk about it. He already knew what his bomb could do.

In addition to the device on the cart, several teachers thought they heard the man mention other explosives nearby which could be detonated anytime for "effect."

Since no one questioned his bomb-making ability, Young apparently felt it unnecessary to detonate one. He never did show off the blasting caps left in the hallway. They were there if he needed them.

It was most fortunate that none of the hostages directly challenged Young's ability as a bomb expert. He had a great deal more to impress them all with as an explosives expert was to later reveal.

The hostages noted that Young seemed very much at home with his guns. They also sensed the truth: he had handled them almost all his life. At times he seemed to be waiting for someone to challenge him in their use. If anyone did, he would be ready.

Rubble is all that remains of the once-threatening bomb cart. The device's design was intended to destroy the entire south wing of the school. (Dan Dockstader photo, Star Valley Independent.)

By now the members of this unusual little congregation were facing the full reality of their predicament. While it was incredible, unbelievable, it was now seeping in as very, very real. And as the afternoon waned on, there seemed no way out of it.

Teachers noted the children gathered in little groups with heads bowed. "Let's have a prayer. Pass it on," one of Mitchell's sixth graders said.

Allyson Cornia, lean of body but sturdy in spirit, was selected by her twelve-year-old peers to voice a prayer for the group. "Father in Heaven, help us, please help us if the bomb goes off. . . ."

Allyson turned her tawny head to see that the man with the mean look was still there. So was the strong smell of gasoline and the bomb. Somehow, Allyson and the others around her began to realize they should concentrate on being patient. They must make no mistakes which might make the man with the physical show of power unleash it on them. They could only take a deep breath and place their trust on some power outside themselves.

If the Youngs noticed any of these prayers, they said nothing of them. David, who had often written that God exists only in man's mind, seemed little concerned.

Here was the godless versus the godly. Who would win such a diametrically opposed confrontation? It was like no other modern standoff any of the teachers could remember reading about.

Several times during the day Moore would feel a temptation to "take Young on" with a headlock. How dare this self-styled egomaniac do this to these children! Yet, what good would it do to get Young if a single kid got hurt? It went completely against his grain, but Rocky would not upset the intruder again.

Not all of Young's hostages saw the confrontation between him and Moore. Those who did now knew, if they hadn't before, that the man before them was armed and hostile.

For the present, the huddled hostages looked at each other and wondered more than ever about their ultimate fate. Hope had not fled, though it was fading. They had only been here less than an hour.

In the meantime, Excell had telephoned authorities several times in obedience to David's instructions. Police had now taken over the responsibility from the EMTs and cordoned off the school grounds.

As word spread through town, a crowd of anxious parents was slowly building at the edge of the yard entrance.

No guns were seen among the onlookers. There was no way to storm the building without endangering the lives of the hostages. Was waiting outside also dangerous? What was going on inside?

Those in the town hall knew more than anyone else outside the school building, and they lamented their own Niagara of questions. By now every conceivable form of emergency help was being dispatched in the tri-state area. Everyone was busy setting disaster plans in motion.

Kevin Walker could see the telephones were too tied up for him to call local EMTs. He reasoned that using the 911 code might alert the wrong people in the besieged school. He would take the time to notify everyone personally by telephone.

Kevin walked home to call them. He met his wife, Glenna, at the door, but hesitated to share all he knew with her. They had three children in the school building.

Maybe before she found out, Kevin thought, the man could be persuaded to put down his arms, defuse the bomb, and give up. There were times in the universal history of terrorism that it had happened. Weren't would-be suicides sometimes talked out of their senseless plans?

When Glenna did hear her husband summoning EMTs, she thought it might be a mock drill. Being on the emergency team was new to her. She told Kevin, "I don't like them making it so realistic with the children there!"

Later, waiting with the community's populace, she heard on her radio of lawmen being summoned in from all over the West. She realized her husband had been dead right. So, this was all true! If a neighbor hadn't stopped by, Glenna would have been on the way to Kemmerer to take her niece, Jana, for her learner's driver license. In a way it would have been nice to be gone.

"What kind of people would kidnap and threaten someone else's children?" she asked her husband. Now that she knew, he could only put his arm around her.

If the growing crowd had known the awful truth, that the Youngs planned to trigger the bomb anyway, they might have felt more inclined to take their chances right now. They could rush in and end this ordeal without the horror of waiting and not knowing.

Had that happened, with the guns at David's disposal, would violence have erupted before its time? For now, it was probably better that the law authorities hadn't fully scrutinized Young's diaries nor made them public.

In the meantime, the hostages inside had no idea who might be criminal accomplices among the many people near the building. One teacher, hearing a helicopter overhead, wondered if it was piloted by lawmen, news media, or more terrorists. Did the Youngs have confederates waiting to join them?

"I never did dare look out the window," Kam admitted. "I thought there might be people out there ready to shoot anyone who did."

Doris alluded once to having other accomplices at the doors. That might have been true if the Youngs' helpers had not rebelled. It wasn't true, but the hostages had no way of knowing it. They could only imagine the worst.

Part of the horror was that those inside the building did not know precisely who the enemy was. They didn't know his strength. This unknown added greatly to their terror.

With the afternoon school session half gone, the Youngs were, indeed, physically and psychologically in control of their hostages.

List of Hostages

Afternoon Kindergarten

Sam Bennion
Paul Clark
Heather Cory
Linzie Jo Conner
Jodie Eggleston
Jamy Ferrin
Trini Jo Himmerich
Julia Jamison
Joshua Jones
John King
Jody Pope
Bret Taylor
Gina Taylor
Joshua Wiscombe

Grade 1A

Jolene Buckley
Fawna Eastman
Carl Grandy
Nathan Hartley
Hilary Larson
Joni Larson
Travis McKinnon
Jermiah Moore
Emily Murdock
Collin Roberts
Shawn Stahl
Ryan Taylor
Katie Walker

Grade 1B

Shelley Burton
Burton Clark
Jennifer Cory
Billie Jo Hutchinson
Chad Hymas
Brenna McNamara
Kevin Nate
Shiloh Pope
Heather Prows
Jennie Sorensen
Meaghan Thompson
Jeromy Lamb
Jay Metcalfe

Second Grade

Clark Bedell
Nancy Bennion
Cameron Bird
Brandon Brooks
Jennie Buckley
David Burton
Melanie Chadwick

Third Grade

Andy Bagaso
Jamie Buckley
Matthew Buckley
Justin Chadwick
David Clark
Joelle Dana
Ranelle Dana

Second Grade

Michelle Coates
Wade Cornia
Tareesa Covert
Jodi Dayton
Carl John Eggleston
Jason Hartley
Austin Henderson
Jamie Himmerich
Nanette Holden
Chad Madsen
Kellie Miller
Tina Morfeld
Levi Murdock
Karee Thornock
Ryan Thornock
Willie Wathen
Byron Wiscombe

Third Grade

Hyrum Esterholdt
Jenny Ferrin
Cindy Hartley
Billy King
Heather Larson
Joe McNamara
Chad Mitchell
Kristi Moore
Scott Mower
Aaron Roberts
Joey Sweat
Michael Thompson
Karalyn Thornock
Rachel Walker

Fourth Grade

Rusty Birch
Jerry Dayton
Dustin Eastman
Ricky Himmerich
Lana Holden
Adam Hymas
Sandy Hymas
Jeana Jamison
Joe Mackey
Jaime Metcalfe
Monica Morfeld
Jamie Taylor
Jason Thornock
Kimberly Thornock
Stephanie Wiscombe

Fifth Grade

Amy Bagaso
Janaan Bennion
Elisabeth Clark
Shaneil Cornia
BranDee Hess
Jeromy Jamison
Amber Larson
Colton McDermott
Joanna Metcalfe
Brad Shane Nate
Lori Nate
Angie Nostaja
Adam Prows
Justin Sweat
Michael Taylor
Leigh Ann Thornock
Travis Walker

Sixth Grade

Kent Cassels
Christy Clark
Tammy Coates
Allyson Cornia
Drew Cornia
Celeste Excell
Brenda Hartley
Brandi Himmerich
Paul Lazcanotegui
Kimberly Madsen
Bobbie Jo Miller
Brian Nate
Greg Nate
Cameron Roberts
Heidi Roberts
Anna Stewart
Kyle Thornock
Kamron Wixom

Others

Eva Clark, parent
Kathy Clark, preschooler
Sandy Gonzales, UPS driver
Cynthia Cowden, teacher candidate
Kris Kasper, student teacher
Gayle Chadwick, media aide
Verlene Bennion, teacher's aide
Pat Bennion, substitute teacher
Tina Cook, secretary

Teachers

Janel Dayton
Kim Kasper
John Miller
Jack Mitchell
Jean Mitchell
Rocky Moore
Gloria Mower
Carol Petersen
Kliss Sparks
Max Excell, Principal

Cokeville Elementary Students absent May 16:

Chris King, first grade
Vern Setser, third grade
Julie Anderson, fourth grade
Wendy Bartschi, second grade
Mandy Taylor, third grade
LeaKae Roberts, fourth grade

Morning Kindergarten students:

Josh Anderson
Amanda Birch
Candice Bird
Zack Bird
Alex Dayton
Jessica Dayton
Chris Esterholdt
Mindi Hymas
Sandra Metcalfe
Julie McKinnon
Ben Pieper
Brittany Swenson
James Thompson
Krista Thornock
Phillip Stoker
Dain John
Jared Sweat
Regina Tso

The Bomb is Real

"There is absolutely nothing any mortal being can do. We are utterly helpless. Even if we stormed the man he could shoot a child or explode the bomb as he falls down."
—Sixth grade teacher Jack Mitchell

When Young placed his bomb among huddled children, the adults with them struggled against impending panic. They must think this dilemma through.

First, they anguished over their own gullibility. How could they have been so trusting as to bring the children in here and place them all at the crazed man's mercy? On the other hand what was there in anyone's past experience to cause suspicion?

Certainly they would be more wary in the future—if there was a future.

Another factor, almost humorous if it were not so utterly hopeless, focused on the money. Young said he wanted two million dollars for each child—this in a town that didn't even have a bank!

Exactly how much total money, at two million dollars each, would it take to satisfy the hostage-takers and win the children's release?

Newspapers reported the Youngs wanted 300 million dollars. However, this was a rough estimate based on 150 children. How many precisely were there?

At one time, Young had ordered teachers to take a count of their students, adding it up so swiftly in his head that hostages were amazed at his mathematical acumen. Yet, Young never mentioned to Principal Excell any final figure demanded for ransom. It appeared the count

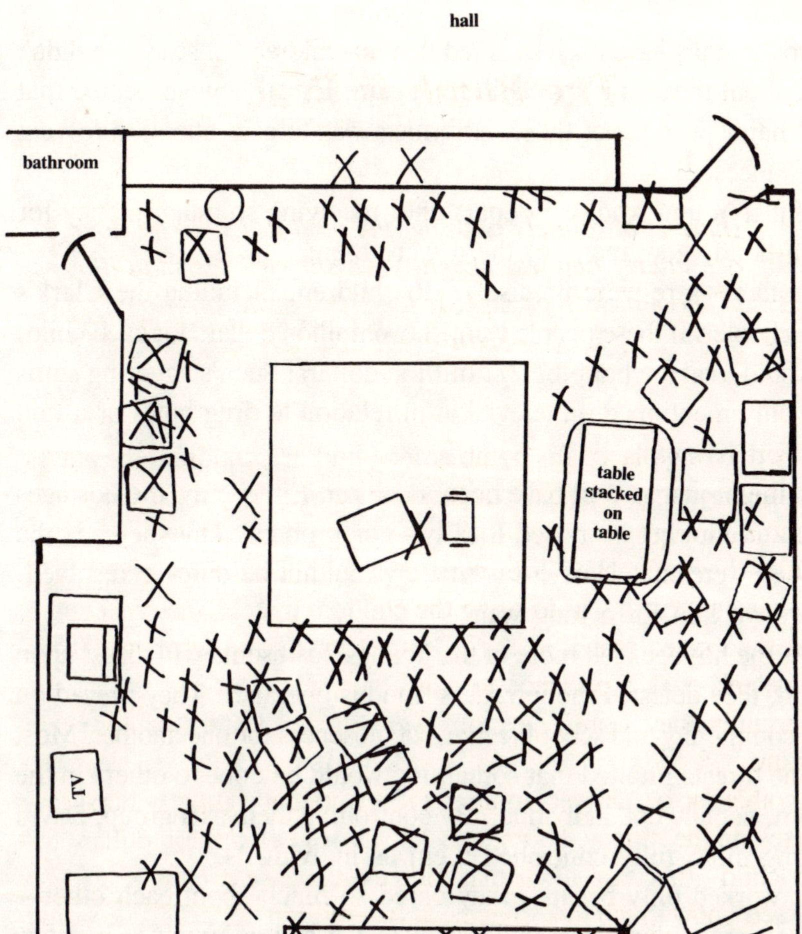

Classroom designed for 35 students became a frightening prison for 154 hostages. With arms and legs overlapping, the hostages waited out the diabolical plot of David Young, seven years in the planning. Each X represents a hostage. David Young is shown in the large square. (Drawn to scale)

was to know if any children escaped, not for any amassing of money at all.

Young must have been satisfied that no children got away. He didn't talk about the number of children again. Excell now suspected that the major purpose of these extremists was to gain attention to vent grievances.

But if Young wouldn't depart until receiving so much money for each child, how many of them were there?

In fact, there were precisely 136 children, including the Clark's preschooler. If these people wanted two million dollars for each child, it would total a whopping 272 million dollars! Such staggering sums are only mentioned on television in relation to drug busts or a raid on Fort Knox.

It might just as well have been a trillion. Either way, the hostages knew it couldn't be raised locally—nor probably anywhere. If the money were mandatory, this matter wouldn't be quickly resolved. They were in for a long wait.

As the hostages felt more of the Youngs' loathsome will thrust upon them, they detested the intruders' modus operandi. They preyed on the community and school feelings of closeness for one another. Most of the threats implied that something would be done to others in the room, not any one individual. By controlling them as a group, David Young more fully controlled them as individuals.

It worked only because they cared so much about each other—and in particular, these children who yet had so much to live for.

This was a community which wanted to trust and love and find the best in other people. Hating only hurt. It wouldn't help their cause to hate the man who held this unfair advantage over them.

While David Young considered their caring about each other a wholesale weakness to be exploited, how should they feel about him or his wife? Many took the attitude they would try to avoid wasting any animosity on him at all. They would merely try to survive. In the meantime, they would try to put their feelings about these interlopers on hold.

But the situation was far worse than any of the victims' initially optimistic appraisals. Princess told authorities at the town hall that her father talked of more than the ten days wait mentioned to Excell. She said David was prepared to "wait thirty days if necessary for his demands to be met."

In addition, Young had apparently taken some notes while working in Cokeville about the various family members, such as who, belonged to whom, friends who wouldn't want each other harmed. That was sinister enough in itself. Worst of all, the hostages had no inclination of Young's diabolical writings to enter a reincarnated "Brave New World" through the portals of death, taking them with him.

If they had understood this, many of the adult hostages would have felt little hope of ever emerging alive.

Looking back on it, survivor Jean Mitchell said she was optimistic about escaping, but "I was simply naive about it then. I had no idea, nor did anyone else, what the two had in mind for us. If he only wanted the money, the bomb would suffice just by looking like a bomb. It didn't have to be the real thing."

A boy told his classmates in childhood faith, "Do you think our Heavenly Father would let us all die?" A teacher said she "thought they could outlast the two." Much of this optimism was typical of life in Cokeville. Residents faced many challenges with that kind of positive attitude. After barely eluding a rodeo bull, a local cowboy might say, "Aw, he missed me a mile."

It was fortunate that most of the hostages had no idea of the real odds in this day of crisis. They did not fully know until later how potentially deadly their trial by terror had been because they did not know of David's plans for them.

On one occasion, he talked of "what we'll do when we get the money. . . ." The hostages who heard this thought he meant David and Doris. They did not connect it to the children.

The crowded prisoners faced a most severe challenge even with the little they did know. The facts they had were terrible enough. They knew the guns were real. They didn't dare doubt the bomb could be quickly detonated, and David had already proven he had a hair-trigger temper.

For Principal Excell, it all presented a special problem. He must report to the Youngs on a regular basis about how the negotiations with authorities were going. What could he say now to stall these people? How long would they accept excuses? Could he continually placate the pair enough to keep them from erupting into a violent rage—further endangering the children? Certainly they wouldn't be here at all if they were mentally stable!

Max Excell, principal of Cokeville Elementary School, just after bomb explosion. (Tim Kelly photo courtesy of Salt Lake Tribune)

Nothing in Excell's years of administrative training or on-the-job experience had even remotely prepared him for anything like this. It was time for a cool, steady head.

It was not a bad dream you could just awaken from; it was happening in real life. One of the toughest facts of all was beginning to sink in: while he felt an intense fury at what the two "revolutionists" were doing to the children, he must not show any of those negative feelings. The Youngs might take it out on the children.

He would have to suppress the desire to grab one of the guns in the classroom and turn it on the intruders. Even thinking about killing them was too risky to contemplate any further.

He was trapped physically and psychologically. He must not allow even the muscles on his face to betray any of his feelings. At the same time he must display visible courage. The children were looking to him for an example of how they themselves should behave, and to a certain extent, every teacher as well. The personal challenge of the situation loomed almost as staggering as the demanded ransom money.

Even if adults did not ruffle the Youngs, how could the children avoid doing it? Within the hearing of fifth grader Amy Bagaso, Young said, "Don't move or pull any tricks. If you do, we'll kill you."

Each child feared doing something wrong which might harm a friend. What little thing might cause an act of senseless shooting?

In their homes and in the school classroom most felt a security in knowing what they could and could not do. Now the rules of correct behavior had changed. No one was certain what the Youngs might decide constituted a shootable offense. Young was both judge and jury and firing squad.

The teachers also wondered what it might take to cause a reprisal against the person closest to the man with the guns.

In time, some rules did seem to emerge. They also changed with his whims. Were they allowed to talk freely? Would David's wrath be unleashed if a hostage inadvertently said the wrong thing? Some matters had to be discussed to keep the children from bothering the hostage-takers. Confusion reigned.

To be sure, the children had been thoroughly taught at school to be obedient, but what were they supposed to obey— and whom?

At one point several children told Doris they had a headache. Could she do something about it? Doris knew just what to do. She stood in the center of the room. "Now listen, children," she said in a louder-than-usual voice, "just don't think about it any more."

That was it. Ordering the children to behave for the Youngs' selfish purposes particularly rankled Jean. How could these pompous people come in and "legislate" what small grade schoolers could feel and do?

Jean knew that as soon as the numbness and shock wore off, the youngsters would no longer sit there stacked like sheep in a truck. They were yet-developing souls with feelings, not mere robots to be controlled by pushing a button. How much more so with the threat of death at their elbows—for who knew how long?

Meanwhile the man sat there as if on a throne, refusing to talk about anything, most particularly anything involving common sense.

If there was one thing Jean and the other teachers had taught the students, it was to have open minds. How could a grown-up in their midst declare himself omnipotent? Freedom was only a word now. How she missed it!

She looked over the children's little arms and legs overlapping almost from wall to wall. She worried about those pent-up emotions come the dismissal bells at 3:25. They had always signalled time to go home.

What about nightfall when the expected presence of mother and father always offered soothing solace from the day's tribulations? Those childish emotions might explode by then even if the bomb hadn't.

It was a concern whether the teachers could keep their own feelings under control forever. It was after 2 p.m. How much longer could everyone walk this man's narrow line?

At one point David turned to Jack Mitchell and asked if a particular sixth grader who was wandering too close to Young might be the kind to cause trouble later. It was as if Young felt a paranoid personal threat. Teachers thought it almost laughable, if it weren't so serious, that a small boy could threaten Young's delicate tolerance threshold. Jack promised Young the boy would not misbehave.

Young was not completely satisfied. "He'd better not." It was said with a casual ugliness that ate into the soul, Jack thought.

As 2:15 neared, several teachers could see that many of the children were beginning to feel more deeply traumatized. Several of the tougher kids who hadn't shown fear in their eyes before were struggling with the viselike predicament. Others could force a smile no longer.

Teachers had never imagined that their students would be required to undergo such prolonged anguish as this. Not only were their cheerful countenances gone, but teachers worried the children might lose their very will to try smiling again.

If that happened they could never forgive this man for that.

These were tough kids who didn't break easily, teachers told themselves. It all seemed endless. What sort of toll was it taking on the children's once optimistic spirits? The combination of this man and the clock ticked away their hard-won pride and confidence in themselves—the pride and confidence these same teachers had worked so hard over the years to instill.

Some children reacted incongruously to the crisis, at times making up mock television scenarios about how they would emerge triumphantly. At least the latter was a brave front to be applauded as long as the Youngs didn't become provoked with it.

Students moved around aimlessly, trying to find something to occupy time. That was all they had. The question of "how long" was too much to contemplate. Young, sitting there sphinxlike, would say no more on the subject.

Mitchell made it clear how much depended on the older children holding up. He looked into the faces of the sixth graders. He saw in their eyes that they were still the plucky kids he had known during all of his teaching years here.

"No one asked for this thing that's happened to us today, but let's be an example to all the others. You are the oldest students. We need you to be brave! We all feel fear here." He hesitated. "For awhile . . . we must not show it. I'm counting on you. I know you can do it." Then they heard a loud whisper from the side. It was Rocky. "That's right kids! You can do it!"

The twelve-year-olds needed to think about it only for a few seconds. They circulated quietly from one young child to the next, smiling, giving them a little tap on the back, telling themselves they would get out of this somehow and then trying to convince the others of it.

The two teachers nodded at each other. These were their kids. They were not going to be intimidated by the bomb; they would just respect the fact it could kill all of them instantaneously.

Some of the smaller children stopped crying.

"We'll get out of this somehow." Eva heard the sixth graders say. The words sounded full of encouragement. The innocent confidence and uncomplicated faith of a child was in itself a wonderful thing. Eva told herself she must replace the awful fear she felt with some of the children's optimism.

For a time, the heartened children summoned up a sparkle in their eyes. Their renewed spirits brightened the faces of teachers.

Some found new reason to be less than optimistic. When Doris told the children "we will do nothing to hurt you," children noticed that the man looked annoyed at her. Apparently he didn't agree.

Jack could hold back his feelings no longer. He stepped forward. "We've got to get the children out of here. We'll have them out by 4 p.m.!"

Young's violent reaction came swiftly. Mitchell watched in horror as Young made a gesture toward the gun in his belt. It was obvious he could do so instantly and still set off the bomb with his other hand.

Jack sat down. As he did so, Jean noticed the look of anger subside on David's face. Her fourth grade son Chad, sitting nearby, grabbed at his mother. Jean felt both deep agony and relief in his hug. The intensity of her son's anguish penetrated her inner depths like an arrow. Why did the pair have to put these children through this?

Any hope of reasoning with the man had fled. The man understood only physical force. What could anyone present do to combat it?

Viewing the entire situation with analytical actuality, Jack concluded in his thoughts: "There is absolutely nothing any mortal can do. We are utterly helpless. Even if we stormed the man, he could shoot a child or explode the bomb as he falls down."

Then something else happened to plummet the hostages' already sinking morale. Doris began telling David every word that police were saying outside the building.

She had commandeered an EMT radio from another room. She asked Jack how to use it, but he played dumb. Being a ham radio operator, Mitchell knew full well how to operate an EMT radio. But he didn't intend to show Doris how to do it. Determinedly, Doris managed to tune into the police channel anyway. She was listening to every stratagem police even now discussed outside the school.

She also heard Wyoming Highway Patrolman Brad Anderson report to the town hall that he had set up a command post where he could look down the school's south hallway from a Main Street back yard.

A smug feeling might have passed through David's being. From the beginning, Young had told Excell that "local lawmen are nothing." He himself had been a cop. It would be difficult to put anything over on him.

The hostages did manage one minuscule victory. It accomplished absolutely nothing to change the prisonlike drama they found themselves in, yet it allowed a shred of hope to beleaguered souls searching for any improvement in their odds—any improvement, however slight.

When Excell next returned, Jack motioned him over. "Tell the police by telephone to get off the radio! They'll have to communicate some other way. These people can hear everything they're saying outside."

A few minutes later, the channel was silent. Doris now had nothing to report to David about the police. Teachers looked at one another. For a long time they had no reason to smile. Now for brief seconds, they did.

Many of the teachers tried to look blankly at Young despite the turmoil in their hearts. It would not be wise to reveal any of their thoughts. For one thing, there was no way of knowing precisely what went on behind those dark, brooding eyes, the morose expression. It was better not to know. The only way to ensure calm was to remain completely inconspicuous and draw no attention.

Indeed, Carol Petersen realized she dreaded any repeat confrontation. To guarantee it, she dared not move.

Janel Dayton felt it would be dangerous to look away from her "barricade assignment" by the restroom.

Earlier warned with a gun to stay out of the way, the usually effervescent Rocky Moore knew it would be best if he did nothing further to antagonize David. It was that way with all the hostages.

One didn't even know for certain if it was acceptable to breath some fresh air by the window. There might be snipers out there waiting to shoot anyone looking longingly through the open panes.

For a time the wall clock ticked away unnoticed. It couldn't be seen from all parts of the room. It seemed to Jean that from where she sat the hands loomed larger than ever.

Nearly 2:30. What was going on outside? From the growing concern among townspeople came a rumor bringing, if nothing else, a feeling of moral support from other communities. Word was received that certain citizens in nearby Montpelier and Randolph had somehow raised almost two million dollars.

It was not the asked-for total amount. Yet, it might persuade the "bombers" to take the money and leave the children behind. Whether the rumor was true or not, it evoked a feeling of closeness with those other communities. People who didn't even know the Cokeville kids' first names were trying to gather money in their behalf.

In the end, it did no material good, "But," said one mother, "it buoyed our spirits to hear other people cared. We were not alone in this outrage."

Back inside the school, there was yet one person not trapped in room four. Several times custodian Rentfro had stepped from the kitchen to ask what the hallway commotion was about. Twice he had looked into the eyes of a woman who seemed to be ushering him away. He had even looked inside the room and been told to "forget it." Going back to his work, Rentfro thought it all strange, but then he dismissed it as a mock drill of some sort.

He questioned why the telephone kept ringing, with no one answering.

Now he saw the principal hurrying toward the school office. He stepped out into the hallway. "Delbert!" Excell exclaimed. "We're all being held hostage in Mrs. Mitchell's room. Get over to the town hall while you can. Tell them to be sure they keep everyone away from the school building! We can't risk anyone trying to get in."

Rentfro looked at his friend and next-door neighbor quizzically. "You're joking!" But there was something heavily etched on Excell's face which told him his boss was deadly serious.

The custodian hurried out of the building, found no one stopping him, and ran to Town Hall. There he relayed his boss's message, giving lawmen a description of the Youngs and their location in the building.

Then he had a strange feeling. He almost wished he was inside the room with his daily pals, the kids. He felt a horrible frustration not knowing what was happening to them.

As the afternoon wore on, the high school track team, competing in a regional meet at Casper, Wyoming, was notified of the crisis. "We had no more heart to do anything but finish up quickly and get home," one athlete said. "Our brothers and sisters were in that school." It was a silent bus during the seven-hour drive back to Cokeville. "I think others did as I did. They prayed, then they prayed again," another student commented.

On this particular day the senior civics class was taking a tour of Utah's Point-of-the-Mountain Prison south of Salt Lake City. As the class talked with prisoners and heard metal doors clank shut,

Andra Birch remarked she would "be glad to get back to Cokeville where I didn't have to think about problems with crime and criminals." When she arrived home, she learned her little brother was one of those being held hostage in his own school.

By now rumors were flying. Erroneous information was to have one of the most psychologically damaging impacts of the early afternoon. While some radio newsmen like Ken Rand and Robin Spurling kept listeners informed with eyewitness accounts just outside the school, others tried to guess what was going on. Some guessed badly.

Before the track team left Casper, they were informed on the air waves that grade school principal Excell had been killed. Max Excell's son, working in Idaho, was told the same thing. Although threatened with his own death, and that of his pupils, Max was still very much alive. He was only looking into the face of death with 153 others.

Time. Was it an ally or an enemy? The intruder wasn't showing any sign of giving up. He looked no different than when he walked in. The clock ticked toward 2:45.

Time. The school bells—they have to be disconnected! Jean thought, the bell going off always signalled the children it was time to go home, and now it would simply remind them they couldn't. The younger ones would not understand. They had been here all afternoon in this prison, and they would not understand there was no end to the pain. They would try to walk out on it—and David Young. It was no longer pain. It was madness. There was no time to think about that. The bells. . . .

Jean finally managed to flag Jack's attention. Jack asked for permission to leave. David studied him, then voiced no opposition. By now he did not concern himself about anyone returning. Didn't everyone know his rules?

Rushing to Tina's office, Jack located the switch and turned the bell off. He was back so quickly it seemed too easy for such a vital accomplishment. "It's done," he told his wife.

Eva looked at the clock. Nearly 3 p.m. How much longer could her brood of six children, including little Kathy, keep their emotions under a blanket of pretense that nothing was wrong? What would Lowell think when she did not arrive home soon with the groceries? They had much work to do. Yet thinking of that now was trivial. There were worse things to think of.

Why had it seemed there was once enough room here? The children had no place to put their feet except in someone's way.

It wasn't long before one boy began to quarrel over who would have the "funnest toys." He grabbed another boy's construction block. Teachers and older students looked on anxiously. All knew the children were just being children. That was normal. However, these were hardly normal times.

Townspeople outside inevitably began assessing their community's seeming capitulation. Wasn't this the town with unique grit and special self-reliance? Why weren't they doing anything to halt this intimidation and traumatizing of their children?

They wanted the lawmen to just let them look inside the classroom to see what was happening. They were told one word. Wait. Wasn't that the word sent by the hostages themselves through Excell and Rentfro? "Wait."

Agony, then more agony. Nothing was too much for them to handle. There must be some way they could help.

"Yes," a sheriff's deputy answered. "Wait . . . wait."

The same thing struck those inside. Maybe someone could try to do something. Anything, even accidentally tripping over a child's leg, could be misconstrued as a signal to set off the bomb. No one was willing to take on the burden of having a child killed or maimed for life. Difficult as it was, waiting was the most heroic thing anyone could do. It was, thought, Jack the only thing to do.

Eva told herself that when there is nothing a person can do, it's a special time to rely on God. If there was ever a time when— for all of this community's self-reliance, it needed help—this was it.

This was a test to see how they would humble themselves and admit they couldn't do it by themselves.

In the meantime, the hostages noted that the ever-alert David never relented from a watchful surveillance over his captive kingdom. Those hawklike eyes missed almost nothing.

He personally monitored everything with the same mathematical precision with which he earlier added up the number of hostages teachers gave him. He, David Young, was very much in charge. He didn't have to tell the hostages anymore. They knew it.

Over to one side, John Miller watched for any change in the afternoon's incredible fortunes. So did Gloria Mower, who might have escaped so easily earlier, and media aide Gayle Chadwick. They could be grateful no one had done anything to trigger the bomb. How much longer would they have to wonder if everyone in the room lived or died?

Jay Metcalfe was only seven years old. His world was one of simplicity. He did not understand all this strangeness going on around him. The boy could no longer fight quiet tears. Doris handed him a tissue to daub at his wet cheeks.

Some teachers said Doris conducted herself like a social director. She made certain things ran smoothly. One decision she seemed to have trouble making was whether to wear her glasses. When she didn't, she wasn't sure where to place them. At times she seemed like a grandmother who shouldn't be here.

In the interim, job-applicant Cowden became convinced that if she and the children survived, she wanted to work here with them. She felt an intense yearning to help these youngsters overcome and laugh and grow. She wanted to help them learn and gain confidence.

"I loved the children for their determination to make the best of their circumstances. They wanted to do what their teachers told them. I fell in love with them," Cowden said.

Several children near her again began to pray. She held their hands and prayed with them. The young ones pleaded, "We are doing our best; we've done all we can do. Dear God, we need some help. . . ."

They haven't given up hope, she thought. "Neither can I."

It was a day to forget, but Jeremiah Moore remembered it was his birthday. Permission was asked to sing "Happy Birthday" to him. David not only allowed it, but he and his wife joined half-heartedly in singing part of the song.

The settling effect of the music brought approval from David, and he allowed other songs. Kliss Sparks stood up to lead them. She called enthusiastically over to John Miller. "Which ones do you suggest?"

Thinking of the smaller children, Miller offered, "I Have a Dog Named Boo" and "Teddy Bear's Picnic."

"If you go into the woods today you better go in disguise, . . . because every bear who ever was there will be there today for the picnic . . . " Some of the grown-up boys didn't feel like singing "baby" songs. But if it was helping the youngsters, then singing "baby" songs was the very least they could do.

The singing seemed to relax the children. For several teachers it was difficult to force out the words, but for several precious minutes some of the smaller children almost forgot why they were there.

When some children remembered, their zeal for singing eroded. It was fun for a few minutes, but it didn't fit. It didn't make any of the anxiety really go away.

After the singing, sixth grader Greg Nate realized his parents were out of town. He didn't even know if they would be able to find him if he got hurt. "They'll find out somehow," his cousin Brian Nate, another sixth grader, assured him.

"What if I get killed?" another youngster wanted to know. "Your parents will find out then, too," a young voice answered.

There was too much time to think about what could happen. Teachers couldn't keep the children too occupied to think about reality forever. It was inevitable that they would pause for a second and then begin to think again. . . .

3 p.m. The children needed something more to do. They talked more loudly. They began to wander. They sought release for their spirits too long bridled.

Jack watched some push steadily toward Young's desk.

David stared at them, then at the teachers. Young made a motion to clear the kids away.

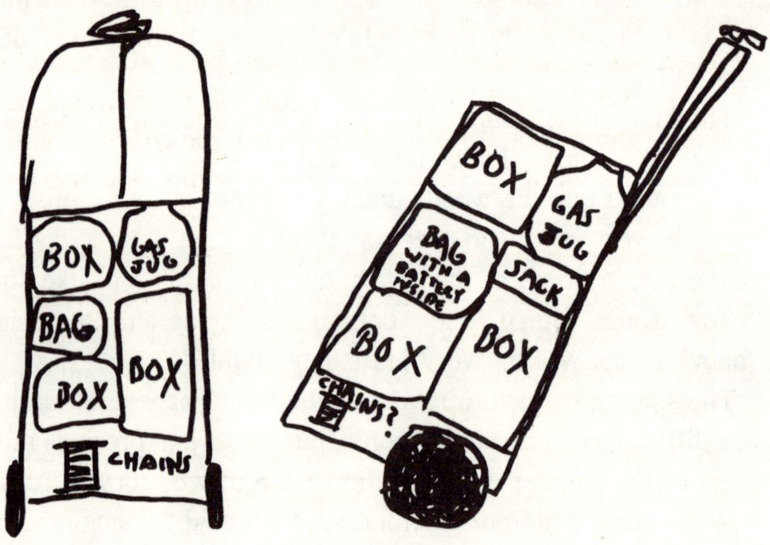

Child's-eye view of the bomb which threatened his life. It could have ended it. (Drawing by Kamron Wixom)

Jack knew he must find some way to keep the area around Young and the bomb cleared, not only for now, but once and for all. He had an idea. From the nearest desk he took some masking tape. He taped off what he told the children was a "magic square." Working quickly to keep the children away, he left a wide berth around David and his grocery cart.

"Don't go across this line!" Jack told the children. "If you do, you're out of the game!"

The forbidden area was roughly ten feet square in the south-central sector of the room. This zone would figure prominently later in investigating the events of the horror-filled day. For now, it was a place you simply stayed away from even if it did make an already crowded room much worse.

Older children tabbed it the "Line of Death." Younger ones were warned not to go near it. All of them now stayed behind the tape. Young looked satisfied with the arrrangement.

Here, too, was temporary relief among the rising and falling tensions for everyone in the room.

When wadded tissues from tear-streaked faces were tossed inside Young's newly-created "forbidden" zone, one teacher kept busy for a time cleaning them up. It might appear to be condescending, but she wasn't doing it for the man with the bomb. She was doing it for the children.

Kamron tired of the construction blocks in the center of the room. He and Brenda Hartley "built tanks to cross an imaginary line of death and get the bad guys." Seeing a group of their classmates gathered around Doris, he said instead, "C'mon, Brenda, let's go see what's going on over there."

Tired, and trying to settle into a normal routine, the children were asking some practical questions. One of the boys said he felt hungry. The group queried Doris about food.

"Don't worry," she responded almost sympathetically. "When the time comes, we'll send out for it."

"How long will we be here, anyway?" asked twelve-year-old Drew Cornia. The question, as usual with Drew, had something of an intellectual ring to it.

"Ten days. Maybe more."

The boy paused. Then finding his sense of humor, he said, "If you're going to hold us here ten days, I hope you brought us some toothbrushes."

"I hadn't considered that," Doris said with a trace of a smile.

The conversation was so congenial and friendly at this point, almost reaching comic relief, that some of the children wondered if the ugly business were finished. Could they go home now? Doris issued them a warning.

"Don't try to go anywhere unless we tell you!"

Brenda wandered off with one of the girls. Kam noticed a tray of magnets on a table near the door and busied himself with them.

By now, Young was growing concerned a child might sneak out the north doorway to the hall. Jack Mitchell was assigned to guard that door. He might as well get comfortable. He slipped his shoes off and sat on the floor of the opening with his feet propped up on the door frame. He might as well settle in for a long wait; they might be here forever.

The stress dissipated at times, but it reached new heights when Young decided the room was too warm. He determined to remove his jacket and his sweater even though it required lifting the same wrist with the shoelace trigger.

It was a moment of agony for the children, especially as they watched the man pull his sleeve down to the shoelace.

At one precarious point Young seemed "stuck." His wife assisted. Some said they thought they saw David detach the trigger from his wrist—and rapidly snatch it up again. Others said David merely pulled his sweater on top of the trigger without untying it. In any event, he kept twitching his wrist. Children watching held their breath.

"I could not hear anyone breathing," Kam Wixom said. "It was as if we had turned to statues. We didn't dare do anything until he quit moving his wrist around."

When the garment was finally peeled to the wrist where Young let it stay, only then did some children feel it was safe to resume breathing again.

Not all of the children felt comfortable afterward. A girl began crying. A classmate next to her suggested she think of it as "just another practice drill like the ones we do every week." His reassuring tone seemed to comfort her. Within minutes she regained her composure.

Several times as late afternoon wore on, David showed marked signs of confusion. All along, teachers feared the man's instability where he might set off the bomb by mistake almost as much as on purpose.

Young became boastful. He gloated to Excell, "People pay attention when you're holding elementary school children."

It became more difficult than ever to determine the mood Young was in. Excell tried to explain to him that there was an epileptic boy among the hostages who might require medicine.

Young then told Excell to order a doctor to come into the room. Since there was none in Cokeville, the word went out to locate one. Young never asked about the doctor later at all. If he had, would the physician be allowed to enter and leave without adding to the hostage total? The group never did find out.

When it was discovered a ten-year-old diabetic hadn't taken his insulin, a teacher suggested, "why don't you just let him go?"

Young answered, "If we do, we'll need two twenty-year-olds to take his place." It seemed to several bystanders that he answered with some slight show of sympathy, "I understand. I'm a diabetic myself."

He was telling the truth. Young's diabetic supplies were in the hallway with a stack of firearms. He had taken his insulin that morning. He now had nothing to fear about his condition. He would just take another injection again that evening. Investigators would later discover many other things about Young's medical condition.

Was the tension beginning to overwhelm the man with the bomb? Was that in the hostages' favor or against it? While it was understood that teachers must return or forfeit a life fourth grade teacher Kliss Sparks asked if she could go in the library to get more books for the children.

"You can go," he said more menacingly than usual, "but if you don't come back, one of these kids is going to die."

Kliss, who had asked calmly enough, thought Young was becoming more oppressive. Previously, he simply nodded his head at similar requests. She left and quickly returned with books and projects to help keep the youngsters' apprehension level down.

At one point, Young glowered at a child approaching too closely. When there were no arguments against his rulings and judgments, the ruffled Young relaxed again.

He lapsed into a more lenient mood. A little girl sitting near Carol Petersen had a sore throat. Jack Mitchell was allowed to go to his room and get some throat lozenges for her. Earlier, Jack had not been allowed to look for the EMT radio Doris wanted.

No one stopped to reflect upon it at the time, but a frequent factor in such hostage situations, often described by lawmen, is for individuals to attempt to curry favor of those in power. The purpose, of course, is a promise of special treatment. There was none of that here now. In fact the opposite seemed to be in effect.

High school music teacher Miller, who had left his class "just long enough to borrow a movie projector," turned to Tina Cook. "If someone has to go with them when they try to leave the school, it might as well be me. I don't have any children."

Senior citizen Verlene Bennion, always thinking of the children, suggested if someone must die to appease their captors, "It should be me. I'm the oldest here and have lived a full life. The children have too much to live for. Maybe we can find some way to persuade the man to let these little ones go. . . ."

Mrs. Clark, earlier noting the ways a lone hostage might elude the captors, concluded that everyone seemed to have entirely rejected the idea of individual escape.

It's got to be all of us. It won't do any good for one to get away . . . not unless every one of us here can make it out alive, Eva thought.

During the later afternoon, she noticed more heads bowed. The man who did not believe in prayer continued to pay no attention. If Young did notice any prayers, he must have thought them to be no impediment to his purposes.

Outside police were finding it more difficult to restrain frantic parents from pushing too far onto the school grounds.

"We've got to see what is going on in there," a parent said.

"We're trying to find out ourselves," a sheriff's deputy responded. "We'll let you know as soon as we know. For now, do you want to be the cause of some child being killed?"

That cold question caused some mothers to sob in their husband's arms.

During this time, Gwen Petersen had received a call from her married daughter, Cheryl, who lived on the opposite end of the valley. "My three girls are being held hostage at the school! We've got to get down there!"

Gwen had never heard such anxiety in her daughter's voice. Only when she heard a radio announcer describe the grimness of the matter as she looked into the school yard did Gwen realize this was not just a "few transient druggies after spending money."

Arriving at the school, Cheryl was so anxious to find out what was going on she hadn't taken time to put on her shoes. What she saw was lawmen moving around, "crouched down" in an apparent effort to avoid being seen from inside the two small classroom windows.

"I had three granddaughters in there," Mrs. Petersen said. "Now all we could do was muster the faith they would eventually get out in one piece."

As a correspondent for several regional newspapers, Gwen could still not get a grasp of the situation. What kind of story was she going to be writing here? Until she knew, patience—and faith. It was what she had always taught in her early morning weekday religion classes.

Elsewhere, a father had a different solution. He could restrain himself no longer. "I'm going in!" he shouted at state highway patrolman Brad Anderson.

Anderson warned him to get back behind the police cordon. "Oh, no you're not! You're not going across this line."

"But I've got a son in there!"

"So do a lot of other people."

"How long will I have to wait?"

"No one knows," Anderson retorted honestly. "How can anyone know?" He hunched his shoulders.

But the man was not satisfied. "I'm going in!"

Later, he did just that. Police officers temporarily mistook him for David Young. The father found himself looking down the barrel of Patrolman Anderson's service weapon.

Patrolman Anderson hadn't brought his bulletproof vest with him. It was at home, half a mile away. Yet, he couldn't leave his vigil on the school yard. Seeing a neighbor, Anderson asked him to rush home and "tell my wife I need my vest."

It wasn't a wife's everyday request. But within minutes Kayleen Anderson had brought her husband the bulletproof vest. Only then did she realize the life and death drama occurring at the school and with her husband.

Josh! she remembered. He could have been in there!

Earlier her six-year-old son, a morning kindergartner, asked if he could return to the school. He had left a toy there from his "Show and Tell." It was his little brother's. Now Jeremy wanted it.

"If I don't go now," Josh told his mother, "we'll have to wait until Monday. I can go there at one o'clock when they get back from lunch." The boy could be persuasive.

She had allowed him to go the school to retrieve things on other occasions. This time she simply told him "No."

She wondered to herself why she had been so adamant, but for the time being she forgot all about school.

As 3:10 came and went, Jean tried to clear her mind. A new problem loomed. The children were running out of coloring book pages at a time when they needed to be busy more than ever. Jean asked permission to leave "just to make copies on the machine in the faculty room," she said. Young granted the request.

"You'll be back," Doris reminded her. "You have too much to lose."

Jean didn't want to give even the slightest impression she would try to escape. She knew both David and Doris were keeping track of emotional family attachments. Besides all the students, she had her husband and son back there. The last thing in the world she wanted to do was be tardy in returning.

Yet she was. When she reached the copier she realized it had been off for two hours. It would require four minutes to warm up. Four minutes—an eternity before the green light went on! She could only hope the Youngs wouldn't notice how long she was gone. Battling panic, she knelt down. How could a person feel so helpless?

What else can we do? she pleaded from the sincerity of her soul. We've tried everything! Please help the children to do what we cannot do for them. She felt better as she released the terrible anguish of the long afternoon.

When Jean rushed back into the room, she felt David's eyes fastened on her.

He seemed even more nervous than ever now. The calm exterior he had exhibited during the last two hours was crumbling. It seemed to Jean that Young was becoming "dangerously restless." She looked at his wrist. The shoelace was in place—for now.

It was 3:10. Jean felt better as she saw the children busy with several new projects.

Noting the children's growing restlessness, Jack and student teacher Kris Kasper had been allotted time to bring a television set from the media center. A crowd of children, particularly the little ones, clamored eagerly in front of it. They began watching a cartoon called "Transformers."

A young fan explained, "Cars turned into robots, then into animals and different things. Each of the characters makes war with the others. They have explosions and a big shootout."

Somehow the children became engrossed in the program without connecting it to their own threatened violence. Several became so absorbed they settled down on the floor to better see the action. Travis explained philosophically, "Hollywood explosions don't hurt anyone."

''A relative calm had developed about a program of guns and killing,'' one teacher said in amazement. ''But as long as it was make believe and it kept the children occupied, we felt a calming effect ourselves.'' For a short time peace reigned.

A number of children were to later talk of a most unusual phenomenon, an event not fully explainable in mortal terms—yet it was credited with saving their lives. They testified of receiving a "special message" that the bomb would go off before much longer—but incredibly enough—they and other hostages would not die if certain instructions were carefully followed.

These experiences, the children later stated with sobering intensity, were to have a most profound bearing on what happened in the next fifteen minutes. They were credited by the children as having a direct effect on what happened not only in the next few minutes, but for the remainder of their lives.

Travis seemed suddenly determined, for some reason, to leave his friends in the northwest corner of the room to talk with his two sisters over in the southeast corner. To get there he had to pass by both hostage-takers and the bomb. Several hostages stared at him. When he reached Katrina and Rachel, they quickly left their friends to relocate by the windows.

It seemed strange, but it was a strange day. Then Travis rejoined his friends over by the door.

3:15. Children began wandering. It seemed Young no longer had the will to threaten them as he had. Jean kept an eye on the clock—3:23, 3:24, 3:25 . . . time school would normally be out. The buses were always on time. She waited. No bell! No buses!

Kamron worried that his bus driver, Ed, might be taken hostage when he came to pick up his riders. Now he need no longer fear for him.

However, Jack and Jean had another major worry. Danny and Billy frequently came over from the high school to be with "Mom and Dad." What if they showed up? No one in the room had any inkling the high school had been notified what was happening here. She hoped against hope neither of her children would walk in. If they did. . . .

None of the hostages had attempted to peer outside the classroom. One reason, of course, was a fear of snipers. The other was that David scowled at anyone approaching the windows.

If the hostages had scrutinized the scene outside those windows, they would have known police were keeping anyone from nearing the school building. The buses couldn't get through. Neither could Danny and Billy if they had tried.

By now those conveyances were taking only half their usual cargo across the valley. Passengers and drivers shared the trauma of not knowing what was happening inside the school.

High schoolers poured off the buses and down roadways to release a rush of incredible news onto stunned parents.

3:35 came and went. Adult hostages exchanged more grateful glances. Every minute was another minute of life.

The children kept looking at that clock—should they have all been removed a long time ago?

David looked at a sea of hostages which he no longer effortlessly controlled. Were his muscles tensing?

Several teachers later described the feeling within the room. "Something was about to happen. You could feel the unbearable tension mounting. It seemed like someone was going to die. You couldn't tell who." Jean told herself, Things cannot continue as they are!

The clock ticked toward 3:45 as relentlessly as if it was ticking time off their lives.

Jean had been proud of the children all afternoon. They had done everything asked of them. Now for their own sakes, she wondered if they could just muster the same discipline again.

It might be far too much to ask. The Youngs had already pushed them well beyond their normal day's endurance level.

Eva looked again at the man. His confidence was ebbing! Something strange was occurring. She was not certain what it was.

Early in the afternoon, Eva feared that many hostages were going to die. Now she had a strange feeling of buoyancy. Had a gloomy look settled over the hostage-takers? Through the afternoon, Jean felt animosity toward Young because of his evil edicts to the children. She hated what he had done to the children, but she knew it would do no good to let her mind dwell on that. Young wasn't worth it. She would let someone else deal with his fate, whatever the outcome here.

Not far away, Eva was thinking somewhat the same thing. It would be psychologically harder on the hater than the hated. "Let the Lord take care of this man in His own way," Eva finally resigned herself.

Someone with more wisdom than she had would have to deal with the man holding these children, she told herself.

Shortly after 3:45, Young arrived abruptly at the saturation point. He called Doris to his side, then he quickly began changing the shoelace bomb trigger from his wrist to hers.

Young had given his wife no instructions earlier in the afternoon about the device, and he gave her none now. She simply obeyed David's will as she had done all along.

It was the last thing she was to do for her husband. Doris Young had only a few minutes left to live.

With the trigger in place around his wife's wrist, precisely as it had been around his own, David walked to the end of the room. He wanted to enter the bathroom. Janel noted that a boy was still inside. Young would have to wait! At that time, Jean decided to try cutting into the tension. It was a bathroom with small facilities, constructed for the children.

"You'll just die when you see the inside," she told the man holding them hostage. He saw no humor in it, glaring at her more coldly than ever. Then, he stepped inside the door to the child's restroom.

Eva felt it peculiar he did not quickly reappear. It seemed as if he was now leaving the entire hostage matter to his wife. Somehow, the room's many occupants felt safer that way. One boy even remarked, "I feel safer with him gone."

However, the boy had no way of knowing what was about to happen. It would finally put an end to the day's awful suspense—and bring on an entirely new wave of terror.

The clock ticked past 3:50.

At this point, Jean saw that the children were becoming more noisy than they had been all afternoon.

"Children! We need quiet time," she said over the mounting uproar.

Suddenly, Jean began to feel suddenly ill. "I've got a headache," Jean said in Doris' direction. She placed her hand to her head.

"So do I," Jean heard Doris say. In that second, Doris raised her hand to her own forehead. It was the hand attached to the bomb trigger.

In an instant, a great orange ball of fire and choking black smoke crackled wall to wall. Jean heard a deafening roar. She felt herself blown toward the door. She could not see her hand in front of her face. The lights went out. The fire alarm started clanging.

She heard the cries of children's voices. Then—utter pandemonium!

The Children Were Screaming

"I turned back to locate Kathy. Then I saw the woman burning like a human torch. I had to pass by her to find my baby."

—Mother fleeing explosion

"We're all dead!" Tina Cook exclaimed. The bomb's first shock waves pounded at her ears and eyes.

Eva Clark felt lifted several feet out of her chair. At the same time, she saw an orange fireball engulf Doris. With it all came the fury of the concussion. It was like sitting directly on top of a sonic boom. The sound of the blast drove into the body's very core. It pummeled into the soul, unleashing its most primitive survival instincts. Eva had never known fear like this.

Then came a renewed consciousness, a sudden realization—what they had feared all afternoon was happening! It swept into their inner thoughts even as it instantaneously overwhelmed them.

With it came a terrible darkness. It seemed like an evil shroud, holding them prisoner. Yet the darkness lasted only for a split second.

Fire arched over the room, followed by the ominous smoke. It swirled thickly enough one could grab a handful and stuff into a pocket.

Eva heard children screaming. How many had been killed already? How many were unable to shout at all?

Air. That most precious of all things, a single gulp of air! It was only one of many immediate necessities for survival.

Had some part of the body been blown away? It was difficult to tell in the nightlike blackness and the paralyzing limbo of the moment.

With the searing heat of the blast came the sound of the fire alarm bell. Above it came more screaming crescendo too shocking and powerful to hold back.

Within the chaos came the booming command from Jack Mitchell. "Run! Get out of here. Run!"

Not every teacher heard the cries of terror. Janel Dayton wondered why she could hear nothing. Had she been permanently deafened by the explosion?

She had no answer. There was no time to think, only to act on instinct. She began clearing away the south exit barricade she'd been required to guard. Was David Young somewhere nearby with his guns? She must get the children here through the barricade quickly.

Finding herself nearly free of the smoke, Mrs. Dayton looked back to see Jean Mitchell lying on the floor. She pulled at Jean. The other teacher was alive and trying to stand up, but she couldn't, and Janel could not pull her to her feet. Then the smoke seemed to close in on her. She plunged through the door into the hallway, around to the room's opposite door. Where were her first graders? She felt the wave of hysteria engulf her now when she realized she did not know whether a single child was in there waiting for her help before it was too late.

Were they all dead even as she stood there peering into the wall of smoke? Missiles of spewing flame could forever silence a child's cries and do it quickly.

Within the room's confusion, several teachers felt a strange numbness. It was as if emotions were blown to the ceiling with the bomb's force.

One of the room's occupants, Carol Petersen, had a mixed feeling of both silliness and terror. She had been sitting on the floor with children curled across her lap. When they seemed swept away, she tried to stand up. She could not. Their circulation having been completely cramped, her legs had "gone to sleep." What a silly way to die! she thought.

Like most troubled with such a temporary paralysis, she knew the feeling in her legs would return, but would it be soon enough? Was something as ridiculous as this going to prevent her escape? It was imperative she elude the smoke very soon.

Then it dawned on her that she had reason to feel utmost elation: the bomb had blown, and she was yet alive! She had survived the worst of it. Now she must find a way to drag her legs from the room.

Over in the southeast corner, a large group of kindergartners and first graders had been watching television. Now, a great shower of fire descended on them. In the pandemonium, clothing and hair caught fire. Some of the children attempted to beat out the flames with their bare hands.

Many children along the taped line were grasped by the inferno's fiery fingers. Elsewhere in the room, others were burned almost at random by the napalmlike splashes. Christy Clark felt her skin "on fire."

In the scramble to avoid the conflagration, a child thought he stumbled into the body of an adult. It might be a teacher dying or dead. Realizing it might be the woman who had held everyone captive, the youngster crawled toward what was, hopefully, an exit somewhere.

Kam Wixom and Travis Walker, near the doorway, escaped into the hallway unscathed. Walker landed on his knees from his hasty leap out the door, but he quickly regained his legs to race for the school entrance.

Tina Morfeld tried to catch a breath as the bright flashes leaped around her. The biting heat scorched delicate tissue in her throat and lungs. In the next 36 hours she would hang balanced between life and death.

Billie Jo Hutchinson, near the "line of death," was faced with a wall of fire before she could move. Like many others attempting only to escape, she was in so much shock she did not feel pain. Not yet. For now, her only conscious thought was to flee—get away from the trapped room with its trapped emotions.

How many were maimed or crippled somewhere in the thick darkness, unable to move, perhaps knocked to the floor unconscious—or worse? Which children not yet dead needed help first?

Teachers probed around for the feeling of human flesh. But how much time was there to look? Was there another portion of the bomb yet to be triggered by the furnace like heat?

The incongruity of shattered glass surrounding children's modeling clay symbolizes the trusting world of an innocent child vs. violence of terrorists. (Ravell Call photo courtesy of Deseret News)

Rocky Moore stationed himself by one of the two small windows which was barely large enough for an adult to crawl through and began grabbing the first children he saw. His adrenalin flowing, he was surprised at how quickly he stuffed them through the opening to freedom.

In their shock, some were slow to jump up and run. "I looked out and saw them stacking up like a cord of firewood," Rocky said later.

Visualizing Young showing up somewhere with his guns, Moore pleaded with the children, "Run, run, get away from the building!"

Then Moore noticed they stopped at the edge of the lawn. They had been taught to wait here in fire drills.

"Get off the school grounds, get out of sight!" he screamed at them again.

As Moore looked at the youngsters inside the room, he was horrified to see their blackened faces, some with clothes glowing. Several ran toward him with their hair afire. There were no towels or blankets in sight. Teachers had to smother flames with hands and arms.

So far, Rocky had seen only hostages who had been on his side of the room. As he continued to throw children out the window, he had no idea if anyone elsewhere had survived. One thing he was certain of, anyone left much longer in the acrid smoke would be overcome and lost for good.

By now children who had been on the opposite side of the room began emerging from the northwest hallway door into daylight. However, most of the children had been seated near the television set and the southeast corner. They struggled to the windows. For some it was the only dim light they could find. Out in the hallway, Jack looked for Jean. Chad would probably be with her.

"Have you seen Jean?" he called to a figure running down the hall. Jack did not know that Jean had been blasted toward the door, and was already somewhere out of the room. For now, he could not find her.

While some were stunned and confused, others were running without realizing it. Kindergartner Johnny King ran into the schoolyard crying, "I don't wanna die! I don't wanna die!"

Later, he collapsed at the foot of his aunt, Judy Himmerich.

"I don't know how I got out in the hallway," Kamron said. "And I don't know why I turned north to those doors. I just found myself running."

Outside, he shouted, "I'm alive! I'm alive!" He added, "I thought I was running fast, but I guess my legs were starting to go rubbery.

I saw a little first grader tear past me toward Main Street," Kam recalled later. "Being panic-stricken helped him run like I'd never seen him before."

Those heading out the south door were slowed to a crawl. The barricade of chairs and tables looked like a mountain. John Miller attempted to scoot children ahead of him.

Then David Young's morose face appeared at the open restroom door. He held a pistol in each hand. Both were leveled at Miller's upper body. One was a large pistol, the other a .22. The face did not change expression. Yet those eyes. . . .

Miller turned to run, but there was no place to go. He heard the report of a pistol. Then he felt a "dull thud." Not certain he had actually been shot, Miller continued to the outside entrance. There in the afternoon sunshine, he felt the elation of escape.

It didn't last long. As he ran, he began to feel dizzy. Then the band teacher collapsed near Main Street at the edge of Robinson's yard. He fell almost at the feet of Mrs. Dayton who was trying to catch her breath.

Kamron arrived just in time to see Emergency Medical Technicians running toward Miller. Finding blood from a bullet wound below his right shoulder blade, they loaded him into a waiting ambulance. He was rushed toward Bear Lake Memorial Hospital in Montpelier.

Kam saw the blackened face of Brenda Hartley. Startled, he looked closer to see that she was not burned as much as covered with soot. The plastic decoration on her T-shirt had melted.

A young boy was trying to cry, but he was in too much shock to let the tears flow freely.

Meanwhile, seeing no more children to help through the window, Rocky Moore attempted to crawl through himself. As he prepared to crash on the ground, something held him back. He feared someone's hand or that Young was standing behind him. This time would he pull the trigger?

Moore looked around, but saw no one. He felt frantically along his belt. It was caught on the protruding window latch!

On the other side of the room, Eva had not been far behind Miller when she realized Kathy was not at her side. She must grope directly into the conflagration. "I turned back to locate Kathy. Then I saw the woman burning like a human torch. I had to pass by her to find my baby."

Eva realized Doris must have taken the bomb's full force, but for now, she had to locate her four-year-old. Poking around in the room, Eva thought she saw Kathy's small form. Then she heard the most wonderful sound she could ever hear. "Mamma!"

Dragging and pulling Kathy upward, Eva pushed for the room exit where her other children were waiting.

As she approached it, she faced a final obstacle, the man who had threatened to shoot people all afternoon. A few feet from Eva, Young still held a pistol in each hand.

"He could shoot me right here and now!" Eva realized, but she saw a surrender in his eyes she had not observed earlier. "I will never forget the man's face. It had the look of defeat. He knew his evil scheme was done. I had seen that look before in a movie about the devil losing his power. His will to continue was shattered."

Would the mood change? Eva turned her back toward him, shielding her children, and hurried out the door. She heard no shot—then she was finally at the end of the hallway.

Some of the school children also escaped with a story of intensified emotion. Six-year-old Joshua Jones said he "had been coloring a panther in his book" when the room went dark. "I climbed through a window but my tennis shoe got stuck."

Hanging upside down for a moment, Joshua worried that he had "lost all that money Uncle Bill gave me. There were three nickels and a penny." Joshua felt the pain of burns only after riding his bicycle home.

Meanwhile, still struggling to extricate his belt, Moore could hear ammunition exploding. Thinking it must be Young returning to shoot children, he battled blind panic.

Unknown to him, however, the bursting ammo was from that placed on the shopping cart with the bomb that seemed a sadistic move by Young to injure those who survived the blast. Hundreds of cartridges lined against the wall with the firearms were now triggered by soaring room temperatures.

Moore pulled again at his belt. Thinking he felt a hand on his leg, he frantically jerked again. Something loosened from the window latch and he tumbled to the grass in a heap.

It seemed he had been stuck for hours.

Looking back through the window, he was amazed to find more children arriving. From the outside he began to pull them through. As he did, he also saw something which greatly lifted his spirits.

Cynthia Cowden, who had been on the far side of the room, loomed in the window frame. It was his first indication that anyone on another side of the bomb had survived. These children coming through now must have been over there! Then he saw student teacher Kris Kasper round the school building corner. Kasper had also been elsewhere in the room. Many of them must have been temporarily blinded by the smoke.

During all this time, no one had a chance to check for injuries with those children thrown out the window. If a youngster broke a leg or arm as he fell, there was no time to worry about it now. At least they were alive.

Although few knew it at the time, the gasoline incendiary which ignited the blasting caps and gunpowder thrust most of its violence upward to the ceiling. From there the explosion powered to the walls, then plummeted straight down their sides. Anyone near those walls took the bomb's hottest, heaviest combustive effects.

One of those to feel the worst of this impact was substitute-teacher Pat Bennion. Nevertheless, she remained near the east wall windows lifting children through. The abrasive action on already seared flesh was to exact a painful price. Only later did she realize how badly burned she really was.

She developed infection in her wounded arms, possibly due to the damage done while lifting dozens of children through the windows. She did not return home that evening, nor for several more. Hospital officials carefully weighed the possibility of transferring her to the University of Utah Burn Center. Recovery would be slow and painful. But she survived.

One of the last to leave the room was white-haired Verlene Bennion. Her greatest desire at the moment was that each one in the room might live at least as long as she had. She would be treated later for severe smoke inhalation, and second degree burns on her arms and back.

Many children ran directly for a home in town without even looking back. Lowell Clark, alerted by his high school daughter, Beverly, watched the chaotic scene with a crowd of some two hundred parents. He was unaware that his wife, Eva, was inside the bomb-blown room.

He saw children with bewilderment in their faces running blindly to the nearest adult with a familiar face. Others were not so selective. They hugged anyone on the street.

Some children, their faces blackened, were not immediately recognized by parents. Townspeople just grabbed any youngster and comforted the quivering child until medics could determine the extent of injury. Only after reaching loving arms did the child's trial by terror finally begin to subside.

By now, radio stations were describing the evacuation. Radio station KMER, Kemmerer, with Ken Rand telephoning from a house near the school, called it a "scene of carnage" unfolding before him. Out of breath, he explained that he had just heard the bomb explode while at Town Hall, and raced closer to the schoolyard to make his report.

Lowell Clark found five of his six children being led from the besieged building by his wife. Lowell thought she appeared like a mother hen with little chicks. How had she gotten in here ahead of him? He would find out later. For now, he simply blurted out, "Where's Christy?"

Eva thought she was with the crowd outside. She had also expected some comment from her husband about her own well-being. That luxury, the conversation with her husband she had yearned for all afternoon, would have to wait until late that night. Only then did Lowell learn his wife had been one of the hostages.

For now, both parents frantically asked around if anyone had seen Christy. No one had. She must still be in the bomb room! Emptiness engulfed Eva. Had she saved five children, only to lose the sixth?

In the meantime, some children fleeing the school headed for backyard fences. Cheering parents helped a number of them over the patchwork of wire and wood. Older boys scarcely stopped as they scaled the obstacles.

Homes on Main Street bordering the school had been evacuated by town hall officials moments after learning of the powerful bomb Young carried. These homes were now turned into temporary treatment centers as technicians triaged victims outside. Those not needing hospitalization telephoned home for parents. But most of the valley's parents were already in town trying to sort through children to find their own. Some did not find them. Many were unaware that badly burned children were already enroute to hospitals. In some cases, parents couldn't locate their children until hours later.

As teachers escaped, they agonized over any children who might have been left behind in the dark confusion. When they escaped from the building, these teachers were besieged by anxious parents asking, "Where is my child?"

The answer was heartrending. "Right now we don't know! We don't know!" was all the teachers could tell them. The teachers were busy finding out. Kliss Sparks could be heard above the shouting. "Fourth graders—over here!" Several students volunteered to look for the others Mrs. Sparks couldn't find. Jack Mitchell was assembling his sixth graders, smiling as each one was located. Where were Brian and Drew? Jean took mental count of each pupil in her first grade class. Some were still not found.

There was a fear that some children, once safely out, might have returned for shoes, books, or some personal belonging.

It's terrible! Jean told herself. We wait and wait all afternoon to get out of there. Now that we're out, we have to wait some more to see if everyone made it.

Escaping the immediate threat of death and the ordeal of imprisonment, those who had made it were now beginning to feel the effect of burns. "Do I have blood on my back or something?" one fleeing child asked another. His shirt was not burned, but looking under it, one could see a growing area of scarlet flesh. Many victims were grabbed by paramedics and cooled down by neighbor's garden hoses to halt the corrosive effect of the burns.

At the time of the explosion, Excell was in his office where a newspaper reporter had just asked him what was happening. He remembers yelling "The bomb's exploded!" into the telephone, dropping it, then deciding he had better notify the town hall. "The bomb's exploded!" he called into the receiver all over again.

Sheriff's deputy Earl Carroll didn't need to be told. Those at the Cokeville Town Hall heard the explosion and in the ensuing seconds heard a horrible sound. The children were screaming!

Excell grabbed a fire extinguisher from the wall. Looking at the huge cloud of smoke bursting from within room four, he gave up. He ran outside. The first people he saw were law officers running toward the building.

Holding frantic parents back in the entrance area for nearly two hours, lawmen could now see it was useless. Parents broke from the police cordon toward school entrances in a wall of anxiety. Cursing and then cursing again, someone yelled, "I'm going in there after that SOB myself!"

Lawmen heard Excell tell them to hurry inside. "I can hear ammo exploding," Excell yelled. "They must be shooting the children!" But before emergency officials could enter the school house, they had to first convince parents and townspeople to stay out of their way.

"We've got enough lawmen and firemen here to do the job," an officer yelled across the pandemonium. "Now everyone else get back!"

One of the officers, Patrolman Brad Anderson, knew he must get in quickly. The gunman just might be fanatical enough to kill as many as he could before dying himself.

Lawmen had only a sketchy description of the hostage-takers. How could anyone tell for sure what they looked like?

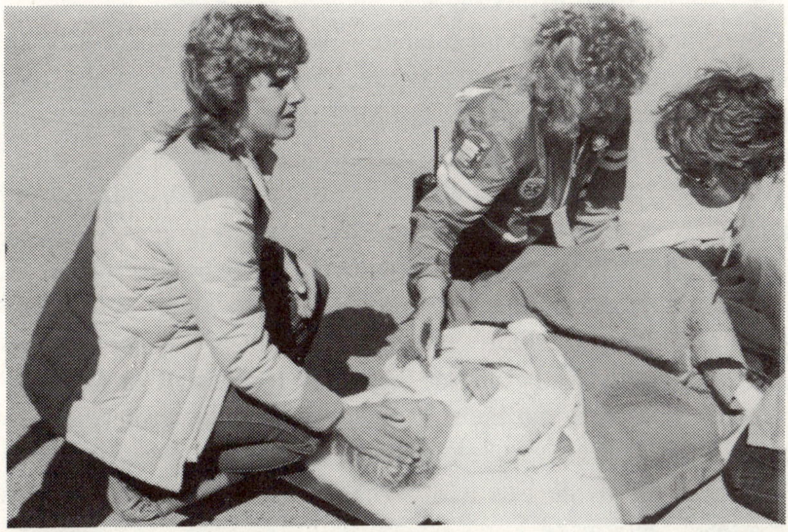

Neighbors and paramedics comfort injured child after bomb explosion sends hostages fleeing in terror from their school classroom. (Dan Dockstader photo, Star Valley Independent)

In a previous case, Anderson had been given a description of a "short man" which so poorly fitted that of the actual lean, tall murder suspect that lawmen almost had to let the man go even though he had been captured while hiding.

Now Anderson was faced with an armed terrorist in a smoke-filled building lurking almost anywhere among dozens of rooms, and without an accurate description of him at all! A mistake in identification or a hurried one—either way, someone could be dead.

Anderson checked the heavy metal plate in the bullet-proof vest, making certain it was in place. He gave his shotgun to another officer, preferring to draw his service revolver instead. Sheriff's deputy Greg Goodman joined him, and the two lawmen stepped through the school's double doors into the hallway.

Thick black fumes engulfed them. It was nearly impossible to breathe.

They heard the clanging of the fire alarm bell. Above that din .22 caliber shells were exploding somewhere.

Covering each other with their revolvers, they traded duties and inched ahead. Then they saw a figure, shrouded in the smoke, moving directly toward them. He had long hair, medium frame, older clothes. Sure enough—he matched the description!

Anderson had to scream above the fire alarm to make himself heard. "Hold it there!"

"Don't shoot!" the figure called back. "Don't shoot me!"

Was the man just stalling to get out a gun? Anderson wasn't about to take any chances. "Don't move! Get down on the floor. Spread out your hands and feet. And stay there until I get a good look at you!"

Anderson peered into the mist, his eyes burning from the acrid smoke.

The man did as he was told. When his face focused into view, the officer recognized him.

The face was one he had seen before, outside. This was the father who said he "was going inside to find his boy!"

Lawmen warned him to stay out of the school. He hadn't. Now, he was lucky to be alive.

No one bothered to ask the father how he got in. Anderson surmised it must have been through one of the east wall's open windows, the same ones the children crawled out.

Unknown to his father, the boy was already home. He had grabbed his bicycle and pedaled into town. He was nearly swept off his bike by his overjoyed mother when she saw her son alive. He was later treated for burns.

Disgusted, the lawmen now ordered the man before them to get out and stay out. When he did, some townspeople looked at him warily. Not everyone knew him. Was he the gunman? He had to locate someone who recognized him.

Inside, Goodman and Anderson now groped down a hallway which grew heavier with smoke as they neared the besieged room. What happened next could well have been the most tragic event of the day.

While Goodman and Anderson entered the south hallway, other lawmen crept through other entrances. City police chief Cal Fredrickson had turned back from a trip to repair his car in Logan when he got word of the crisis. He entered the school building still wearing his civilian clothing. So did sheriff's deputy Earl Carroll.

All felt a hurry to stop David Young before he harmed anyone else. He could emerge anytime from almost anywhere. He had shot John Miller. He could kill with any one of his dozens of guns. Yet in their anxiety to halt the terrorist and his weapons, lawmen had no idea where their colleagues were located after the explosion.

As Fredrickson and Anderson advanced, each saw the shadowy figure of the other. Aware that hesitation meant death, both men drew their pistols. Police Chief Fredrickson recognized Anderson's state trooper uniform. Anderson, who saw his Cokeville neighbor often enough to recognize him even in the smoky atmosphere, put down his gun.

Deputy Goodman, a resident of Kemmerer, didn't see the Cokeville police chief all that frequently. Anderson watched in horror as the two officers tilted pistol muzzles toward each other's heads. Neither one had as clear a view of the other as did Anderson.

"I could see that shooting in 'self defense' would be plausible for either side," Anderson stated. Fredrickson carried a Smith-Wesson .45 caliber service revolver capable of great destruction. It was pointed directly at the deputy's head. The deputy's weapon was pointed at Fredrickson.

Anderson now had to do something in a hurry or one of his colleagues could be killed. He shouted over the alarm bell, "Don't shoot! Don't shoot!"

Had either of them heard him? "It's Cal!" he shouted to Goodman, the closer officer.

Anderson waited tensely. Did the deputy say something? "No, it's not!" the highway patrolman seem to hear in the clamor.

For an instant the tension was thicker than the smoke. Then Fredrickson backed away. Both put their guns down. Anderson felt tremendous relief. For the time being, at least, no one was going to be shot.

As yet, none of these officers had peered into the room itself. Moving toward it now, Anderson opened the door. Goodman propped a chair against it.

Anderson had already decided that rushing into the center of the room would carry the best odds. It would be less dangerous there than peering around the corner. The gunman would be looking toward daylight of an open door, the lawmen into pea soup.

As the door opened, both men heard a shot inside. Before either could do anything, layers of smoke poured out. Anderson had never known breathing to be so difficult. The fumes were piercing, unavoidable.

He lay back, gasping for breath. There was no way to go in there without an air pack. Pondering the next move, lawmen heard another shot inside the room. The door spring began pushing at the chair, forcing it away completely, then slamming shut. At least there was less smoke rushing into the hallway now.

The lawmen decided to wait for more of the smoke to clear away. Attempting to enter was useless until they could breath.

Someone at the far end of the hallway turned off the alarm bell. Carroll had located the proper key.

The officers could converse normally for the first time in many long minutes. Being able to talk quietly removed some of the tension.

Even so, no one actually let his guard down. The gunman could still emerge from the near door at any time.

Suddenly they heard a voice boom down the hallway. "We've found one subject dead in the bathroom!"

Unknown to Goodman and Anderson, Sheriff's deputy Randy White had already located an air pack and was in the room ahead of them. He was the first to locate David Young. White had entered through a hallway a little ahead of the others. White said in his police report that he saw no one moving about in the room. Seeing the lavatory door, he pushed it until it opened a crack. Watching carefully for any gun poking out the door, he slowly peeked inside. A man's body was slumped with a leg pressed against the doorway.

He was certain that Young was dead; but as a precaution the deputy placed his handcuffs around the man's wrists. He also removed all weapons in the bathroom, including those on Young's body. Examining the body any further would be a job for the medical examiner. He hadn't better disturb it.

Not knowing White was in the building, the other lawmen were not certain it was all over.

"I had to personally convince myself the man was really dead before beginning the next chore, that of looking for bodies," Anderson said. "I eased into the classroom, over to the bathroom door, and tried to open it. Something was propped against it. I pushed harder. Then I saw him.

"A man was hunched over against the wall, his legs against the door. I saw fresh blood on his face. After studying him for a minute, I knew he was dead.

"That part of the ordeal was over. Now we could check the room rubble, the corners, and the closets for bodies.

"I had read many reports of children hiding in fear in such places following fires and explosions. Other lawmen and I now began searching all such little hiding places."

Outside, Excell received word the building "had been cleared." Such notice had not been given to several lawmen inside. Fredrickson and Carroll, concerned Young might be holed up anywhere, began a thorough search for him.

Rounding a corner to help look for children who might be too badly burned to move or dead, Excell surprised the two law officers. He, too, looked into the deadly business ends of a pistol and a shotgun.

Looking once again into the misty hallway, the men put their weapons away. One phase of the day's work had ended.

While this search for the gunman was happening inside, another dramatic event was occurring outside.

After several waves of hostages cleared the windows, volunteer firemen moved close enough to shoot a steady stream of water into the room. As they hooked up hoses, EMT Kevin Walker thought he heard two shots. It was dangerous to get too close, but the crews wanted to extinguish the fire and cool down the room for survivors still inside. It appeared too little water was getting through the two small windows.

One EMT moved to the larger upper windows, only to find they were stationary and wouldn't open. He located a metal pipe near the window and broke the glass. Then he wrestled out the steel frame with his bare hands.

As firemen hosed down the smoke-filled room, they thought they saw an adult woman's body on the floor near the far wall.

At first it appeared she might be overcome with smoke inhalation. One paramedic thought she could be saved with mouth-to-mouth resuscitation.

"But we soon realized the futility," EMT Walker said. "Air being breathed in was escaping through a hole in her head. She had the top of her skull blown off."

In the blackened room, fireman Allen Burton feared it was his sister, kindergarten teacher Kim Kasper. The body was pulled through the window, and carried in a blanket to the lawn. Later, adult hostages looked at the woman's face more carefully to make certain identification. "That's the woman holding us hostage," they told them. Some eyewitnesses said Doris was dropped unceremoniously right where she was.

At that point everyone realized the risk they had been taking by going back into the room. No one yet knew where David Young might be.

The events were becoming more involved. The police were inside making a thorough search.

Eva and Lowell Clark continued their own desperate search for Christy. They split up to cover more area. If she were still inside the school building, they wondered if police would let them back inside?

Before making a final decision about reentering the building, Eva heard welcome news that Lowell had found Christy. He left word with a friend to tell his wife.

She was burned—it was not known how badly—and taken by ambulance to the Star Valley Hospital. Lowell had located her in time to accompany their daughter in the ambulance.

Relieved at last, Eva arranged for a ride to the hospital fifty miles away in Afton.

After the screaming and running inside and outside the school subsided, one lawman was taken to the hospital for smoke inhalation. Patrolman Anderson was treated for smoke inhalation by EMTs for nearly an hour on the school grounds.

Many parents were just arriving, asking which hospital their son or daughter had been taken to. Was it Montpelier, Kemmerer, Afton, or Logan? Who had been taken where? Children from one family might have been taken to different places. Did parents have to decide which one to visit first?

Sheriff Deputy Ron Hartley learned that all four of his grade school children had been taken to Bear Lake Memorial in Montpelier.

Badly burned Billie Jo and Tina were immediately hospitalized. In time, 79 hostages were taken to hospitals; the most critical were transferred to the University of Utah Burn Center in Salt Lake City.

With it all, one question remained. Had any victims been taken to the morgue?

Children's bikes are lined up as usual on a spring day. This day, however, is not typical, as lawmen gather to dismantle a bomb. (Tim Kelly photo courtesy of Salt Lake Tribune)

Along one side of the school building a row of bicycles belonging to children remained unclaimed. Were the owners still somewhere inside the building?

As for Doris and her husband, they would not have to be dealt with by any human tribunal. Few acts of terrorism have ever turned out so fortituously for lawmen.

No jury would decide their punishment. For better or for worse, it had already been meted out.

As yet no one knew if the Youngs had succeeded in taking any of the children with them into their "Brave New World." Lawmen were still sifting through a blackened room. Patrolman Anderson and other lawmen held their breath as they uncovered each pile of rubble. Under each one they expected to begin a body count.

The Miracle

"To say it was a miracle would be the understatement of the century."

—Richard Haskell, sheriff's bomb expert

As lawmen, firemen, and others picked through the room rubble, their first impression was that of total shambles. The walls were still upright, although much of the ceiling tile was blown out. Debris littered the room everywhere. Everything was black, except for one strange place on the east wall about the size of a human figure with its arms partially outstretched. In the smoke-stained walls, this almost white area stood out in contrast.

At first, it appeared the reason for this white area was that the blast spent itself on some person, leaving the place behind it thus unseared. If so, who was that person taking the brunt of the bomb's force? Doris had been in the center of the room.

Speculation on that could come later. Looking for children's bodies in the darkened corners and beneath the piled up debris was the major concern right now. Obviously property damage was extensive. An estimate of room destruction was later placed at $50,000. With that kind of wreckage, how could anyone possibly escape alive?

Patrolman Anderson groped through everything on the floor. Every back pack or abandoned jacket made his heart jump. Was it the body of a little child?

Finally lawmen and other searchers turned over the last of the flotsam and examined the far reaches of the last closet. Only then did the unbelievable truth jump out at them: there were no bodies in the room. Everyone was out!

In time, poring over hospital lists and talking to parents, every one of the 154 persons in the room was accounted for. Even then, the dilemma continued to unravel. Colleen King, already at the hospital in Montpelier to visit her sick father, was told to stand by; her sons had been burned from a bomb explosion in Cokeville. They were being sent to the hospital. Only after waiting one-and-a-half hours did King learn she was at the wrong facility. Her boys had been taken to the hospital in Kemmerer.

Gina Taylor manages a courageous smile from her hospital bed, although bandages swath burned face and hands. Doctors wonder if she will lose sight in her right eye. (JM Heslop photo courtesy Deseret News)

Gwen Petersen completed an earlier scheduled visit to Montpelier, but this time it was to visit her granddaughter Jamie. Other parents were gone most of the night with children. Some parents learned their children had to be sent to the hospital in Logan. The most severely burned were Billie Jo Hutchinson, Tina Morfeld, and Fawna Eastman. They were transferred to the University of Utah Burn Center in Salt Lake City. It appeared several more like Gina Taylor would require extensive burn treatment. Her parents were told she could lose the sight of her right eye. She might also have permanent facial scarring. These families lived with these fears for several days.

Yet it was an inescapable fact: a miracle had occurred. All were alive!

Back at the school the lawmen, no longer seeking victims, looked for more explosives. Blasting caps were discovered. Spectators along Main Street heard the popping of explosives as they were deliberately detonated in the safety of a specially-built container. Weapons were removed and taken into evidence.

Then the bomb, with its remaining components and wiring, was carefully examined by explosives expert Richard Haskell from Rock Springs, Wyoming. Haskell, from the Sweetwater County Sheriff's Office, had become familiar with almost every type of bomb during his military service as well as through his duties as a lawman. He had examined many types of explosives: those made by criminals, by miners to loosen ore, by almost everyone for every reason. The so-called "deadman's bomb" that Young used was a familiar one.

As he dismantled the remains of the device, Haskell found something strange. The two wires which were to have detonated two blasting caps and fill the air with exploding gunpowder were severed, cut cleanly, as if snipped with wire cutters. When battery current could not reach these two caps, it prevented the device from putting substantial amounts of the gunpowder and aluminum dust into the air.

"That," stated Haskell, "would have caused an explosion which would have caved in the walls and blown up everything in the room."

Haskell also found that gasoline leaking from a slit in the plastic jug made a partial paste of the granules and kept them from becoming airborn. The bomb was designed to kill everyone, he concluded. But in those two ways the device was thwarted from venting its full force as Young intended.

It was not likely that the wires could have been cut by pulling the cart around. They would have just been loose, showing no signs of being severed. The explosion itself would have melted or fused the wires rather than cutting them cleanly.

Haskell issued this statement: "I don't know how the wires were cut. My only official conclusion is that I can't begin to explain it." At one time, he stated to television reporters, "The whole thing just appears to be a miracle."

Asked later about the use of the word, Haskell told the authors of this book, "To be more specific, labeling it a miracle is the understatement of the century."

The flying bullets didn't seriously injure anyone in the dark and crowded room. But that wasn't particularly surprising. Haskell said the slugs and shell casings flying around loose, rather than channeled in a gun muzzle, could cause minor flesh wounds, but wouldn't kill anyone. They didn't carry enough velocity outside of a gun barrel to likely penetrate far into human flesh.

"Could they put out an eye?"

"That is always a possibility."

Most of the shells were found embedded in the ceiling although several slug marks were noted about three feet high in the walls. Some children had sharp cuts in their skin which could have been caused by the cartridges or shell casings. There were few such incidents, however, because nearly all of the ammo fired into the ceiling tile. Why most ammo fired in that direction instead of at different angles around the room was not known.

Some survivors wondered if they weren't spared serious injury by the fact that nearly all ammo fired upward. However, Haskell meticuously reiterated that he didn't think the ammo would cause serious injury unless striking an eye. He was far more concerned about what the bomb's powerful force could have extracted in human life and injury.

Certainly the exploding ammo did strike fear into the hostages. All knew Young had several guns in his possession and had threatened all day to start shooting at the slightest provocation. Young wasn't in the classroom proper, yet with a few steps he could begin shooting at anything that moved. Some, including Principal Excell, thought at one time that Young was doing just that.

There was speculation that heat might have detonated any blasting caps left intact, particularly the two on the cart which didn't explode. But Haskell said this would occur only if they had been on the same shelf near the three caps which did partially blow.

"The two caps were on a lower shelf. If Young had placed them up with the others, they might have also been detonated by the heat. Fortunately for the survivors, this was not the case."

What about the force of the blast which did detonate—would that have been enough to kill most of the people in the room?

"Looking at the room, I'd have to call that a second miracle. There are almost always people killed near a blast of this magnitude. Add to that the small children crowded so closely together in a small room and the likelihood of being overcome by smoke inhalation. . . . It makes me wonder why we didn't find nearly 150 bodies in there."

Haskell repeated several times the odds against anyone not having an arm or leg blown off even if they survived. "The whole thing is even more astounding in that no one was maimed or crippled. All of the evidence points to the opposite happening."

Lawmen who described it a miracle included more than Haskell. Sheriff's investigator Hartley, who had four children in the room, said, "I've seen too many things like this in my work. Rarely is there anything even close to a happy ending in hostage situations like this. There are so many seemingly 'lucky' factors here it taxes the mind to suppose they all came about by happenstance."

Scrutinizing all of Young's writings with his avowed intention of killing the children, and with the man's fanatical zeal in doing what he determined to do, investigator Hartley was even more amazed that the tunnel-visioned man had been stopped short of what he plotted.

Haskell and others examining the bombed-out room list these fourteen known factors that prevented death or permanent injury to the hostages:

1. Two bomb wires were somehow severed before the electric current was set off.

2. The blasting caps which did not detonate were placed on a lower shelf from the others, thus preventing them from being triggered by the bomb's heat.

3. The soft ceiling tile absorbed much of the overhead blast.

4. The two windows were open, venting much of the bomb's initial concussion.

5. The two doors were also open, which had a further dampening effect.

6. The tables and chairs had been moved from the center of the room, which allowed the children to quickly escape the closest force of the blast's fire.

7. No one was sitting or standing directly against the walls to take the main combustive force of the blast as it plunged down those walls.

8. Because of the 10 feet by 10 feet masked-off area none of the hostages were adjacent to the bomb and its immediate concussion when it detonated.

9. David Young for some reason selected a plastic jug which leaked; then, somehow, he did not take notice of that fact when he filled it with gasoline. Further, he did not see or smell the problem throughout the long afternoon—even when he was sitting or standing next to the leaking jug.

10. Doris's body apparently absorbed much of the explosion's fury. She was standing between the bomb and the hostages.

11. The children had a drill just the week before in the school cafeteria "on how to escape a fire quickly from a single room."

12. Princess gave an early warning with details about the guns and bomb. She briefed legal, medical and other authorities on what to expect. Civil Defense workers "just happened" to be on hand to coordinate it.

13. The hostages wisely chose to wait out the dilemma rather than risk being shot trying to escape or rushing the Young himself. To have done so would have left them more exposed to the close-in, maximum explosive force of the bomb.

14. Despite the dense smoke, the teachers did just the right thing at the right time at the windows and doors to evacuate all the children from every part of the room before anyone succumbed to the pain, fire, or lack of oxygen.

After looking at the bombed-out room, Haskell concluded over and over again that, even in the partial explosion which did occur, it was "unexplainable" that no one died in the concussion, flames, or confusion of so many people in such a small area.

In addition, there was the "amazing coincidence" of Miller being shot with the smaller pistol—even though Young held a more lethal one in another hand. The bullet penetrated near, but not into, his heart. He was out of the hospital in two days.

There were many individual incidents of "good fortune" in eluding death. Some of the recoveries, like that of Billie Jo, were not without weeks of mental anguish before the patient was declared out of danger. Yet all made it.

Medical officials said they "almost lost" Tina Morfeld because of her internal injuries, but she perservered.

What appeared to medical technicians as lifelong impairments such as Gina Taylor's badly burned right eye, turned out much better than the most optimistic people had dared hope.

Lawmen fortuitously escaped death and injury, considering what could have happened in the smoke-shrouded school as they were searching for an armed and hostile gunman.

Later, as lawmen unraveled Young's journals and diaries, the hostages began to realize how fortunate they were to be able to talk about their ordeal. Few wanted to nurture a "festering enmity" against David or Doris Young. The psychological healing process would take long enough as it was, without their harboring any hatred for their captors. Nor did very many want to harbor any long-enduring feelings of self-pity. It wasn't practical in a community like this.

It would, nevertheless, require a mental miracle for all to immediately reconcile their feelings with the selfish or sick David Young. Some would never forgive him, nor did all feel any particular reason to try. The fact that the Youngs were dead made it easier to forget. The guilty are not always so quickly punished.

In time, some stated outright that they softened their earlier opinions toward David Young. Principal Excell said that at first, he "wanted to get my hands on a gun and kill him for what he was doing to the children. I felt it even more when I thought he was shooting them after the bomb went off. Now after all that we have learned about him, I can only feel a deep pity for anyone like that."

Pity. That was a growing feeling of 154 people toward the man who sought to kill them. They were, as they looked back on it, increasingly grateful just to be alive.

There are a number of questions unanswered in this chapter. Generally speaking, science does not like to deal with unknowns. It is part of our human nature to seek a plausible answer to every question. Nevertheless, some answers are difficult to explain.

Not having a human explanation for something which should be explainable is Webster's definition of a "miracle." Specifically, the Webster's New Collegiate Dictionary says "Miracle—An event or effect in the physical world deviating from the known laws of nature, or transcending our knowledge of these laws."

While there was much "deviating from the known laws of nature" attested to here in this 100 per cent survival of the Cokeville hostages, the hostages themselves offer some answers for their "miraculous" survival. They will be explored in the chapters ahead.

The Spiritual Message

> *"Mommy, the angels saved us!"*
>
> *—two hostage girls*

When the children ran from the bomb explosion, some had a simple explanation why they survived. Unabashedly and without hesitation, several talked of "angels" appearing to them.

Seven-year-old Katrina (Katie) Walker told her fourteen-year-old brother, Shane, the first family member she saw after running from the explosion, "They saved us. I said a prayer, and they saved us!"

"Who saved you?"

"The angels. They saved us."

When Katie saw her mother, Glenna, a few minutes later, the girl repeated, "Mommy, the angels saved us!"

Mrs. Walker patted her daughter on the head. "Yes, we all have much to be grateful for, dear," and held her closer. Certainly Mr. and Mrs. Walker, along with all parents of hostage children, had a benign feeling this day for everything pertaining to deity.

However, Mrs. Walker did not realize that her daughter meant what she was saying literally. For the moment, an anxious mother felt only utter relief. She had been following the hostage crisis all afternoon along with her EMT husband, Kevin. Now, finally, Katie was safe. The Walkers learned that their other daughter, Rachel, nine, "was going to be fine," but she was being treated for burns at the hospital.

With the girls and eleven-year-old Travis safe, Glenna no longer felt it necessary to talk about the unhappy ordeal. However, her three children did. When everyone in the community was invited to talk with psychologists about the traumatic event in their lives, the Walkers joined other hostage families in group and individual discussions. Katie and Rachel told Dr. Vern Cox they had tried to talk with their parents about the "angels saving us."

Travis, too, wanted to pour out something deep within which was troubling him. Dr. Cox told the parents what their children had been telling him.

"Why haven't they been telling us, their own parents?" Mrs. Walker wanted to know.

"Have you been listening to them?" he asked her. "Really listening?"

Mrs. Walker realized maybe they hadn't. When they did, they heard something which sent an electric awakening into their souls.

"They were standing there above us," Katrina told her parents matter-of-factly. "There was a mother and a father and a lady holding a tiny baby, and a little girl with long hair. There was a family of people. The woman told us the bomb was going off soon, and to listen to our brother. He was going to come over and tell us what to do."

"She said to be sure we did what he told us," Rachel added.

"They were all dressed in white, bright like a light bulb but brighter around the face," Katie told her mother.

"The girl had a long dress," Rachel added, "which covered her feet, and she had light brown hair."

The girls were talking quietly but firmly about people who had not been in the room before. Whatever the heavenly definition of angels, they were talking here and now about divine messengers as plainly and openly as their parents had ever heard them talk about anything. There was no apology or self-consciousness in their faces. It was all as real to them as their own parents standing there listening to them.

"The white figures standing above them moved around to another part of the room just before the bomb went off," Rachel told her mother and father.

It was while we were talking to the Walkers about their roles as EMTs in the hostage dilemma that they told us about their children's unique experiences.

We asked about spending an evening talking with the children ourselves. At first the family was concerned about it being "too frightening" or "stressful" to recall the May bomb survival experience all over again. It was also, up to that time, a personal family conversation.

With our request, Katie told her mother, "The woman made me feel good. I knew she loved me. I want to talk about it." Rachel and Travis agreed. They, too, had a warm memory of the "ordeal."

We had talked with the Walkers several times after the hostage incident, but the interview on December 28, 1986, was easily the most remarkable and memorable.

It had been more than seven months since the event, yet the children remembered details as if it had happened just a few days before.

Our daughter Cindy and our son Kamron visited the Walker home with us on December 28th. The children were having so much fun playing tag that we watched for several minutes. Then Kevin and Glenna called their children to come over and sit down. Katie climbed onto her mother's lap. Then began one of the most soul-stirring evenings anyone could possibly experience.

"What did you see?" we asked Travis. "Can you describe it to us?"

"I didn't see anything, nothing!" he emphasized. "I just heard a voice. It told me to find my little sisters and take them over by the window and keep them there. I did what I was told. I looked around and found them and told them to follow me over by the window."

His face seemed absorbed. I had known Travis for five years and I had never seen him look that serious before. "I told them to stay there and not move," Travis emphasized." At the same time, he was calm. He said it as calmly as if he was recalling a little league ballgame score.

"Did they respond?"

"They were playing with their friends, and I didn't think they would want to leave them. I knew they had to come with me. They got their coloring pages and I took them over by the windows."

"Did they stay right there?" my wife asked.

Both girls quickly said "Yes.

The objective newspaper questioning techniques of three-and-a-half decades were coming out in me.

"Was it a male or a female voice?"

"I don't know," Travis responded. It had never occurred to him before. "It was a voice. It told me what I had to do."

"This voice was unmistakable?" I asked.

Travis politely ignored the question as if it wasn't even applicable.

"But . . . I didn't stay there with them. I was also told to help them through the window when the bomb went off. And I went back over with the other boys where I had been, by the door. . . ."

Glenna interrupted. "That was when he told Dr. Cox how terribly guilty he felt—that he had not been by the windows with his sisters when the bomb exploded."

Travis had not struck me in the time I knew him to feel particularly guilty about anything. He was mostly just a happy-go-lucky, All-American boy.

"Travis isn't the kind to feel so guilty. And his sisters don't always do what he says, either. But they did this time," Glenna said.

"Did you say a prayer while you were a hostage?" we asked. The three of them looked more serious now. Yes, they had.

We asked Travis if he remembered what he had said in his prayer. He looked away. The words gushed out, "Heavenly Father, we need your help. We can't get out of this without you. Please help us know what to do!"

There was a long silence. Then Travis looked at us again. "I should have gone over by the window with my sisters. That's what I was told to do. I didn't do it."

There was no consolation for Travis in the weeks following the hostage crisis. Mrs. Walker said her son did not sleep well for weeks. "I had never seen him so upset."

His sisters seemed to have forgiven him. They smiled. Even Rachel, who had been burned.

The girls seemed content to discuss their experience for a long time. They were as completely engrossed in talking as everyone else in the room was in listening.

"How did they come into the room?" they were asked. "Was it through the main door or the door by the bathroom?"

"Through the ceiling," both girls said at once.

"Where were they standing?" I asked.

Katie held her hand about two feet off the ground, just below her waist. "They were about this high off the ground."

"Could you see all of them, their entire bodies?" I asked.

Rachel nodded. Then she said, in deep thought, "Except for the little girl. She had a long white dress. I couldn't see her feet."

"Was there any color at all in the clothing they wore?"

Rachel shook her head. "They were all dressed in white."

"Had you ever seen any of these people?" the girls were asked.

They did not answer immediately. "The man looked something like you, Mr. Wixom. He looked like somebody we had seen before," Rachel said.

I wrote Rachel's comment down precisely as she said it. Personal comparisons or not, it was a time for utmost and careful accuracy.

"What about the woman?"

"The lady who talked to us had brown hair, curly like this," Katie said, gently touching her mother's hair.

"Was it someone you had ever seen before?" Katie shook her head, "No." Kevin suggested looking at some old photos of family members, both living and deceased. They sifted through photos for several minutes.

However, Katie did not require a lengthy look as she picked up an old picture in a locket. She didn't talk for a moment, but there was a certain enlightenment in her face. She studied it as if enjoying the recollection of a happy memory. "She looked like this, only she didn't wear glasses."

Moments later, Rachel returned to the room again. Studying the tiny photo she declared, "That's the angel! But without the glasses," she said emphatically.

At that moment, no one could say anything. There was not anything to say. It was simply a time for thinking.

A picture came into my mind of 135 school children saying a prayer, a powerful plea for divine intervention, all at once. Katrina, Rachel and Travis were among them.

I looked at the faces of the two girls once again. My wife and daughter and I felt a certain warmth, a "closeness" filling the room, along with the Walkers. It was a time when a person could feel as if the physical realm didn't exist—only the spiritual.

No one could be in the room at that point and not feel certain these two girls were completely convinced of what they said.

Katie looked and studied the face again, but said nothing. There was a trace of a lingering smile.

Shirley Ruth Thornock died when Glenna was only sixteen. "My mother never lived to know my family," Glenna said.

Another photo, this one of Kevin's brother who died in 1961, "looked like" the man who was with the "family of angels," the girls said. But they hadn't looked at him that day as closely as the woman who was doing the talking. They couldn't be sure.

There was no explanation for the others mentioned in the group. The girls had never seen nor known any of the others they described, including the little girl with the long brown hair.

The term "guardian angel" was never used by any of the Walkers. They simply talked about them in the role that some people do, of "messengers from across the veil" who were credited with helping to save their lives.

As for the definition of angels, it was not given, except that the people who appeared to them were not in the room until they appeared "from the ceiling."

I had to ask a question I'd often heard. "Did they have wings?"

"No!" the two girls said without hesitation. "They looked like we do, but all dressed in white," Rachel emphasized.

"Did she smile at you?"

Katie pondered the question for a long time.

"She sort of smiled at me with her voice."

"Did she make you feel you were going to be safe?" I asked.

"She said we would be if we did what our brother told us," Rachel replied.

"Travis, did you feel that you would be protected when the bomb went off?"

"I knew, somehow, we would be if I followed directions. When I heard the explosion, I just forgot about part of what I was supposed to do. I was so close to the hallway, it was easy to get out there . . . it was a minute later when I thought about my sisters."

"Were all the angels there when the bomb went off?" Kevin asked them.

"I don't know. The smoke from the bomb covered them up."

By now it was the girls' bedtime. We had talked for more than an hour, including some time the girls left to play games.

We asked them one more question: "Where were you sitting?"

The girls located in the southeastern part of the room near the corner until Travis came over and moved them. They named several other children and a teacher who were nearby.

It didn't seem to concern the girls whether anyone else saw the same people in white standing overhead. They didn't even seem to think of it. They just explained what happened to them.

There were others in the hostage room who related that "messengers" appeared to them as well. Some families felt it was a "personal matter." There might be people in the world who have hardened their hearts, people who would not understand or believe.

One mother said some people would not comprehend what the children were saying or know what to do with it.

Several other parents said their children specifically gave details of someone they didn't know appearing to them in the hostage room. These families specifically requested their names not be used.

As for the Walkers, all of them discussed their own personal feelings. Mrs. Walker said, "The children know it happened, and they want to share it. They feel they have a responsibility to share it so others can benefit from it. What others do with their experiences or feelings is up to them."

Kevin explained, "It was the children's decision. They stand behind it. We stand behind them. Where would we be—where would any of us be—without the courage to testify of such a spiritual happening?" he asked.

Later, I asked Glenna, "Are your children better behaved now; do they try to be more obedient, more helpful since this incident?"

"I wouldn't say that!" Glenna laughed. "But they do seem to have a much closer relationship with each other than ever before."

Miracle or not, human nature does not miraculously change without conscientious and diligent effort, it would seem.

"Everyone involved in the investigation of David Young's bomb knows something strange and unexplainable happened," Eva Clark stated. "No one has any plausible idea at all how the children safely escaped. I think it is time to listen to them, the hostage children themselves, and let them tell us the reason they all survived. We can label it 'divine intervention' or whatever we want. Whatever we call it, many of these explanations from the children help everything fit together better."

Another hostage child willing to share his spiritual experience in surviving the explosion and its aftermath was six-year-old Nathan Hartley.

Nathan was sitting near the taped line before the bomb detonated. He told his father, veteran sheriff's investigator Ron Hartley, what he saw. "The lady helped me get out alive," he said.

"I've been through it all with hours of interrogating suspects and prisoners," Hartley said. "I'm especially trained to detect lying or manipulative answers for personal gain," Hartley said. "I asked some more questions."

The first grader continued: "A lady told me the bomb was going to go off very soon. She told me how to save myself. She said to go over by the window, then hurry out when I heard the bomb explode. She told me that I would make it if I did exactly what she said."

Nathan said he had never seen the woman before. Later leafing through a family album, the youngster stopped his father. "That's her!" he exclaimed abruptly.

It was his great-grandmother, Flossie Elliott. She had been dead for three years, the boy's father stated.

Did the Hartleys feel any concern about relating their son's unique experience? "It happened," Mrs. Hartley said.

"I'd rather face people now than explain later why we didn't say something about it—either here or in another life," Hartley emphasized. "We can't back down from personal convictions."

What about the entire idea of divine intervention? If it is to happen, why not a providential Deity halting David Young and his idea altogether? One parent answered these queries this way: "Everything we read on the subject, whether in the Bible or anywhere else, tells us man has his free agency. The way I see things, it would not be consistent with it that a bolt of lightning hit a person with criminal intentions enroute, in this case, to the school building. Young's bomb went off as he intended it. But the intervention preventing innocent people from being killed—in answer to fervent prayers—also occurred."

Christians would point out that in allowing man free agency, God even permitted the crucifixion of his own Son.

In addition, there are many people, including little children, who are killed every year. What about them? Why some die and others don't isn't known. Perhaps in the Cokeville case, it was the power of prayer preventing so many young children dying before their time. Perhaps it was to mitigate, if not wholly eradicate an anti-God force. The only explanation is that of the children, that it did happen as they explained it.

It is interesting to note that sincere prayers preceded most of the spiritual messages or assistance hostages said they received. Rather than being shocked or frightened by the experiences, all seemed to be bolstered by them. One may even ask a question, "Has anyone in the history of spiritual events testified that spiritual enlightenment was forced upon him against his will?"

Someone elsewhere may conjecture miracles as happening in a different manner. Certainly it was not the way Hollywood would have depicted it. On the other hand, the results were even better than Hollywood could have imagined.

There were also the many "feelings" of divine intervention. Many parents had heard the adult hostages say they "felt like something—some extraordinary influence—entered the room" just before David relinquished the bomb to his wife. It was noted by many that Young's behavior seemed more nervous and uneasy. At the same time "we had a feeling that somehow we were going to make it," one teacher explained. Several teachers like Jean Mitchell sensed a change in the atmosphere of the room as the day progressed.

Eva Clark was intrigued with the sensation she had during the more than two hours she was a prisoner. "I was scared," she said, with no reservation. "I was really scared. He had made sure we adults understood that he would not hesitate to shoot us. I was sure we were going to die. For about an hour and a half, time seemed to drag by, if not stand still altogether. But the last hour or so, after praying over and over, was entirely different. I felt peace. I knew we would make it.

"Interestingly, that space of time seemed to fly by. Something came over me and told me to be patient for a little longer."

Several months after the incident, Travis and Kamron discussed their first impression of the takeover.

"It was like the room was smoky or something, just a little. It was like someone had been smoking a cigar in there."

"Yeah, I remember," Kam responded. "It was like on a cloudy day and they hadn't turned the lights on inside. Only the lights *were* on, at least the one light in the middle right over the 'magic square.' Later, just a little while before the bomb exploded, the light from the middle of the room was brighter. It seemed a little more yellow or orange—a warmer light than before." The boys were not certain what to make of it, but it seemed strange to them, as they explained it. There just seemed to be no cause and effect reason for it.

As a teacher pointed out, it had been made clear by the Youngs there was no other option. "A time bomb set to go off in so many hours, if demands were not met, would have given us something to work on. All we could do was wait or force something to happen. No one wanted to take that responsibility. There was simply no way for any of the hostages to get out. We had to rely on a power higher than ourselves!"

"After several fervent prayers, there was a way," Mrs. Mitchell stated. "But the only way out was the way it happened, with the bomb exploding first."

After talking with hostages about being helped by angels, I spoke with several psychologists about their professional experience with "unexplainable occurrences." One of them, Columbia-educated Dr. Craig Peery of Provo, Utah, has talked with a number of people over the years on this subject of spiritual experiences. Some he believed; some he didn't.

His questions were: Was there a discussion about angels prior to the event? Was there some collusion as a group getting together and discussing it afterward before coming forth with their comments? Was there some worthwhile and beneficial reason for the described happening? Was anything predicted, and did it come to pass?"

For those who can "feel by the spirit" the truth of a matter, it was not a necessary discussion. But for others more comparable to doubting Thomas, the psychologist suggested analyzing each stated experience.

Several factors should be emphasized. It all happened without any previous discussion on the subjects of "getting help" or of angels. Not only did no one know when the bomb would explode, there was no human way of knowing if it would. Yet the children were told it "would happen shortly." This information about an eminent explosion gave them a peaceful, rather than unsettled feeling. All of them felt they faced a crisis ahead, but that they could meet it.

Furthermore, all this happened not in some dark room alone at night, but in a crowded room in the bright light of mid-afternoon. Children spoke of it independently of one another, not after any discussion among themselves.

By any procedure of analysis the testimonies of the hostages are simple but most powerful.

Words used by the post-bomb investigators were "unexplainable" and "miraculous." For some these words are a signal to dismiss them. To do so one would have to also dismiss many other accounts of extraordinary occurrences, including those discussed in such books as *Life After Life*. It seems clear that there are many happenings in this life not easily explained from a standpoint of the physical world only. To label all of the unexplainable as untrue would be as closed-minded as people during the time of Columbus holding to a flat world contradictory to known facts—therefore, false—also convenient. It is an invitation, instead, to learn more.

As for a post-earth life, it has always been intriguing to me that a number of past surveys indicate that many people who do not even attend a church believe in life after death. There were those who would always believe, some who never would, and a good many in the middle waiting for some sort of evidence. Yet it seems that adults are often less capable of seeing that evidence than children. As much is suggested in the Bible: "Whosoever, therefore, shall humble himself as a little child, the same is the greatest in the Kingdom of Heaven." (Matt. 18:4)

One problem with adults is that their habits become more deeply ingrained. It apparently becomes more difficult to make changes, whatever the evidence. Yet in the May 16th incident, all of the teachers felt they had witnessed the necessary evidence. For some, ideas and habits of a lifetime were obliterated in a single day.

One who had "seen enough" was Rocky Moore. Moore had long joked that he would believe in a God only when he saw his personal "burning bush." He had used the expression every time he wanted to avoid a religious discussion. Now, he wanted to talk about spiritual experiences.

"What was it that saved you from the bomb?" someone asked Rocky several months after the crisis. Moore was concentrating on his beloved Panther team from the sidelines of the high school football field. They were in trouble at the moment. Moore whirled around.

"I'll tell you what happened," he said with his back now to the game. "God was looking out for his kids."

"And you were saved because you were with them?" a bystander wanted to know.

"Exactly."

"Did you see your burning bush, Rocky?" a child who had been one of the hostages asked.

The mountain man's jaw jutted. "You bet I did!" Moore nearly shouted. "That's enough for me or anybody. And don't you forget it!"

Rocky's white teeth smiled through his red beard. After falling from the classroom escape window, Rocky carried his sprained arm around in a sling. Now it had healed. Rocky seemed as feisty as ever, but almost contentedly ecstatic with memories of the experience. "I don't see how there could be any more atheists left in this country," he shook his head.

An interview with Jack and Jean Mitchell in their home produced a longer conversation. At the outset Jean emphasized, "The explosion hurt many people. But it seemed to be an act of God the way things turned out. If the children had gotten any more restless, I'm afraid

Young would have begun shooting. It would have been worse, looking at the final outcome, than what actually did happen."

Once agnostic, Jack looked the authors squarely in the eye when he said: "I know this. There is no other explanation for what happened. It was divine intervention. A higher power stepped in. We could do nothing for ourselves. There were prayers answered in there. I'll never doubt the power of prayer again."

It was a statement Jack repeated in three different interviews over several weeks' time.

He reiterated how he felt when he was nearly shot by Young. "It was obvious to me he was about to begin shooting if anyone pressed him any farther. He'd reached his tolerance level. It didn't seem he would need much more provocation to start firing."

Jean recalled vividly her minutes in the faculty room obtaining copies. "It still seems like I was in there for an eternity. It couldn't have been more than five or six minutes, but I'll never forget how I felt the peace I received as I said that prayer. This isn't the kind of thing you go through every day."

Jack and Jean, as well as the other hostages, think of themselves as just "doing what was needed to survive." Part of surviving—along with cooperating as a group in protecting one another—was praying. For Jack it couldn't have been easy. "I hadn't said a prayer in many years," Jack repeated several times.

In effect, the Mitchells, like many others, found faith in themselves, and in their future.

Leaders of churches throughout the country sent letters to Excell praising the school's "spiritual strength." Even the most hardheaded pragmatist would admit that with Young's weaponry and fanaticism, there wasn't much hope of every hostage walking out of this one alive.

One woman in Virginia, seeing the map of the crowded room and reading of the explosion's magnitude, stated: "None of the hostages were experts in bombs, yet it would appear they couldn't possibly have done more things right during and just after the explosion."

Haskell concurred. "Somehow everyone seemed to know what to do to get out alive."

Within an hour after the explosion, a nation's press descended on the Wyoming hamlet. Many of these people, accustomed to seeing tragedy and fear, expressed surprise at the tide of optimism and light-hearted spirits they found. "It had been an afternoon of sheer terror" said one newsman, "I marveled at the way everyone was already bouncing back, especially the children."

There were almost as many versions about what happened before, during, and after the bomb chaos as there were survivors. "Things climaxed in different ways for different people with the explosion," Jack Mitchell stated. "But one thing everyone seems to agree on. It's unbelievable we all got out of there alive."

The Mitchells showed the authors pictures they had taken of the strange "human-sized white mark" on the east wall.

"What do you make of it?" they were asked.

Both hesitated. "I've never been much for symbols," Jack said. "In fact, as I said, I've really bordered on atheism. I haven't found any particular religious significance in anything. But I have to wonder about this mark. It is the only place where soot didn't blacken the wall. I don't have any idea what could have caused it. I don't think anyone does. Still, it has a special importance in reminding us, not just that we survived the bomb, but how we survived it."

Two days after the ordeal, churches in the Cokeville area were filled as never before. Through letters and conversations flowing into the town, it seems it was not the only place this occurred. Prayers were offered in behalf of the community from everywhere.

"I guess the whole world has a little child in their lives somewhere. To think this affected so many children touched all of us," one woman said with intense feeling.

Upon hearing of the unbelievable fact that all the lives were spared, one young woman announced to friends: "That does it. I'm going to church on Sunday until further notice."

Part of the Sunday crowds were due to an LDS mission "farewell," always a crowd-gatherer. Max Excell was called to comment on his son Rick's departure. But Max could not help referring to the deliverance. "This was to be a special and happy occasion today, looked forward to for many years," he told the crowd. "But it couldn't have been if someone wasn't looking out for us at the school. I didn't see any angels," he said, his voice cracking with emotion, "but I felt them there."

Over at the Catholic and Episcopalian services down the street, ministers looked at some new faces. Stated Jack and Jean, "Just to be sure, we went to all the church services—all of them—on the first Sunday after the hostage crisis."

As for personal feelings about the childrens' extraordinary experiences, I remembered as a teenager a line originating from W. Somerset Maugham's "The Razor's Edge." It was: "The dead look so terribly dead when they're dead." Indeed, I was the skeptical type.

People wanting to believe something wasn't good enough for me, no wishful thinking now. What was the truth—life after death—or not.

After my grandfather died, my grandmother, Ada Hart of Preston, Idaho, related at a family gathering that her husband had appeared to her a few nights before. She said he had given her instructions on raising her large family. To me such statements were impractical, for impractical people who sat back and dreamed about life rather than living it.

But Ada Hart was as practical a person as ever lived. She had to be to make ends meet on her little farm. She had to work eighteen hours or more a day to survive, especially after her husband's years of ill health. She ran her life with the precision of a computer programmer, in the days before there were computers. And she always told the truth.

Her statement was irrefutable. Those who knew her did not scoff. Some who did not know her, of course, might doubt. It required courage to share the experience.

In later years, my grandmother confessed to me that sharing this "revelation" was a burden in some ways. While she knew it happened, she had to be prepared to answer many questions. She had precious little time to sit and talk. She shared the story unselfishly because she knew it would benefit many others. Her decision to do so blessed many for decades as they sought to build a more spiritual life.

This was the same reason given by the Cokeville hostages for sharing experiences so powerful that their lives will never again be the same.

A Time Of Coping

"The burns had healed; the rest hadn't."
—Mother of a hostage child

High School students gather with sixth graders near edge of school yard only yesterday besieged by bomber. There is only one thing to talk about. Media vehicles lining streets indicate normalcy has not returned. (Photo courtesy of Max Excell)

Three days after the citizens of Cokeville had been torn apart by terror, they pulled themselves together at a community counseling session.

The high school gym frequently held the majority of the town's population witnessing athletic events, dance programs. In two weeks, it was scheduled to house the graduation ceremony for the fifteen seniors of Cokeville High. Now it was the gathering place for an unprecedented town meeting. The subject: How to Cope Following a Disaster.

Dr. Allen Lowe, the district school superintendent, assured the listeners that "you have the prayers and support of many. There were many heroes to come out of the tragedy last Friday, including you and your children. Our purpose is to rebuild, restore, and strengthen."

He said the school room would be rebuilt for the next school year. Those who would feel a financial strain from medical expenses should know they would receive help through insurance as well as other offers of money. "Other regional school districts and the state want to help," he told the crowd.

The audience was somewhat subdued, yet there was excitement in the air, too. The shock was wearing off. People talked over "where they were when the bomb went off." Never had so much happened in such a short time here. Never had so many of these people felt so many emotions. Many felt anger.

In an effort to prevent feelings of self-damaging hatred—which could possibly overwhelm the hostages and their families—one person attempted to Christianize negative emotions. He suggested the hostage-takers "didn't really want to hurt you."

"How can anyone say they didn't mean to hurt us? They hauled all that crap in to kill people. . . ."

Rocky Moore took what he called a "realistic" attitude. "I wish David Young was here right now. Take away his guns and I'd like to have my hands on him—right now."

"Do you hate him?" Rocky was asked.

"You bet I do. I love hating him."

At least Rocky could talk in a positive way about the negative man who held him and the others hostage.

It wasn't as easy for Tina Cook. A man stepped up to the receptionist's desk and seemed to be stalling; she panicked. Finally, he asked for Mr. Excell. He was just there to check out some playground equipment. A woman fished around in her purse for something; Tina imagined a gun. At last the woman produced a card. She was selling something. Mrs. Cook sighed with relief. Tina also had a nightmare. She saw David Young walk up and thump on the counter. "Here I am, Mrs. Cook, and you didn't think I'd come back, did you?"

Whenever she turned off the lights, the school receptionist saw those steel grey eyes resembling a snake. Tina couldn't get the man's arrogant superiority and the fear she felt that day for the children to go away—not for months.

Other families seemed to have enough problems without the Youngs' coming to town. One family was out of work; now they were burdened with the expenses of driving to the hospital daily to see their daughter who had been burned in the explosion. They had only a hope of someday being reimbursed for their lengthy travels. School health insurance didn't promise to pay for such expenses. There was no time now to look for employment until their daughter was out of danger.

Another man, with a daughter being treated for burns, later had a car wreck and had to be taken to the hospital himself—about the same time his wife went to the hospital to give unexpected birth to twins.

A parent reminded lawmen and their families, in a group counseling session, that most of the community's crime problems had been caused by former local peace officers. There was, of course, David Young for a starter. One hopeful candidate for the marshal's job had predicted, when Young got the job, that the man would cause problems. When someone later told him that a former law officer had taken children hostages, the losing candidate was heard to say: "David Young, right?"

Another town policeman was convicted several years before for raping and killing his landlady while he was on drugs. Still another officer before that was released under a cloud of child abuse charges although he sued the city for so stating. There had been practically no other major crimes in the entire area for decades. It was a time of coping, for the lawmen as well as their wives and families, when local citizens reviewed the record. "Where do we go from here?" the parent asked within the public meeting.

With that reference to former law officers causing problems, there was a heavy silence. Then Deputy Hartley's wife, Claudia, made a teasing comment to her husband about being a problem to her. She said it loudly enough to be heard by several people around them. Knowing the devotion Hartleys felt for each other, the crowd laughed. The comment and the laughter rippled through the crowd. The tension was broken. Then Colleen, police chief Cal Fredrickson's wife, stood up.

"If I have anything to be jealous of in my marriage, it's the dedication my husband feels toward you people in this town. You are very important to him. He'll do anything for you."

The people knew it was true, and the feelings of appreciation and support began to soar. There was applause.

At this meeting, Max Excell gave a report on the condition of those who were still hospitalized. At the University Medical Center in Salt Lake, Tina Morfeld was serious but stable. They had been very worried about her Saturday. Doctors said, "We almost lost Tina Saturday with her internal injuries." Billie Jo Hutchinson was serious but improving. Fawna Eastman was scheduled for probable plastic surgery. At Bear Lake Memorial in Montpelier: Christy Clark, satisfactory; Ryan Taylor, satisfactory; Pat Bennion, serious but stable, considering possible transfer to Salt Lake with infection in her arm. At Logan Regional Gina Taylor, Jay Metcalfe, Jodi Dayton, and Jenny Ferrin were "Doing very well—can't keep them down." There was a cheer and more applause. "In fact, all the fathers are there with them trying to keep them settled. The dads are in worse shape than the kids."

There was laughter—healthy, healing laughter. Three of the four fathers were high school teachers.

About a dozen psychologists were introduced and their backgrounds and specialties explained. They were there to listen and to help the town understand. Questions began slowly at first, then came in rapid succession.

"My child won't talk about it, yet it seems that he hurts inside. If we ask why, he changes the subject. What should we do?"

"Be supportive and open. Let them know they can talk about it freely when they're ready."

"Some of the things I'm hearing from my child are gross and aggressive."

"Just listen. Some language or behavior may seem inappropriate for a while. Don't let it shock or disturb you, but broaden your tolerance level to help them work through their feelings."

"Were they 'bad' people?"

"Like machinery, people can sometimes go awry. These people **did** bad things. . . ."

"My child saw his father pull a rifle out from the truck today and was terrified."

"Such reminders will initiate fear. This hunting community will have a lot of that."

"My son doesn't really know what happened. When people talk about it, he isn't sure he knows what happened, and he was there."

"My daughter says she will never go in room four again."

Many teachers struggled with their own emotions. Janel Dayton talked about yearbook photographers nearly giving her a heart attack by taking an impromptu flash picture in her room. Another time a grandmother walked right in her room unannounced to fetch a grandchild. "I'd never seen her before," Mrs. Dayton said. "She could have done that in the past and it wouldn't have mattered, but things were different now."

Some old-timers said they would wait out the day when the pain would go away. "Every good thing happens in due time," John Teichert stated.

Many hostages and family members who had read their Bibles reread them.

"How long will we see these behavior traits, these problems?" townspeople asked psychologists.

They were counseled: every person will move at his own pace. Traumatic events have anniversaries. "A year from now, for example, people will probably show increased anxiety."

Some hostages responded with a sense of humor. One could drive to Evanston 70 miles away and order a T-shirt printed with "Cokeville's a Blast." In trying to gain understanding and forgiveness, one could always use a little levity to light the way.

Scriptures and poems, uplifting sayings from literature, any source of optimism and strength were used as a road map to locate trails to the summit of forgiveness and its lofty view. From there, hopefully, once the fog went away, the correct future course below the peak would no longer be blurred, but focus clearly.

School district officials suggested that teachers begin working with therapists the following Tuesday to learn how to best help their students start school again. It would be important for the teachers to talk through their problems before attempting to help children with theirs. One thing teachers wanted to convince the children of was this: you have experienced a severe trial, and you passed it with flying colors.

Teachers were also given a boost when they were praised for heroic efforts, particularly in keeping themselves and the children calm in the face of danger. They were applauded at the coping meeting. The children were praised for obeying teachers and summoning up a brave front for each other. Peace officers from other areas, who had come in to assist, lauded the entire community for its discipline. "You were a great example," officers repeated.

Someone stood to commend the EMTs for their work, then another spoke words of praise for law enforcement. Everyone was thanking everyone.

"In the eyes of professionals around the country who have handled very serious situations, you are to be commended," said Dr. Nohl Sandahl, head of the team of psychologists. "They stand in respect for how you have come out of this situation. You did things right."

School district officials recommended not entirely cleaning up the "bomb room" until students had a chance to look it over once more. It was open for tour all day Sunday, two days after the bomb exploded. Except for a tarp thrown on the floor in the room's southwest corner where Doris' body was found, everything was left just as it was when the children escaped from it. There was even a pair of shoes left behind. Some asked if the owner was blown right out of them.

Tentatively, children with their parents relived the scene within the blackened room.

"This is where I sat."

"I was coloring right here at this desk."

They were putting the pieces together in their minds. Several therapeutic touches were seen. Someone had scrawled a belated message in black on the wall which read "help." Others wrote their names in the soot.

Nearly all the children asked if they had to return to the besieged classroom. When they were told "no," they did so anyway. They didn't want to see the room again, yet said one child, "I had to."

"Reestablishment of ownership is an important part of the healing process," school psychologists told parents and teachers.

When would school resume? Summer vacation was just around the corner. School officials felt that no matter how little work was accomplished in the final few days, it was important for the children not to wait three months before returning. At the same time, psychologists felt it necessary to ease students back into school sessions. Students were invited to return when they felt up to it. Most returned for a few hours Wednesday, then half a day Thursday, and all day Friday.

Returning to what she enjoys most, being a first grade school teacher, Jean Mitchell helps her class with the coping process. Moving into a new room, the class works to reestablish their close-knit unit by discussing, "Where were you when the bomb went off?" (Dan Dockstader photo, Star Valley Independent)

In time, some even settled down to hear the rest of the interrupted stories like "Tom Sawyer."

Counseling would be made available on a walk-in basis as needed throughout the week and for as long as necessary. "We hesitate to put a time limit on it," officials explained, "as each victim works through his fears."

A person did not have to be present in the classroom to feel the trauma of it, the counselors explained. "Families and people who were outside of the town when things were happening will still have some very real and important feelings that need to be worked through," they added. A sonic boom was a big thing in the community for some time.

Adults were counseled to show confidence. Children can handle what parents can handle, townspeople were reminded.

Newsgatherers asked Mayor John Dayton what he predicted for the town's future psychological recovery. "This is a town which pulls together. We'll make it."

Teyana Smith, a former resident, stated, "It's like one big family there. Everyone will help each other."

Within a few days, the children seemed to come a long way psychologically from the moment they ran in confusion from the burning school building. One witness called it "mass hysteria." But others said that "under the circumstances, it was just what you would expect, children running and yelling."

Patrolman Anderson reported that most of the children he saw were "happy just to be alive. Some were looking for friends and laughing at how frightened they'd been."

At the hospitals, the administrators and physicians, prepared for a wave of victims, found most children "highly cheerful" despite painful second and third degree burns. "By golly," said one physician, "their attitude appears to be helping their recovery. I was amazed at how quickly all of the burns I saw healed."

Rod Jacobsen, BLM Hospital (Montpelier) administrator, said "everyone noticed right away" that the kids were not feeling sorry for themselves or harboring self-pity. "They just wanted to do what had to be done."

As people consoled or congratulated each other, one person was virtually forgotten for a time. She was the only one in the entire community who had actually lost a loved one; Bernie Petersen had lost her mother. Bernie was also afraid she had lost all her friends. "My own mother doing something like that? I kept asking myself why she would endanger children's lives that way. Could I have stopped her? I felt guilty—but I had no idea."

She paused. "We loved living here in Cokeville. My husband was born and raised here. This is his home. Must we move because of any feelings of animosity toward us? Would that solve anything anyway? How could we run away from our own thoughts?

Some people in town had to work through animosity in their own minds. It was difficult for them to be reminded of the horror they experienced at the hands of people with perverted philosophies. It would take time.

Some neighbors "just didn't know what to say" to the Petersens. The first to find the words were parents of one of the most seriously burned children, the Morfelds. Bernie was assured they did not blame her for what happened. More encouraged, the Petersens mentally wrestled with their feelings. Then they made their decision; they would stay.

Within a few days, many families realized how much they must help one another psychologically. Counselors from around the country, including some who had worked with survivors of the senseless McDonald's Restaurant massacre in San Ysidro, California suggested to parents they just listen to their children.

"Don't even think of what you are going to say next. Simply listen, even if you say nothing."

In one of the many ironies of the entire dilemma, the very thing which had lured Young to the community—strong family ties—now began to mitigate and dissipate what the Youngs had wrought in Cokeville. Young had been defeated by the same love and family togetherness which he had supposed to be the most vital factor in his favor.

There were some coping complications which didn't surface until later. This was often more true with the parents of hostages than the hostages themselves. A number of adults were traumatized by waiting and wondering about what was happening inside, then thinking about it afterward.

It was also difficult to tell how well all of the hostages were coping in the months which followed. Some children remained in shock. No one knew what was going through the minds and hearts of each child.

There were those who took the attitude, "Let's not make too much of this whole thing. The kids are lucky to be alive. Now, let's just forget about it, and get on with our lives. The sooner we do it, the sooner the kids can do it."

It wasn't always as simple as that. Psychologists helped many older students, who felt guilty about not helping rescue brothers and sisters, feel better by asking them," What if you had gone back into the burning room; wouldn't you just be in the way of people trying to get out quickly?" As the children answered that question, many of them realized it was, indeed, unselfish to care so much; yet they did the right thing by getting quickly out of the way.

There were some special problems to overcome with younger children. Those aged six and seven were just beginning to build a sense of confidence and order in their lives. Now both were, if not shattered, at least shaken. Trust, in particular, was on shaky ground. Love and obedience were suspect. "We did what the adults told us to do and we got hurt. What did we do wrong?" A feeling of guilt and "not measuring up" crept in.

One kindergartner who ran from the school shouting, "I don't wanna die, I don't wanna die!" collapsed on his bicycle at his aunt's feet. There was little logic then. There was only fear.

Other children who had been some of Jean Mitchell's "best huggers" began to hold back. They were now aloof, sharing less love. She sorely missed their expressions of simple love. Yet one can't force such a thing. She wondered when love would return naturally.

Perhaps the children were feeling betrayed by the world of grownups who let this thing happen. Jean was fearful about the youngsters losing trust in their teacher. They had obeyed her, now this happened. She was not sure what she could say to them.

Meaghen Thompson is one of Jean's best huggers, but fear and distrust have become part of some of the children's lives since David Young tried to force his "superior intellect" on unwilling hostages. Love strong enough to overcome those fears will be Jean's top priority now. (Ravell Call photo courtesy of Deseret News)

One kindergartner's personality changed. Not even her own family members could find the old enthusiasm in her. "The burns had healed. The rest hadn't," her mother said. Outgoing no longer, the little girl shut herself into a shell, hiding anytime she saw someone with a beard. When her father talked with such a man at the door one day, she ran for a back bedroom. Hearing a firecracker at a family party, she disappeared and couldn't be found. After a long search, family members found her cowering in the barn.

A five-year-old watched his father carry the body of a woman from the smoking classroom. His father "took good care" of the woman. Then, the boy saw it was the one who tried to kill them. How could he pass it off as if nothing had happened?

One youngster said he was "awfully, awfully mad."

A boy told his father, "Daddy, the man lied to us."

Another said, "I saw the lady blow up. . . ." He could not find the words to say more.

A teacher, who wanted to exhibit Christian love "even to those who despitefully use you," found she could not entertain such feelings toward David Young. "I hated him," she concluded, "and that's that." Then she added, "Well, at least I hated what he did to those trusting and loving children."

Among the mental hurdles faced by parents was the urge to never let the young ones alone again, even to send them to school. But, of course, they had to do so. Parents couldn't overburden their children with twenty-four hour security. They couldn't just hold and hug their children for the rest of their lives.

The tangle of emotions was not quickly sorted out. A common bewilderment among most of the hostage children was why Young picked them as the targets of his ugly outlook on life. What had they ever done to him?

A custodian who had a child held hostage said she could not work in the building any more after dark.

Principal Excell said it gave him "an eerie feeling" to turn a key in the school door when alone several days later "with the memories so fresh in my mind."

A strange quirk in the crisis aftermath was that those who were absent on the "hostage day" didn't feel 100 per cent relieved they missed the ordeal. Psychologists called it "survivor's guilt." Perhaps because of an empathy for those who suffered through it, those absent (including teacher Briant Teichert who had been at the track meet) talked a little tenuously about wishing they had been there. No one envied those who had been burned. Yet they wanted to know first hand what happened. They wanted to help share in the burden. As for Teichert, he said the thought of substitute teacher Pat Bennion "being harmed while taking his place was just unbearable."

Pat's husband, Sam, had a particular burden to overcome. His wife had been hospitalized for several days. There was serious concern about her well-being for a time. All three of his children had been held hostage. His widowed mother was injured when she remained behind in the room searching for children. He had been threatened with the loss of his entire family. Such a threat is not easy to dismiss.

There were only six children absent during the ordeal, but they sometimes felt they had missed out on the most discussed thing to ever happen in their community. Morning kindergartners, eluding the incident by half a day, felt the same way. It was considered a good thing by many that only half the five- and six-year-olds were taken hostage. That age has a lot of "squirmers," a parent of one admitted.

"I don't like to think what might have happened if the ordeal had gone on much longer," one teacher observed.

There were other types of mental stress with the families of the lawmen. The wife of a peace officer had rushed up to friends outside the schoolhouse shouting, "My husband has to go in there after the gunman!" The thought was mirrored in her countenance: If there is no one dead in there now, will there soon be?

Her husband did not die. He nearly witnessed other lawmen being shot, then he was treated for nearly an hour by EMTs for smoke inhalation. Another law officer was taken to the hospital for treatment. Several stopped to think about their lives being ruined by either shooting a fellow peace officer or vice versa. Such things happened all the time in the newspapers. However, when it happened to your husband or father, it was altogether different.

It made bystanders realize the terrible risk a law officer is called on to take. The trauma is often worse for the wives and family members who can do nothing but wait and imagine the worst.

Shortly after their successful escape, the children showed a strong inclination to forget the grim and serious. They were looking for opportunities to turn their energies elsewhere. One occasion was a Little League baseball game of "alumni" thirteen- and fourteen-year-olds against the current practicing team of nine-to-twelve-year-olds. On Saturday morning it was nearly cancelled. Parents didn't know if the kids would be up to it

The kids voted a resounding "yes." However, there was now an unusual twist to the event. Some of the children had baseball mitts and shoes in the elementary school building. A police cordon had sealed off the entire grounds. Bomb experts had combed the premises for any explosives, detonating them and removing all the weapons to be placed in evidence, but investigators were still sifting the entire school property for additional clues needed in any possible future hearings.

Learning of their plight, that the children would need to enter only the north wing which was nowhere near room four, a sympathetic sheriff's aide skipped the red tape. When the aide hesitated, a boy piped up, "Come on, we need to get our minds on something else."

"Go get your mitts," the aide ruled. This quickly done, the game began.

Taunted at being "over the hill and out of shape" at the ripe ages of thirteen and fourteen, the alumni nevertheless defeated the still emotionally shaken regular team comprised of the previous day's hostages. It mattered little, according to one youngster. "It just felt great to think of something else."

Travis Walker wanted to know if the coach felt his broken hand had healed enough to play first base. "It looks like you're doing better than ever," his coach told him.

The high school playing field is used for a variety of things through the year, but never before as a landing field for newsgathers in helicopters. (Photo courtesy Cokeville High School Yearbook)

Television cameras on hand took footage of the children at play the day after. One boy commented that it was the only time a sports event in Cokeville would ever be on TV.

Several children also observed that the crisis accomplished one thing; "it put Cokeville on the map."

When school opened Wednesday, five days following the hostage crisis, a few of the students returned with parents, but most came without them. "More than I expected," said school district counselor Mike Cummings.

Cummings and local psychologist George Chournos spent the morning watching children arrive, looking for signs of any problems.

"I saw five kids walk up here by themselves real early, and I just about bawled," Chournos said. "I think it's a matter of pride with these kids."

As one who grew up on a rugged western sheep ranch, Chournos said it struck him that "some of these kids really are tough." He thought the therapy of teachers and children seeing each other again "was just as good for the teachers as it was for the children. All of the teachers encouraged their students to talk about whatever was on their minds."

"Where were you when the bomb went off?" Kliss Sparks asked her fourth graders. Rusty Birch said he was right next to the lady on fire. "It took me about three seconds to figure out what was going on. Then I got out of there!"

Rocky Moore asked his students if they were mad at him for throwing them out the windows. "Oh no!" they shouted.

What about the blackened classroom—who would have to use it again? Jean told her principal flatly, "I don't ever want to see the inside of that room again."

Completely renovated, it was first utilized mostly for storage. Eventually, Verlene Bennion volunteered to take her reading classes in there.

By Friday an interesting interlude happened in town—the Ford Brothers Circus. Excell, Mitchells, Moore, and other teachers raced elephants down Main Street. "Oh, it felt good," a teacher said. "For a time I forgot all about everything." Delighted youngsters cheered for their favorite teacher to win.

Some circus rides were shunned because the attendants were strangers wearing beards. Mostly, it was a particularly happy time for the children. It was one of the few times they could ask for money to buy popcorn, peanuts, or cotton candy and hear only the word yes.

"It was fun," one boy said. "I ate everything I ever wanted."

Spoiled kids? "I was happy to give them the opportunity for one night," a father said.

In the incident's aftermath, the Mitchells learned Young had been a graduate of Chadron State College. Coincidentally, the Mitchells had also both graduated from Chadron. Later, they visited their alma mater, picking up a copy of the "Zero equals infinity" philosophy statement David mailed to Chadron with his note scribbled on the bottom.

It felt good to help investigators and newsmen put the pieces of this strange David and Doris Young puzzle together. Some months after the bombing, Eva Clark remarked, "I have a new appreciation of my family and of my freedom. I'll never take those things for granted again, not after nearly losing them all."

Eva talked about Memorial Day, which followed ten days after the explosion. "I was grateful the town didn't have any new little graves to visit," she emphasized.

Memorial Day held an emotional experience for several of the hostages. Local Boy Scouts were asked to assist the American Legion post in commemorating the community dead. The boys felt lucky not to be among those honored, but the traditional twenty-one gun salute still sounded "a little too close" to them.

"I jumped when the guns blew off near me," one boy said. "But we made it. I think we're going to be OK."

Some difficulties showed up later among hostage families. Their lives were beyond their control for a time. Fathers and mothers, in search of security once again, found themselves putting down tougher rules. Mothers jumped at the falling of a pencil. Fathers berated them for being so touchy. Mothers got after fathers for being so insensitive.

Even weeks later, a mother said she cried at nothing. Confessed another, "I snap at every little thing."

Everyone was home now, released from hospitals if not from bandages. Burns were healing rapidly. Physicians treating the young patients couldn't believe how quickly and completely the wounds were responding. They must remain covered with Jobst bandages or gloves for some time, however. Billie Jo Hutchinson would be wearing her cover for at least sixteen months. Still she managed a big smile for anyone who walked near. Her smile was about the only part of her that was not bandaged.

There would be scars on the faces and arms of some of the injured girls, Principal Excell reported when the authors visited Cokeville in December of 1986 and early January, 1987. Billie Jo will probably have some scarring on her face. Gina Taylor once feared she would lose an eye. She may carry a mark below that eye as a reminder of her ordeal, yet she and her parents had coped well. They thought of it more as a symbol of her eyesight and her blessing.

There will be emotional scars. Only time will tell how many and how deep. The sleep was not always peaceful, even after months of healing. Tragedy in the news brought an empathy and a shiver. Yet, it should be remembered that these youngsters were not fearful just for their own lives, but for people they cared for very much: lifetime friends, trusted teachers. In the situation with Eva Clark, parent and students agonized for hours with each other. That concern will probably never diminish. "Nor should it," psychologists told survivors and their families.

Hostages did not want the miraculous aspects to be forgotten. Said one woman, "I think this should be remembered as a miracle of the same magnitude as the parting of the Red Sea."

Certainly, there was a lesson in it, every adult hostage agreed.

One of the most memorable comments was made by Mrs. Cook. "Deep down I don't want to ever forget how bad this was because I don't want to ever forget how good it eventually turned out either."

Many citizens who knew each other only casually learned to help and receive help from nearly everyone in town. It brought about a greater feeling of camaraderie, even in a small community where it already had a head start.

Interviewing them, I tried to visualize the feeling of closeness people felt for those they scarcely knew, including United Parcel delivery woman Sandy Gonzalez and teacher candidate Cindy Cowden. They weren't related to anyone in the valley. I recalled the lesson learned while attending Wood Badge Training for the Boy

Scouts of America just the summer before. Helping each other through many work projects, everyone gained a feeling that no one could be left out. Pulling together must have been a healing balm in the rejuvenation process for Cokeville.

Every conversation in this community after the hostage ordeal seemed to say just that. There was also an unspoken determination to not feel sorry for oneself. "Put your shoulder to the wheel . . . push along; do your duty with a heart full of song," to quote an old pioneer song. "We all have work, let no one shirk; put your shoulder to the wheel."

That approach was the opposite of David Young's philosophy that the establishment owed him something.

An editorial in the Salt Lake City *Deseret News* a week after the incident stated: "Before the rest of the country forgets about Cokeville, a quick word is still in order about how admirably well the little Wyoming community handled itself during the recent ordeal."

The commentary applauded citizenry who "cared for each other." Then, most importantly, came a weighty conclusion about the cause of that ordeal. "If a lesson emerges from this episode, it is a lesson about what can happen to individuals who start nursing a grievance, real or imagined—who convince themselves they are right and everyone else is wrong. . . .As was so graphically demonstrated by the Cokeville madness, people can poison themselves with their own ideas. . . .Surely another lesson is the well known one about the futility of violence."

Later, Wyoming Department of Education's Audrey Cotherman was surprised to find Cokeville "politely refusing" any state aid. "The town is so self-sufficient," she said, "that it has not needed state aid and has done very well on its own resources. Cokeville is the most remarkable community we've ever seen. Those people responded and organized themselves. I cannot praise that community enough."

It was sweet music to residents. Many were still trying to find some way to utilize the lessons of the crisis. Said one mother, "I wouldn't want anyone here to go through that again. But I can see where it has bonded people closer together than before."

Unfortunately, another lesson was to have less blind trust in people you don't know.

For guidelines in psychological counseling given Cokeville crisis victims and their families, Lincoln County School District officials used a manual for teachers labeled "Project Cope." The procedures had been previously used by the Community Services of the San Diego California Mental Health Department.

Although Jeremiah Moore's seventh birthday was not too happy, future birthdays are bound to be better. (Jack Monson photo courtesy Deseret News)

For dealing with ages five to eleven, it recommended a "physical reenactment of the disaster." Another was "to give a patient clarification of what happened."

That was one reason school officials encouraged the children to enter the blackened classroom before it was cleaned up. They could see it again at its worst and later at its best.

For older children, including the twelve-year-olds, it was recommended to "encourage verbal expressions of thoughts and feelings about the disaster; rehearse safety measures to be taken in future disasters; encourage child to verbalize any feelings of loss and grieving."

School officials also noted the document's warning that "performance levels in various academic and other skills might drop off for a time—but parents and teachers should reassure the youngsters competency will return."

The coping period would continue.

"No one without a child in that room can fully understand how much the thing affected us" a mother said. "We thought these things happened somewhere else. When our own children were threatened, we had to face the very real possibility of going through life without them. It had an intense impact which we can never entirely forget."

However, things were getting somewhat back to normal in Cokeville by the late fall of 1986. The boys' football and girls' volleyball teams had taken the state championships. Six of John Miller's music students had been selected for state awards. Rocky Moore was still grabbing tardy students and neck-wrestling them into his room. In some ways things hadn't changed.

A town had triumphed. At the same time, these thoughts by Sherrie Cornia, who had three children held hostage, wrote of the lasting impacts local residents felt:

"I stood silently, staring at the smoke-blackened classroom. The horror of what my children had survived seeped deep and heavy. My eyes scanned the gray walls, covered with school papers and dulled displays; over scattered building blocks and crayons; into tipped-over chairs and empty shoes; around the masking-taped line that had framed the lethally loaded shopping cart; up the broken ceiling panel where the bomb's explosion had found partial escape;

out the windows and doors where heroes had lifted, carried, pushed, and pulled our precious heritage to safety.

"I stepped to the corner and studied the graceful folds of red, white and blue hanging in quiet dignity, altered only by a thin film of black dust, a symbol of freedom that had been held hostage.

"The standard had been tested and terror had failed. Our freedom was intact, our children were alive. Pain would pass, burns would heal. God does hear and answer prayers.

"As reality settled into reverent gratitude, the words of a small son gently echoed through my calmed thoughts 'and Heavenly Father, please don't let it ever happen again.' "

Town Hall is the scene of a press conference conducted by Lincoln County Sheriff T. Deb Wolfley. The room is filled with television and newspaper reporters, lawmen and investigators...

...and the arsenal collected from school and Young's van. In addition to rifles and numerous handguns, cans of gun powder and other bomb components, lawmen also collected three volumes on bomb construction and over a dozen diaries kept by the terrorists. (Ravell Call photos courtesy of Deseret News)

Pistol exhibit from Lincoln County investigation. A number of these were taken by David and Doris Young with them into the classroom.

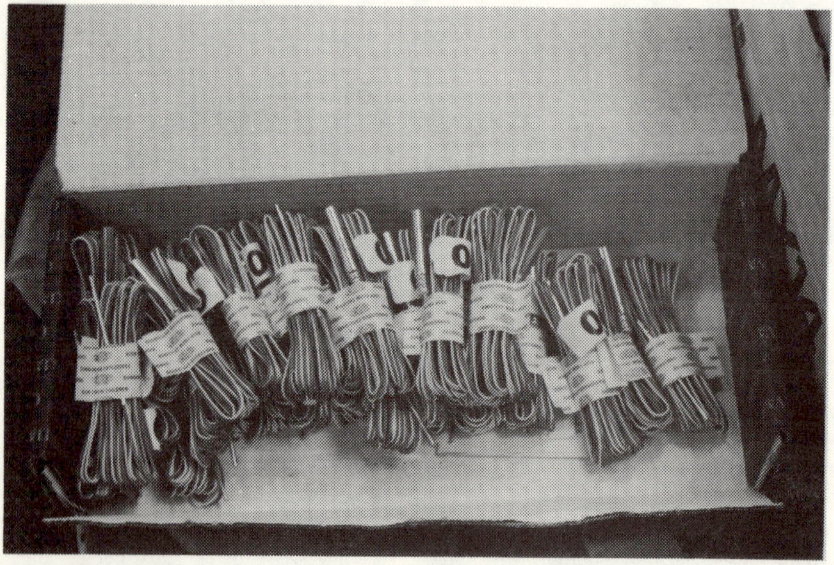

Fine print on these bomb components reads, "dangerous-explosives, keep from children." The Youngs had them along when taking 156 hostages. (Photos courtesy Dan Dockstader, Star Valley Independent)

A Massive Investigation

"David and Doris Young could have each received a minimum of 3,080 years in prison for the kidnapping charges alone."

—Lincoln County Attorney R. Leonard

Within fifteen minutes after the bomb exploded in Cokeville, Lincoln County Assistant Attorney Richard Leonard (County Attorney as of Janunary 1, 1987) was at the schoolhouse to provide legal advice. It would include possible search warrants, determination of justifiable self-defense shooting actions. He would initiate the most monumental criminal investigation in the county's history.

It was, in Leonard's own words, "what appeared to us to be the most extensive act of terrorism ever attempted in the United States. No one had ever held that many hostages or injured as many as in this criminal action, so far as any of us knew."

Leonard emphasized, "I've seen it all; homicides, drug busts, all kinds of things among crimes and criminals. Yet I have never seen anything as potentially lethal and dangerous turn out so positively for so many innocent people involved. It seemed even more so the deeper we probed into the Youngs, their many writings, and into the many depositions that we have gathered."

He also stated that while several people thought the matter of determining who died, when and where, and particularly, how and why, to be an easy one, such isn't the case, legally speaking.

Civilian onlookers heard that the two perpetrators were dead, and that Young apparently shot his wife, then turned the gun on himself.

However, to even determine that much officially, painstaking investigative procedures had to be followed. Along with Leonard, county sheriff's investigators Earl Carroll and Ron Hartley spent days in the schoolroom, talking to hostages, and poring over evidence in the case.

All were veterans at their jobs. Leonard had spent more than five years in the attorney's office, while Carroll had been a police chief in Utah for twelve years before joining Lincoln County. Hartley had also spent years with the county as an investigative officer.

They launched a thorough investigation into everything known about David and Doris Young: their possessions, travels, lifestyle, and particularly their diaries. On nearly every front they discovered some surprises. In the matter of weapons alone, the investigation turned up three guns the hostages didn't even know the Youngs had.

One of them was a .22 caliber pistol Doris carried in her purse. Another was the small .22 caliber pistol David had tucked in the back of his trousers. In all that made four guns on his person. Still another firearm the hostages didn't see was the .44 caliber Bulldog pistol found in the restroom with Young's body. Had he stashed it there before herding in the hostages?

Carroll said it was determined that the .44 caliber Bulldog was used by David to shoot his wife. "He fired two slugs, one of them missing her. Both slugs were found in the ceiling tile." Lawmen concluded Young must have been shooting upward from a low angle in the smoke-filled room. He may not have even known who she was, but simply fired at a figure moving toward him from above.

The act of killing Doris in her fiery hysteria may have been considered by some to be a merciful one, yet so far as Lincoln County was concerned, it was termed first degree murder. The reason: it was committed while attempting to perpetrate a felony, in this case, hostage-taking or, legally speaking, kidnapping.

After shooting Doris, David went back to the restroom where he placed his .45 caliber long Colt beneath his chin and pulled the trigger. When sheriff's deputy Randy White discovered Young's body and determined that he was dead, he and other lawmen followed proper legal procedure in leaving the body precisely where it was.

Custom-made handgun with "DGY-1" proudly stamped on side, is the .45 Colt officers determined Young used to kill himself. (Dan Dockstader photo, Star Valley Independent.)

However, investigators were somewhat miffed at first that the body of his accomplice, Doris, had been removed from the blood-spotted southwest corner of the room where she apparently died. That "screwed up" the investigation of the death of a criminal accomplice.

EMTs then explained they thought they were removing an adult hostage who they felt at first might respond to mouth-to-mouth resuscitation.

No one moved the body of David (except slightly to put handcuffs on "just in case" he wasn't dead) until some four hours later when Lincoln County Coroner Michael Richins arrived. According to Sheriff T. Deb Wolfley, Richins found no diabetic paraphernalia on Young's person or in the restroom where his body was found. Apparently Young did not go in with the intention of taking an insulin shot. His supply was still out in the hall.

Why did a man who so carefully oversaw every facet of the hostage takeover abruptly leave it all to his wife just before the bomb exploded? There was no indication from the autopsy that Young was experiencing a diabetic blood sugar imbalance, just before he died, according to the investigators.

Strenuous physical output could precipitate a reaction, but Young had been sitting relatively still in the middle of the room for over two hours. Investigations show, if a little sarcastically, that Young was accustomed to just sitting and thinking over the years.

There is no evidence to confirm that Young's profuse perspiring and nervousness just before the bomb exploded was due to anything medical. "If he saw or sensed something that upset him," one doctor explained, "it might make him perspire or be nervous, but only as it would with anyone. It did not have to be diabetically triggered."

Why did Young spend as long as he did in the restroom when he previously had been watching intently every move the hostages made? Was it due to any loss of confidence or courage? If he still felt the same urgency to personally oversee everything that happened, why did he seem to tarry inside? (Note: not all hostages agree whether Young tarried or not. Some said he was only in a "very short time, while others stated it was about "two minutes.") Whatever his reason for going inside, it was apparently not medical.

Diabetics who do not correctly control their chemical imbalance sometimes suffer from a severe thirst and a bladder problem. Since David never took advantage of the drinking fountain in the room, thirst was apparently not a problem to him. There is no particular reason to believe his bladder would have been a reason for him to spend so long in the restroom either.

If Young were so stressed that he sought refuge in the restroom, one might question why. Though he was in charge, perhaps the children's restlessness was getting to him. Wasn't he too "brilliant" to let that happen?

In his initial plan, mapped out over a seven-year period, he talked about holding children hostage for up to ten days or more. He must have been prepared for such a thing physically and emotionally or at least thought he was.

Did he suddenly grow nervous sitting by a bomb and deadly weapons? Earlier he had been thoroughly disgusted with his daughter, Princess, for letting the idea bother her.

Had he been in "his own universe" so long he failed to recognize what happens in the real world? Small children held prisoner in a crowded room and the threat of violence made real by the presence of guns and a bomb were bound to create some restlessness in most people.

Yet with all his careful equations and his powerful persuaders to back him up, it seems the wandering children or something did cause him to succumb to tension. Hostages became convinced that it mounted until it became more than David Young could handle.

Some who prayed so earnestly for a higher power to assist them may give a spiritual reason for an anti-God advocate to suddenly falter. Judging from all the hostage statements presented, any open, scientific mind would stop to ponder the testimonies given.

At the same time, it is not the nature of official government investigations to include the words "divine intervention," nor did they.

Personal opinions of investigators did, however, express a feeling that "putting everything together, there are many unexplained things happening here."

The personality profile pieced together of David Young was that of a man with an unusually high IQ, yet a man who was an emotional iceberg, capable of doing almost anything without feeling any compunction for his acts. Anything he did had to be right because he did it.

Not a petty crook, nor a school dropout street thug, Young went about his business with deadly precision. He was highly disciplined when it served his selfish purposes; he wasn't likely to drink too much when he visited a bar or go to a party. He was, as a former lawman once arrested, now quite careful about keeping out of trouble.

One reason was that he remained at home most of the time with his diaries. In addition, he didn't like confrontation with anyone else unless he had the deck highly stacked in his favor—as he did when planning his "biggie" in Cokeville. It was one of the few times he ever got involved with any other group of people.

Furthermore, he did little talking about his plans. The newspaper report of Sheriff Deb Wolfley saying that Young told "large groups" he planned on taking children hostage was news all right, but only to the sheriff. At no time, the law officer said, did he know of or tell anyone that he knew of Young discussing hostage-taking plans.

Workers at the Lazy T Motel did say they overhead considerable arguing from Young and his entourage when they stayed overnight twice just before the hostage crisis. Yet no one heard enough, apparently, to make them sufficiently suspicious to contact the law.

Mayor Dayton always did suspect Young of burglarizing a local store, but the town marshal was never pinned to the crime. The mayor fired Young shortly after that for other reasons and the matter was not explored further.

So far as is known, Young was never officially charged with any crime prior to the Cokeville incident save the single arrest for wearing a concealed weapon. He died while perpetrating his only known felony.

There was no indication from any official investigations that he was an orphan nor that he was abused or mistreated as a youngster. At an early age, however, his intellect and his ego were seldom tempered by any overt compassion for others. With little social contact, there was not much opportunity to determine how far out of line he might have been with the rest of the world.

He was dangerous because of a fanatical compulsion to prove that he was always right. That served him well when he was within the law, but poorly when he was not. In retrospect, it would be a likely reason why Young committed suicide. He wanted no one around to tell him he had failed. He made certain it could not happen.

Young's body was removed to the Kemmerer City Morgue. Dr. William Fogarty, medical examiner for the state of Wyoming, traveled from Jackson to perform the autopsy. No sign of drug use, including marijuana or significant alcoholic intake, was found. It was determined he had taken a few beers on the day he died, Sheriff Wolfley said.

The body was then turned over to relatives, including Princess and Bernie Petersen. They had the body taken to the Crandall Mortuary in Evanston.

It was a time of intensely mixed emotions for the family, according to Cokeville Mayor Dayton. He met at length with Young's relatives in the mayor's office. The man who had so abused their lives was dead. But as Princess indicated, "He was my father."

One of the facts to be determined before the body was turned over to relatives was whether Young had, indeed, committed suicide. Lawmen all testified they had not fired a shot, yet David was "found dead."

Leonard said there are many ways to determine whether someone has shot himself. One is the angle of the cartridge entry, another is powder burns from firing at close range. Based on these factors, the county officially determined that David had definitely taken his own life. Of course, nearly every one had unofficially concluded as much.

Most legal entities dictate that the first person on the scene is the "controlling officer," although it was difficult to determine here who should be considered first. Deputy Carroll was the first to arrive in Cokeville, while Deputy White was the first to see Young apparently dead. With the passage of time, various aspects of the investigation were given to different lawmen, with Carroll in charge overall.

When Deputy Hartley arrived in Cokeville, he had heard nothing of the crisis on his car radio; he assumed a "massive mock drill" was in progress. He was soon told otherwise and taken inside the school building. Later, the Youngs' forty-one diaries and journals were turned over to Hartley, who as of January, 1987, still had them for further study.

Some initial mysteries were resolved, such as why feathers were attached to the Youngs' last two diaries. Did they have some symbolic significance, perhaps something to do with reincarnation? Probably not. Hartley said that the Youngs' birds had died just before they left Tuscon. They may have simply added some feathers while in a jaunty mood before departing for Cokeville.

Hartley said that one thing he determined, after months of intensive scrutiny of the Young diaries, was that David specifically sought children of high intelligence to take with him in his "Brave New World" of reincarnation.

"It was clear in Young's writings that he had an obsession with starting a new world with pliable and intelligent young minds."

Some citizens did say that Young wrote many things down, as was his usual habit, while in Cokeville. It may have included not only information about close family ties, but what was happening at the school. Test scores over the years did show much higher than average national achievement scores from the Cokeville schools, but it is not known specifically what those scores were when Young visited town.

Carroll said that the gun David used to kill himself was apparently his favorite, bearing the serial number (his only custom made gun) "DGY-1" or David Gary Young, one. He rarely used that middle name "Gary."

Did the Colt or .44 caliber Bulldog jam when Young aimed it at Miller? Was that the reason the music teacher was shot with a .22 caliber revolver? It would make a good story that the larger pistol somehow failed to work. Several townspeople said they heard hostages say they saw David working "frantically at his pistol" as they passed by him standing in the restroom. The authors did not find any direct statements from hostages to that effect.

Young may have just impulsively fired with the .22. If either of the larger pistols did jam, they unjammed later, because Young used them both to shoot Doris and himself.

In some news accounts, a .44 Magnum was mentioned as a weapon used at the school by Young. If so, he returned it to the hallway. Law officers later found it there alongside an AR-15 semi-automatic and a shotgun and 30 blasting caps.

Some of the confiscated rifles carried scopes, normally used for long-range outdoor, not indoor, shooting. Why bring them? It was another one of the anamolies in the Young investigation. Another was the fact that Doris's diaries tell of many odd jobs she performed to provide a living while her husband remained home to "think." Yet in the Young's trailer home at Wayan, Idaho, where David lived when working in that area, lawmen found many fancy, expensive clothes. Some were unworn, still in boxes.

Lawmen found a considerable amount of gunpowder, ammunition, and expected to find some guns in the Young's Tucson mobile home. They also expected booby traps, according to the Pima County Sheriff's office, but fortunately, found none. Other bomb components and weapons were found in the Montpelier motel where the Youngs stayed.

Carroll reiterated what other investigators had said about Young's intentions. "It doesn't appear from all the evidence that David Young ever planned on walking from the school building alive."

He had no escape vehicle, of course, after sending his daughter away with it.

In some places the Youngs wrote of "taking children to an island," but careful reading indicated it was part of the couples' "BNW," lawmen concluded.

Leonard said that because of the magnitude of the investigation, many legal organizations entered the case. One was the United States Department of Justice.

In a letter written October 27, 1986, Carroll stated: " . . . This case is not closed out, and the possibility of future prosecutions has not been ruled out. The case has been referred to the United States Dept. of Justice and is being reviewed."

As late as January, 1987 Carroll labeled the investigation "still open-ended." Some citizens might have thought the matter closed when the two bodies were found, "with no lawman firing a shot." But the probe may require years to unravel, Carroll emphasizes. Princess, Deppe, Mendenhall, or Harrison could be contacted for further questioning, he said.

Those who knew of Princess carrying supplies into the school questioned whether she should have been so quickly exonerated. However, she was released into the custody of relatives-by-marriage, Richard and Joanna Petersen of Cokeville. They said Princess was told to remain in touch with the FBI, so they would always know where she was."

Mrs. Petersen also said, "based on the number of long distance phone calls she made in the one night she stayed with us, she was extremely upset with having an involvement with the hostage incident. You also have to wonder how she wouldn't know anything about it."

Learning how upset Princess was, her fiance drove up from Tucson to be with her and take her back with him.

Those listening to her talk of the "big day" coming up, particularly in the Lazy T, felt she knew more than she later let on. She had made the reference, "don't let them in without a warrant," but it wasn't enough evidence to charge her with anything in the legal opinion of the county attorney.

Teachers in the school also said that when Princess ran down the hallway screaming, "My god! My god . . . " they were completely convinced she was either in shock or else a "very adept actress."

City, county, state, and federal agents are still examining the bizarre matter to determine if any other persons, with full knowledge of what they had in mind, might have assisted the Youngs in gathering their bombs and guns.

Deputy Hartley said, in talking to interested groups about the Cokeville incident, that one of the most oft-asked questions is, "How could anyone do a thing like that?"

"That's one reason we continue to study the Young writings," Hartley emphasized. "What we find there may help us deal with individuals or groups who become consumed by hate or bitterness." It may help us understand those who take over the role of God as David Young did, another lawman said.

Early in the investigation, it was clear the many Young writings would not be quickly analyzed. In fact, they were so voluminous "they could have filled an entire car," Carroll told news reporters, and that was with the many abbreviations used by David and Doris. That list of abbreviations required a special section of the journals and diaries by itself.

Prior to the explosion two agents from the Federal Bureau of Investigation in Boise and Denver were hurrying to Cokeville to help with money negotiations with the Youngs. To be more accurate, they were hoping to talk the Youngs out of their extortion threats. When the bomb blew, that wasn't necessary anymore.

It was a federal crime to kidnap or attempt kidnapping, of course, and agents from the Federal Bureau of Alcohol, Tobacco and Firearms were already enroute. Wearing their yellow coats with large black letters "ATF" stenciled on the back, they were very much a part of the scene. They assisted in determining that David Young shot his wife after she caught fire from the explosion.

Was there ever any real promise of governmental or even private organizations or individuals raising two million dollars for each of the 154 hostages? Carroll stated that one county commissioner had suggested raising one million as bait to get the Youngs away from the school. Law officers would have to worry later about how to recover it. As for gathering up millions of dollars, no one involved in the probe saw much chance of actually amassing it.

"Strangely enough," Carroll added, "for all of Young's preoccupation with money, he hasn't got much of it where he is now. He had only eleven dollars in his wallet, and I've got his credit cards."

Much of the material gathered, including tapes made of conversations between Cokeville Town Hall and Excell in the school, as well as with lawmen and emergency vehicles, was still being examined in early 1987. A routine matter, it can determine whether any government employee or other person acted improperly. It also gathers all known facts on hand in case of future hearings and/or lawsuits. Also under review are depositions taken from school teachers who were in the hostage room, distinguishing hearsay from actual fact.

However, there is nothing particularly secret in this information. Town hall officials and a number of school teachers discussed freely what they consider pertinent to the crisis they experienced just after it happened.

Little was ever said about one phase of the investigation: the recruitment of area teenagers to help comb the school grounds. They searched it inch-by-inch for "anything which appeared to be out of kilter" with what was there before the Youngs arrived.

Every discolored or burned shred of paper, blade of grass, or unaccounted flotsam, anything and everything, was flagged with a pink marker on a wire stick. Some of the items could well have been left by kids during recess or lunch hour or have fallen from pockets of firemen and EMTs running toward the smoldering classroom. With hundreds of wires piercing the grounds, the yard soon resembled a giant pin cushion.

All this information added up, by late autumn of 1986, to what Carroll labeled as "a report more than four inches thick." He also said that in an unusual move, the report was copyrighted to prevent unauthorized use of any part of it until released for public access, the precise time unknown. It could very well release no additional information, except in one valuable area, recommendations on how to prevent such outrageous acts in the future.

Leonard stated that his office was prepared, in the event David and Doris had lived, to charge them both with kidnapping. If convicted of that crime alone, both could have received a minimum of 20 years for each of the 154 hostages. That would add up to 3,080 years for each of the Youngs.

Since the penalty for kidnapping is 20 years to life, it could have been even longer. This sentence would have been served consecutively, not concurrently, Leonard emphasized.

Both of the Youngs would have been charged equally as co-conspirators in the kidnapping. David would have faced a first degree murder charge in the death of his wife. He would also have been charged with attempted murder in the first degree for shooting John Miller.

While neither were premeditated, the usual circumstance for this charge is that it is automatic here since it was linked with a felony crime, Leonard emphasized. Leonard explained that this holds true in the commission of a felony no matter who is killed, whether it be a criminal accomplice, intended victim, or innocent bystander.

He added that there would be no way either of the Youngs would have gained freedom through parole. "It just wouldn't have happened under these circumstances," he explained.

It is not necessary, Leonard said, to transport victims anywhere in order to constitute a crime of kidnapping or the taking of hostages. Threat against a person to hold them anywhere is sufficient, Leonard explained. "In this case it happened within the school classroom."

Since a review in 1932 of the famous Charles Lindbergh kidnapping case, the crime of kidnapping was made an offense allowing the involvement of the FBI, if the victim was transported across state lines. In 1956 it was strengthened to be a federal offense twenty-four hours after a kidnapping, whether the victim was transported or not.

With charges of first degree murder and attempted murder tacked on, David's penalty would have been substantially more than 3,080 years. It should be pointed out that these sentences are state statutes only. If desired, the U.S. Attorney's Office could also levy identical charges on the kidnapping cases.

The county attorney also stressed that a claim of mercy killing to "put Doris out of her misery" would not have gotten David out of first degree murder charges. He would have been so charged regardless of any reason given for killing his wife.

There likely would also have been no leniency shown Doris. She entered the school building on her own volition, without any known coercion from her husband. On the other hand, Leonard said that Princess would not have been charged—possibly even if she had remained with her father in the school room—due to the fact her life was once threatened. Deppe and Mendenhall, handcuffed in the back of the van, were clearly not part of the kidnapping-extortion scheme once it became known. At least this was the thinking of the county. Carroll made it clear the federal government has the perogative to reach its own conclusion.

If the Youngs had lived they could have pleaded insanity. "That would have been the most likely defense approach. If I were a defense attorney, that is certainly the only avenue I would think to be open," Leonard said, "at least with 154 witnesses present. But one can't speculate on what would happen." He added, "I think in this case it was highly unusual for anyone to do anything like the Youngs did, yet it does not necessarily follow that either one did not know what they were doing."

Could they have been found innocent by reason of insanity, then released later from a mental institution when declared cured?

"That is slim in this case. But you have to say it is always a possibility. I can't speak for a judge or jury."

Leonard was asked what he thought of the compiled evidence, as he saw it, concerning hostages escaping without permanent injury.

"There are many unanswered questions. From looking over all the facts, I simply cannot see how all of the hostages got out alive."

Leonard also said it was fortunate for his office that little else of a criminal nature occurred during this time in Lincoln County.

The American and Wyoming state flags fly briskly in the spring breeze while the body of Doris Young lies covered (white blanket) in the schoolyard. Meanwhile, lawmen discuss next move.

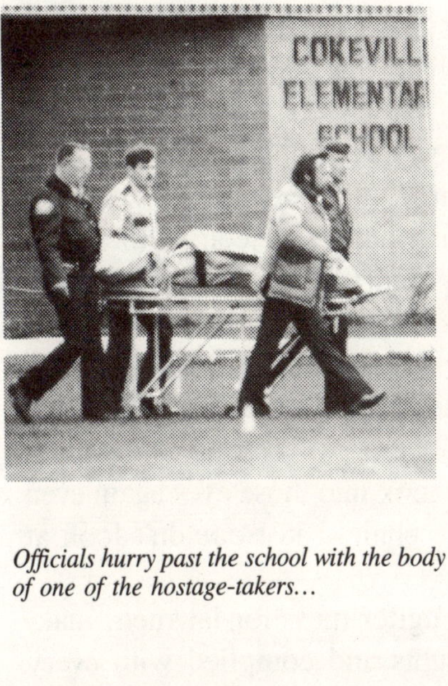

Officials hurry past the school with the body of one of the hostage-takers...

...while others stand by windows from which 70 percent of the hostages made their escape when the bomb blew. Note flagged wires marking possible evidence in the schoolyard. (Photos provided by Max Excell)

"Things were fairly quiet elsewhere during that period, so we could assign just about every person in the department full time to this case."

Charges assessed for kidnapping or attempted murder seem deterrents enough. But when do they actually become crimes that are "chargeable?"

"At the time anyone who talks or writes about it does anything at all toward taking action," the county attorney's office stated. "In the case of the Youngs, that occurred as soon as they transferred weapons into their van with the purpose of taking them into the schoolhouse."

Months after the hostage ordeal, many conversations in the Cokeville area were still punctuated with the question: "If the Youngs had lived, and there had been a trial, how much of a nightmare would it be for the hostages to testify?"

Would any self-styled vigilantes have tried to assassinate David Young? Though many townspeople said they wouldn't fault such a thing, in the eyes of the law it would be murder. That would have been the greatest tragedy of all, a parent or friend of the hostages being charged with a felony, then imprisoned. If so, David Young would have done even more damage than what occurred in the school room.

What about the children—could they have shut off their fears with the knowledge this man might return? "Probably not," said one parent. "His getting what he so much deserved seemed to satisfy my daughter's worst fears about his returning." That thought was echoed in many homes. "Not all problems in the world are resolved as easily," the parent added. Nevertheless, it would be easier to overcome the nightmares just knowing she need never look into that face again, "even in a courtroom."

One teacher confessed, "I couldn't look into those eyes again even if I was putting him into the electric chair. I just couldn't look at that man's face ever again."

In addition, it could have been an uglier mess for lawmen, making certain they read him all his rights and complied with every technicality of law to prevent his being released. If David Young had lived, there could have been a shootout. Even with the suspect being killed, an investigation would have been required into whether a lawman's shot did, indeed, constitute self-defense.

There might also have been potential sympathizers. Some might have claimed Young was not dangerous and did not have to be killed.

"It was convenient the way it worked out," one official said. "That's the best explanation I know of."

One of the many things lawmen and government attorneys attempted to do following the evacuation of the school building was to sort facts from rumors. There was talk of seven blasting caps or more than one plastic jug (one newspaper said five) full of gasoline. However, Haskell reiterated that one jug was enough to ignite the gunpowder and the aluminum dust on the grocery cart into a full-scale bomb, blowing up everything in the room if detonated as designed.

There were other questions. Why did Young, with a reputation for being so meticulous, search a garbage dump for his gasoline container? How could he fail to note the leak in it? Why use such a complicated device requiring substantial human labor to wire together? Law officers don't know.

Perhaps vanity led Young to oversee his bomb personally rather than trusting it to anyone or anything else. Perhaps he thought whatever he did was destined somehow to not fail. According to one lawman, the DuPont blasting caps used are officially calculated to have a one in two million chance of failure. Considering those odds, Young probably felt he was going to succeed in doing precisely what he planned.

One clue concerning Young's supreme confidence might be obtained from family members. Some of them said David just didn't think he "could be wrong in anything he did."

Another relative told Cokeville Mayor Dayton about Young's refusal to end his habit of taking and selling nude photos at every opportunity, even among his own family members. "He just did anything he wanted and thought he could get away with it. Too often he did." The same relative said he had the perfect opportunity to shoot Young. "I had the .45 caliber sitting right there on my table. It would have saved all the trouble and turmoil at Cokeville." Mayor Dayton reminded the man that the greatest tragedy might be a family member serving many years in prison.

Hostages were not so concerned about throwing the book at Doris. Some of them felt she was brainwashed although Doris actually seemed to be more in command than David at the front office counter of Mrs. Cook. Still, the main concern was that David might have walked free from a mental institution. It was a particularly unsettling thought to most of the hostages. It didn't seem vengeful to those who lived through the ordeal; it was just that Young had introduced enough terror into their lives as it was.

Another unpleasant thought, that of Young's taking hostages with him, was a matter of lengthy conjecture for local citizens. There was little possibility he would ever have gotten away although everyone feared for the lives of any children so taken.

"Strange he should select a rural area as safer for him than a city metropolis," one observer remarked. "In the latter, he could vanish far more easily into a jungle of buildings and hideouts. Here, a helicopter or vehicles could have easily followed him in the wide open spaces almost anywhere."

Local lawmen, although possibly prejudiced, felt the same way. A positive law enforcement factor emerged from the Cokeville incident when a long-awaited Lincoln County SWAT team was organized in the months which followed. They were to receive special training by FBI agents concerning bombs, weapons, and tactical methods for dealing with terrorists.

The entire hostage matter raised many questions about future security. One was should a security guard be placed at the entrance of every schoolhouse? It was decided that it would be impossible to halt every person of questionable sanity who approached government property.

Even the shooting of a substitute teacher in Lewistown, Montana in December, 1986 couldn't have been prevented by a guard in the entranceway. The boy charged with the shooting was a student in the school. Any former employee or person claiming business inside would be admitted. This boy had voiced threats to friends about shooting his French teacher because she gave him a bad grade. The woman who answered the classroom door was not even his regular teacher.

In one related matter, television newsmen stated the same psychological approach used by Cokeville school officials in that disaster would be used in Lewistown.

In another hostage crisis involving school children commandeered in a California school bus, a guard or two wouldn't likely have prevented the takeover.

Security guards couldn't stand by every school door or window forever. In addition, guards could cause a psychological problem for children seeing them there on a daily basis.

The Lincoln County School District drew up several resolutions praising hostages for doing everything they could to prevent matters from becoming worse. They assured Christine Cook and others that there was really nothing that anyone could have done to prevent the Youngs from entering the Cokeville Elementary School on May 16, 1986. Such statements helped assuage feelings of guilt several school officials had after the extortion assault.

What about additional "more realistic" fire drills? Would they help children better prepare for the mental apprehension in future crises? School officials labeled the Youngs' actions so unusual that they couldn't likely be expected ever again, but just in case "more drills from a single room in case of fire or emergency" were determined desirable. It was decided by school officials in western Wyoming that everyone, even small children, could face just about any possible crisis.

Townspeople began reading about fires and disasters as never before. One newspaper clipping scrutinized closely began, "Because firefighters find so many bodies of small children . . . they are found dead not from burning but asphyxiation . . . they simply don't know what they are supposed to do in a fire."

It was a certainty that the Cokeville kids had known what to do this time. They might also have been lucky.

Cokeville school officials were always convinced in the ordeal's aftermath that the fire drill conducted from the school cafeteria the week before the hostage incident helped clear the room with less panic and confusion.

In addition, one irony is that faulty wiring in the school earlier in the year may have actually helped children respond to fire drills with more alacrity. The wiring problem had caused minor fires, so there had been extra fire drills during the spring school sessions. Once smoke from the faulty wiring even caused school to be dismissed for the entire day.

"Smoke in itself didn't panic these kids," one parent said. "They had witnessed smoke before. They didn't panic from the smoke when the real thing happened."

One EMT said it took approximately thirty seconds for the children to clear the room when smoke appeared out the windows on May 16.

However, the authors have not been able to pinpoint this as a precise stop watch measurement. One official thought it more like forty-five seconds. "The time it took to clear the cafeteria in the prebomb practice drill was about forty-five seconds," according to Excell. In other words, the children moved rapidly in both school-clearing instances.

A difference should be noted, however, in the escape route. From the cafeteria there are two double doors, one on each end of the room. Escape from room four had some other circumstances to deal with. One was the blinding, choking smoke. Students could not see clearly across the room. Another was the fact that of the two exits in the hostage room, one was blockaded with tables and chairs. Both had only single-wide doors.

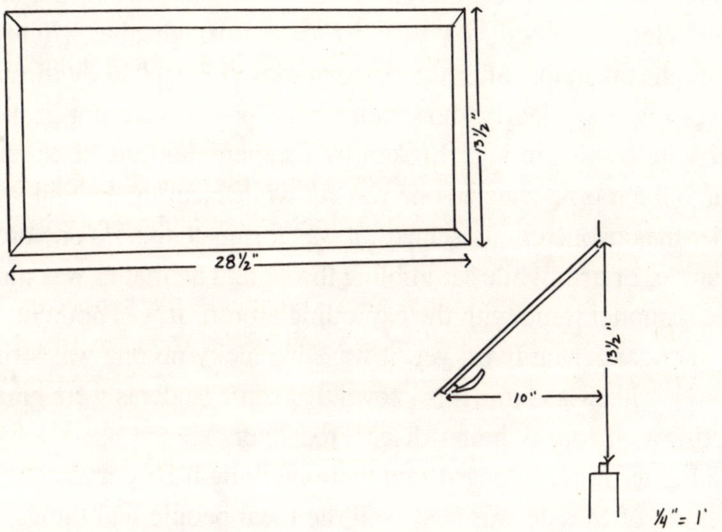

Drawing shows front and side view of escape window.

In the practice drill of the week before, no one had to exit through a window. The window in room four measures thirteen and one-half inches high and twenty-eight and one-half inches wide. It opened at an angle, allowing only a ten-inch clearance from sill to frame.

It is estimated that seventy percent of the 154 hostages made their escape that way. And this in thirty to forty-five seconds!

The school teachers had earlier attempted to convince David the children "would be less restless" in the cafeteria but he would not allow moving the children there. He probably felt in full control where he was. He knew the bomb would have less killing effect in a larger room.

Though it is a diabolical thought, it is consistent with Young's known intentions that he desired maximum killing power from his bomb, and he would find more in the small room.

Some onlookers, including the press, wondered how the children managed to escape through windows, "jagged and broken," without sustaining serious cuts. The lawn below the windows was strewn with shards of glass. However, the glass was not broken when the children crawled, climbed, or were thrown through the windows. Photographs taken just after the firemen moved Doris' body through the lower window clearly show those glass panes were not broken. Higher windows were later broken by firemen shooting streams of water into the room. Thus no one was cut while clearing the windows.

Under the chaotic circumstances, it was fortunate that no one broke a leg, ankle, or arm while scrambling through. The matter was much like the shrapnel issue with the exploding ammo. It was not a major factor in endangering lives, yet, it was also lucky no one was struck in the eye or likewise hurt. It is known that some students were grazed by shells, with marks being discovered later.

On a lighter note, Leonard said that one thing he observed during the evening of May 16 was how well the local people had things under control. "Here were people, in terror of their lives just two hours before, now serving drinks and sandwiches to out-of-town officials. They were bouncing back awfully fast, considering the circumstances. It was gratifying to see them recovering so quickly."

Much should be done to prevent future threats of physical violence before they happen. Considerable time was spent within the community discussing this fact. Threats of this nature may be rare, but they are too serious in their consequence to ignore. Answers aren't easy to come by. The matter is one likely to be discussed forever.

Lawmen and attorneys emphasized that there is no legal prohibition from "writing against" society or government. "The law can act only if some overt action is taken," one lawman emphasized.

There is no law protecting citizens against verbal threat such as was passed a few years ago concerning the president's life. "But maybe there should be," someone opined.

Specifically, there was no law against the Youngs writing venemous or vengeful words in diaries. Their verbal castigations against society or the government were not illegal.

People have been prosecuted for writing against payment of income taxes (The Internal Revenue Service is one of the more quick-to-act government entities). But it would seem one can write just about anything at all in this land of freedom. How does anyone decide when something is an expression guaranteed under the Constitution or when it is actually a threat? "It's the old argument again about what is pornography and what is not," one observer concluded.

It would thus appear that what the Youngs wrote in their diaries or journals, no matter how long studied, will not be considered a crime although there are hostages who felt it should be.

Gun control is an option some people might be willing to consider. But such a measure was not to be condoned in this western community where nearly every family has guns for controlling predators and fetching in a winter's supply of meat. In addition, local hunting seasons bring in considerable revenue each autumn. One citizen suggested that if gun control was started, even against pistols, the restrictive hierarchy "wouldn't know when to stop."

Another suggestion made after the explosion was to pass tougher legislation concerning purchase of bomb components. "Why does anyone need to build a bomb?" one parent wanted to know. "Can't we restrict them to persons clearing land and require data which can be monitored by the law?" That may not be the answer. But local people, having gone through what they did, were asking questions for a long time after May 16, 1986.

In summary, what can be learned from the Young crisis? It has been said that some good can be derived from all pain or suffering. "We will make public all we can which might help discourage a repeat of the Cokeville bomb threat elsewhere," a deputy said.

There were no other similar school hostage crises investigated in the United States in the remainder of 1986. One deterrent might have been the death of the Cokeville perpetrators. They did not gain physically or materially from the incident. From facts revealed in the case, they would never have received the money they sought.

Greater steps of security were, of course, taken by parents and teachers of the hostage community. "We are still understandably shell shocked," one parent said. Another concluded, after months of investigations disclosed just how serious the hostage matter could have turned out, "We are still trying to remain friendly to everyone. But at the same time, we appreciate strangers quickly making their business known."

On February 5, 1987, the *Star Valley Independent* published the report that the official investigation of the Cokeville hostage incident had finally been completed. The article stated, in part, "Sheriff Wolfley has reported that after several months of investigation and follow-up by the sheriff's department and federal agencies involved in the Cokeville School bombing, the case is being closed. Wolfley reported that investigators have reviewed the case with the Lincoln County Attorney's Office, U.S. Attorney's Office and the Department of Justice and that the case is now closed. Wolfley said, 'It's over now, and we can get back to normal and hope that an incident like the one in Cokeville never happens again, anywhere, anytime.' "

The Press Arrives

It seemed too incredible."
—A reader in Virginia

People around the world, learning about the incident in Wyoming, were immediately intrigued with the plight of the children. The story was later voted among the year's top ten in a number of media polls.

This drama was strange enough with the simple facts—but in the early stages particularly—were they all facts?

"It seemed too incredible," a Virginia woman said after getting her local TV and newspaper reports. To be sure, much of the story did seem that way. Much was credible, some was not. One was left wondering, at times, what to believe.

An unforgiveable error circulated by the media was that the exploding bomb killed all hostages; later they reported that only Principal Excell was killed, and still later that only John Miller died. Some newspapers reported that the extortionists were members of Posse Comitatus and/or Aryan Nations, leaving the readers to wonder if these same people might strike them within the next twenty-four hours.

Lesser errors included the following: the ransom demand was $300 million; the woman hostage-taker was killed instantly; the bomb went off when Doris' hand slipped off the bomb trigger; there were three gasoline bombs; the bomb exploded at 3 p.m.

Some minor mistakes not affecting the main story made readers wonder what other "facts" they could not believe: Doris's name was spelled "Dorris;" she wore a blue blouse; she and David "dumped" their spouses to leave Cokeville together; the bombers struck at a school in "Smiths Fork Valley."

When John Miller was shot, media miscues included everything from spelling his name "Jon," to speculation that he had not been shot at all, to assertions that he was in "critical condition" in the hospital, to him dying there.

Perhaps one shouldn't be too harsh on minor errors with rapidly looming deadlines, particularly the television stations eager to get something for Friday night's news. Most of the hostages were not certain about the amount of the demanded ransom money for a time nor the nature of the bomb's trigger.

Several hostage children also had the impression David (or his wife) had to press down on the bomb trigger to prevent it from going off. It frightened many of them even more than they need have been, thinking any small movement or slip of the hand would set the device off. It made things much more "scary," as one child put it, when Young tugged at his sweater. When they saw Doris helping him remove his sweater, they took it as proof of a "delicate hair trigger." As pointed out earlier, there was almost a foot of slack in the shoelace trigger which Doris exceeded when she forgetfully raised her hand to her head.

Many of the media's early mistakes were corrected with second or third reports. But in some cases, a one-shot story left the wrong impression. One of the latter was in a national news magazine. It carried more fiction per sentence than any other account given. Those reading it were given the impression that David transferred the bomb by " . . . handing his wife . . . two bottles of gasoline wired to a battery and manual trigger."

The picture was of a woman struggling to receive two heavy bottles of fuel while, of course, making certain she didn't loosen a wire leading to a battery or trip the clothespin-shoelace trigger. It would have been easier to hand her the trigger.

The same news magazine painted this vivid description: "When her hand apparently slipped on the trigger, she set off the crude bomb.

The blast killed her instantly. . . .reeling teachers shoved children through the blown-out windows, onto the grass outside, where they lay screaming and shivering with shock as their parents fought through police lines to reach them. At least one child had burns over 50 per cent of his body."

Every sentence had at least one major mistake, and as editors warmed to the story, it got worse. To set the record straight, the windows were not blown out (they were open at an angle not catching any shock blast), and if there was some shouting below the windows, Mr. Moore did most of it. Police did not prevent parents from reaching their injured children, only from upsetting the bombers. The worst of the burn victims, Billie Jo Hutchinson, received burns over only twenty-one per cent of her body, according to hospital reports, which was bad enough.

It should be added that police kept townspeople back at two times. One was before the bomb went off in order to prevent the Youngs from harming the children, and later when the building was combed for the bombs which were then detonated in the yard outside the school.

The most irresponsible reporting was the teletype message received by a radio station in Rexburg, Idaho. An employee telephoned to Principal Excell's son, Steve, that when the bomb detonated, "everyone in the building was killed." Knowing Steve was from Cokeville, the caller said, "I knew you would want to know."

"Did you know my dad and little sister were in that building?" Steve asked. With that agonizing news to deal with, Steve answered the phone again. This time it was his mother calling from Cokeville, informing him that all the hostages escaped. The confusion was unnecessary and devastating.

This scrambled message reached Casper, Wyoming, where the Cokeville High School track team was competing in the state meet. One coach learned from a media broadcast that "Principal Excell

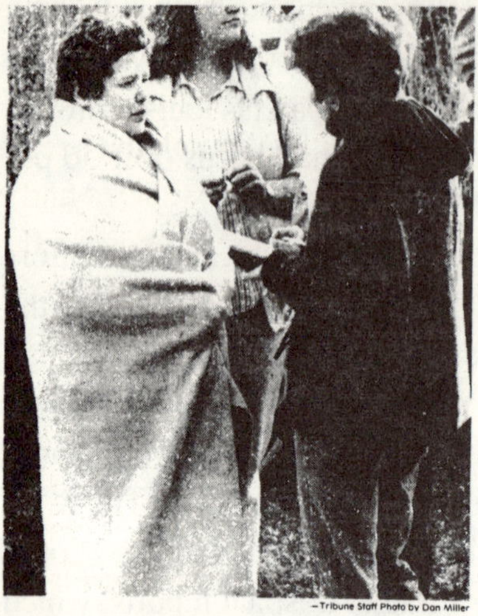

Tina Cook wraps up in blanket against the chill of May wind and shock as she answers questions of reporter. (Don Miller photo courtesy Salt Lake Tribune)

Sheriff Deb Wolfley explains findings of investigations to press. (Dan Dockstader photo courtesy Star Valley Independent)

Media from across the nation question investigators on the bomb used to threaten Cokeville hostages. (Tom Smart photo courtesy Deseret News.)

was dead." Another coach was tuned in to a television channel showing Principal Excell being interviewed after the blast! Fortunately the second coach could relieve the grave concerns of the first coach.

The report which had Miller dying with a "bullet through the back and entering the heart," added to the concerns of many students and friends. Apparently, reporters had not made a simple telephone call to the hospital. A frenzy to be first caused some news media to "shotgun" out the possibilities immediately and worry about repercussions later.

A radio station broadcast mentioned the hostage-taker's name as possibly "Kevin Young," but in time a correction was made. A replaying of the tape made of this period indicated some minor errors during the time everyone was uncertain about what was going on—even those in the town hall.

This is not to make light of news-gathering agencies; some rushed in and out rather quickly. But obviously such heart-stopping news as deaths were more than a little exaggerated.

After getting past the *Las Vegas Sun*'s blazing headlines: "Mad Bombers linked to tax radicals," with subhead, "Ransom sought to fund Posse Comitatus revolt," one did gain some truth from the story beneath it. Quoting Lincoln County Sheriff T. Deb Wolfley it read, "We really can't tell you anything about any affiliation with terrorists, extremists, or right-wing groups. The only comment I can make is that there is a little bit of language [in the diary] that might connect them with a Posse Comitatus group."

The *Sun* then explained, "The militant right-wing group Posse Comitatus, formed in 1973 in the Midwest, opposes income taxes and any law enforcement other than local sheriffs and is critical of the Federal Reserve System and the courts."

The *Sun*'s article of May 18 says that Posse Comitatus origins in Wisconsin "represented a great potential for violence," according to the FBI. Linking the Youngs to that group would have been convenient. It would place them in a known niche. The truth was the

Youngs were in a niche entirely their own. Lawmen never could connect them to any group.

The traditionally astute New York Times echoed the *Sun's* error.

The *Arizona Daily Star* in Tucson wisely avoided erring on the Posse Comitatus matter by writing it this way: "The *New York Times* had linked the Youngs to Posse Comitatus and Aryan Nations. But those familiar with the Youngs said it couldn't be."

That last sentence proved to be a journalistic gem, preventing readers from moving high gear down the wrong track. Lawmen later reiterated there just weren't any such ties.

The Comitatus thing, before being finished and finally placed to rest, reverberated several times. An article in the Provo Utah *Daily Herald* spotlighted a Posse Comitatus member in St. George, Utah who was incensed someone might label David Young as a member of that group. He was quoted as saying, "He's a kook—and that labels everyone in the movement a kook." He called local Posse Comitatus members "damn good patriots," not the David Young type at all.

Poor David Young. No one wanted him.

One of the first publications to fully comprehend the significance of the Young diaries was the Salt Lake City *Deseret News*. In a copyrighted story dated May 31, (13 days after the fact, with time to do research) the story said in part: "Investigators now believe the 'biggie' was much bigger—and more horrible—than at first suspected. Young's writings indicate he was planning on . . . a place where he would rule as God of a new race, a place that could only be reached through death. The ramifications are . . . terrible."

Little more can be quoted because of the copyright, but residents of Cokeville heard precisely that in-depth message from sheriff's investigator Ron Hartley in a public meeting at about the same time the *Deseret News* printed its story.

The gist of his message was just what the newspaper said, "What can be read in the Young diaries was, indeed, terrifying."

At that time the authors asked Deputy Hartley this question: "Do you believe David Young asked for those millions of dollars with the idea he could take it with him into his Brave New World of reincarnation?"

Hartley: "From the investigation, it would appear he planned on taking the money with him to somehow fund his idea. It appeared he also wanted to hurt the government by taking the money away from them before continuing on with the rest of his plan."

Even those actually involved in this event were unsure of exactly what happened. Some children in shock didn't know they had been burned until flesh peeled off with their clothes. In the confusion, it is understandable how much of this false information leaped into news accounts, especially those publications with short deadlines.

One newspaper, with a next morning deadline and very little time to act, succinctly captured the essence of the ordeal in its May 17 lead. The *Salt Lake Tribune* handled it this way: "Terror by bomb and gunfire tore through an elementary school Friday . . . " The next day, with more time to assess what happened, the newspaper carried this headline: "Aftermath of Explosion 'a Miracle.' "

Many newspapers carried the words "Terror" and "Miracle" in headlines throughout the world.

Salt Lake City TV station KUTV did such an excellent job on the early coverage that it was picked up by a London TV network. In London, Stuart Wilson, who had lived in Utah, was startled to see news of a town he knew about. As for KUTV's arrival on the scene minutes before the bomb went off, it evoked semi-serious jokes about "being notified by the Youngs in advance." Part of the legal investigation centered for a time on whether David Young had given someone in the press notification so he could air his political views.

Young said, in his May 13th journal entry, that he sent his philosophy statements "to the press," but those rambling statements probably wound up in the trash cans.

What really happened was that KUTV had a crew in the tri-state corner area on another assignment. They did not have their portable relay equipment with them but they still managed to get footage of children and parents embracing which was the envy of other television stations.

Television satellite was parked along Main Street for several days. Other channels had similar equipment elsewhere in town. (Photo courtesy Cokeville High Scool yearbook)

KUTV added to its positive image by hosting the Cokeville hostage families to a day long summer party at the Lagoon resort a few miles north of Salt Lake City.

If there had been a single death, aggressive or even opportunistic newsmen would have been considered ghoulish or sadistic. In the Wilberg, (Emery County, Utah) mine disaster of the year before, when twenty-seven died, TV press members were castigated, even by their own peers, for asking on Christmas Eve, "How does it feel to learn your husband (or father) is dead?"

In contrast, news crews at Cokeville found an almost joyous scene, with people ecstatic at their triumph from an afternoon of anguish and horror.

Many distant newspeople apparently flew to the scene with a map of Wyoming in one hand and a magnifying glass in the other. They had compassionate questions to ask children threatened with death a few hours before. Generally, citizens of Bear River Valley were impressed with the understanding attitude and sympathy of the media.

There were a few exceptions, however. One mother now laughingly tells of an encounter with a reporter. "Are you from a Salt Lake newspaper?" she asked. Apparently unaccustomed to smalltown openness, the man tried to assume an air of importance and replied, "Try the *San Francisco Chronicle*. . . ."

"I was unimpressed," the mother chuckled.

Some helicopters and private planes landed in the sagebrush-lined airport two miles from town; others found the high school football field ideal. There had never been a mob scene like this in the little community before.

Some newspapers on a cheap budget did not send reporters to the scene; they merely interviewed psychologists about what ought to be done to help the children adjust. One psychologist said he would emphasize "the children were brave enough to survive, that they were winners." It helped appease readers, but it failed to capture the inside story of the ordeal.

Many press members realized early the wide scope of the human drama. They quoted intriguing tidbits like the child who apologized to his principal. "I'm sorry, Mr. Excell, I ran out the wrong door. It wasn't the same one we use in the fire drills."

Another said, "I'm not afraid to go back to the school."

"I don't want to be here," a girl said during the classroom crisis. "Neither do I," her teacher responded.

A first grade burn victim was quoted, "I didn't even feel nothing." Of course, the excitement so challenged his life on this day he probably wouldn't have noticed a broken arm. Not every hostage recalled what he or she said during the afternoon's duress.

As for the number of people treated at hospitals, it was reported, an hour after the explosion, to be approximately seventy. Some of those were treated for smoke inhalation and released without spending the night, including a busload taken to South Lincoln County Hospital in Kemmerer. Reporters often got confused about how many people were admitted for treatment. In this confusion, the press once reported as few as 40 being taken to hospitals. The total figure of seventy-nine was arrived at after counting and recounting.

Few reports had "Doris" spelled correctly with one "r". How the double "r" became inserted into so many accounts is not known.

As for spellings of children's names, all in this book are from the official school list, ostensibly with approval at some time or another of the children or their parents. Several children spelled their names differently at home.

Some maps of the Cokeville area placed it incorrectly 50 miles north of Evanston, Wyoming. Twenty miles off, it was probably close enough for distant publications. Correctly it is just east of the Utah and Idaho borders.

Student newspapers in the region fared rather well in their coverage accuracy. The Utah State University *Statesman* carried articles the hostages themselves enjoyed reading. This was due to their understanding manner in coping with the aftermath feelings.

A cartoon depicting travel to Europe as more dangerous than remaining with weirdos inside the U.S. had a powerful impact in the University of Utah *Daily Chronicle*.

A story in the Brigham Young University *Daily Universe* presented some new insights, including one of a hostage's mother who said the incident "had brought the whole community closer together."

Other accounts focused on teachers telling children to do what they were told by the hostage-takers "so that we won't be hurt." Not every publication pointed out the children were too young to realize just how serious this kind of "hurt" could be.

Volumes were sometimes spoken with the use of a photograph. One of the most poignant and memorable was carried in the *U.S. News and World Report*. It showed a young girl reentering her blackened world of terror, the school classroom. Her face was searching, her footsteps tentative. The caption read "Inch by inch." It was the magazine's picture of the week.

Most townspeople would give the "outsiders" a high mark for compassion on their report card. One newsman bought toys for the children he visited in the hospital. Others let the youngsters enjoy their catharsis by just caring until editors or bosses ordered them home. One journalist, compassion showing on her face, seemed to forget she had a deadline until a photographer reminded her they had a story to file.

There were some selfish competitors as there always are. A newsman called Principal Excell in the middle of the night for an early morning appointment at the schoolhouse, then he didn't show on time. Some newsmen remained too long and asked too many questions of weary hostages.

Many of the children had never talked to newspeople before. The author's son, Kamron, wrote a two-page news release to hand out so that he could continue with his normal twelve-year-old's life. Later, he drew a map of the classroom and approximate location of the hostages in relation to the bomb. It was run only in the BYU student newspaper.

At one point five days after the crisis, the stress of questions and photographers' instructions became particularly acute. Teachers asked the youngsters to vote on how long they wanted to reflect on the ordeal. One class voted a photographer "fifteen more minutes." He dutifully left the children to the things they now really wanted to do.

Many parents recorded what the press did with their reports from Cokeville. Betty Thompson, mother of two hostage children, made a video tape of every word she and others could find on television coverage. A video recording indicates some of these emotional highlights:

—Carol Mikita, KSL-TV, Salt Lake City—"It is a story of tragedy and twisted thinking. . . ."

—David Thompson, also KSL-TV—"How could it happen here? Help was coming in spades . . . the love grows here. . . ."

—Greg Lefevere, CNN, Atlanta—"A town of miracles? That could be right. A third of the town was being held hostage . . . strong family ties pulled them through."

—Randall Carlisle and Michelle King, KUTV, Salt Lake City—"It was an afternoon of terror . . . a man said it was a revolution, he was taking over the school. Then he opened his coat to show his guns. . . ."

—Charlene Brown, KUTV, quoting a young girl hostage—"she was a nice lady but the guy sounded like he was going to kill everybody."

—Sharon Whitby, interviewed on KUTV—"All of the children wanted to know if their teacher was dead."

—CNN, with bomb technician Richard Haskell—"The false ceiling absorbed much of the bomb blast. I can't express how fortunate they are. It's unreal . . . so fortunate. You look in there and wonder why there aren't 150 kids lying in there dead."

Other poignant TV comments captured on TV: "Rah, rah, rah, fifth grader victory!"—Rocky Moore and his class.

—Also from Moore—"I couldn't sleep past 3 a.m. Later I saw the kids come to school with big smiles. Some of them hugged me and I knew right away everything would be all right."

—Jeremiah Moore (a nephew to Rocky)—"They sang happy birthday to me."

—A small boy—"Why did the man shoot Mr. Miller?"

—A young hostage—"They would explode the bomb, and there wouldn't be anything left of us."

Other TV comments:

—"The children returned to their house of terror."

—"It could have been any school in America."

—"No where else in the world have children had to go through this experience."

—"My boy thought his life was over."

—Max Excell—"He knew we would want to protect our children."

—"I didn't see any angels . . . except the children, but they were there in the room."

—"This time it was not just a far away place." (This seemed to echo the feelings of an entire community.)

—Tina Cook—"I kept asking myself if there wasn't anything we could do to keep him away from those children."

—Kliss Sparks—"It was a big load on our shoulders, but we came through it."

There were many possible feature stories; several were used including Miller's feelings, children playing while heavily bandaged or eagerly writing "thank you's" to their teachers.

Absent from most of the reports were criticisms of the way lawmen, volunteers, hostages, or others reacted toward the episode. Usually when such stress is introduced into any community or situation, it precipitates a chain reaction of human weaknesses aggravating further tensions. Given the outcome, with no lawsuits or official complaints, there was simply no one who deserved a bad press—unusual for a story with such negative beginnings.

Some publications noted that the Cokeville citizens turned the strange event to "their own good." It was summed up in the *Eastern Arizona Courier* by young journalist Kathy Jones ("Keeping up with the Jones"): "Despite the recent worldwide attention on the problem of terrorism, attacks so close to home still tend to strike us as somewhat unbelievable. . . ." She then pointed out how the people involved were "bouncing back," if in no other way than to realize how much concern they felt for one another's welfare and for the many friends they had outside the immediate area. It was an upbeat account of an upbeat aftermath.

Some newsmen asked difficult questions: "What will be the psychological effect on the children?" Others were easier: "How will this event be handled by the children at school on the first anniversary?" Consulting the calendar, someone determined it to be a Saturday. "Thank goodness for that," a teacher stated.

One of the best summations came from the *Star Valley* (Wyoming) *Independent*. It told about the community's upcoming Pioneer Day Celebration with the theme, "Miracles Still Happen."

While that was an accurate summation of the community's feelings, the best story about the press itself, good and bad, was probably this one running in that newspaper. It was written by Cokeville correspondent Gwen Petersen. The headline was, "Cokeville bombed with news media."

"It's been a new experience for most of the people of Cokeville to be so closely associated with the news media. Television cameras were on the scene shortly after the bombing tragedy occurred and have stayed throughout the week.

"A satellite truck transmitting live coverage has been parked near the elementary school, and anyone walking down the street has been subject to an interview.

"Residents have opened their homes to newsmen, providing telephone service for calls all over the country. Principal Max Excell received calls from San Francisco radio stations and the *Sunday Today* newspaper from London, and he was interviewed by the three major national networks, plus the *Washington Post*, *Denver Post*, AP and UPI wire services out of Washington, and countless others who were on the scene.

"The incident has received excellent coverage from the media. The people of Cokeville are now looking forward to the time when the news people will leave so they can go on with their lives.

A Personal Connection

Sunday, May 18, 1986

"This is the kind of entry no one—not in her wildest imaginations—figures she would make in her journal . . . Our son is one of the hostages."

—Judene Wixom

Our high school-aged daughter, Jenny, ran frantically into the house from the bus stop. Sobbing and calling almost hysterically to her mother, she gave the terrifying news.

"Did you hear? Don't you know what's happened?" Jenny and her best friend, Carrie Anderson, were confused and grief-stricken. Their faces displayed the stunned disbelief they felt. "Some people with bombs are holding the elementary school hostage!"

"My mind went blank," wrote my wife, Judene, in her journal. "I was annoyed with the girls for going too far with one of their pranks. This was, well, just TOO absurd! They're full of pranks, but their grief was all too real. I had to believe them. I was numb with disbelief.

I sat down with them, trying to comfort them while at the same time trying to sort this out in my head. Nothing sorted.

"I felt so . . . alone, confused, frustrated. In desperation, I fell on my knees and pleaded for help that the children would somehow find the courage they needed to withstand this ordeal. I felt relief—I was afraid to feel assured," Judene's journal entry concluded.

I hadn't seen my wife in five days, and I wouldn't see her for three more hours. For the first time I had commuted home early for the weekend from Provo, Utah, where I was working as student newspaper advisor at Brigham Young University.

The only hint I had of anything wrong came as I approached Cokeville and headed toward my home north of town. A normally conservative neighbor sped past me going about eighty miles per hour. I thought I noted a worried look on his face but figured it was just a personal matter.

Instinctively, I checked my own speedometer and continued driving. It seemed like a peaceful afternoon. There was no particular reason to hurry.

Judene had just watched two ambulances and a police car speed past on the highway in front of the house. As I turned down our driveway, she was conversing with Cindy Dayton, who had been a substitute teacher at the high school that day. Her tear-streaked face showed her desperate desire to just "wake up from this whole thing."

Spotting me, my wife came running up the driveway. As she threw herself into my embrace with more intensity than ever before, I first thought this greeting was the kind I had always wanted. But seeing her face filled with anguish kept me from enjoying it.

"Is everything all right?" I asked, looking into her eyes.

"No! The grade school kids are being held hostage by someone with a bomb. . . .They want millions of dollars. They have guns. . . ." She spit out the scenario in a flood.

"What?" I found myself saying.

"Our son is in there . . . !"

When my wife told me that, I first envisioned an idle threat, a fake bomb. Passersby maybe, who had swallowed too much Percodan. Still it could be a long wait before we were sure. My mind turned to the practical; we would need to take sleeping bags and several days' food to wait at the school yard entrance. If the extortionists also took a child to make their getaway . . . well, it would complicate getting everyone out of this unharmed.

It would do no good to speculate. We had to obtain more detailed facts about this strange dilemma.

"Our son is in there!"

As what she was saying sunk in, the two of us were joined by our high school daughter Cindy, and Joanne Metcalfe, a neighbor who had three children in the classroom. The two mothers shared a hug; it was the only way to express the feelings no words could. Her husband, Jack, had taken his high school civics class on a field trip. Knowing she needed support from someone in this grotesque circumstance, we invited her to come inside the house.

Joanne had called the school. When Max Excell answered the phone, Joanne quickly blurted out, "What's going on there?"

"It's true! There's a man here with a bomb. I can't tell you much more—I've got to go." Joanne had no idea at the time how much pressure Excell was under to make every moment count.

In our living room, there was a heavy silence mixed with confusion although we attempted to not assume the worst. Then Joanne's high school son, Aaron, burst in. "The bomb went off! Boom! I just heard it on the radio!"

The two families headed toward town in separate vehicles. I thought of Kam's smile the week before as he showed me his tree hut, his proud look when he brought in a gallon of milk from the dairy barn on a subzero morning, the last picture he had drawn of a "supercar of the future." The future. . . .

I also thought of the children now being held hostage, the ones I had taught in the honors English class at mid-year. These fifth and sixth graders put out their own newspaper "wondering what we can use for exciting news."

Several of the students had also enthusiastically created stories which might be published in magazines elsewhere. One was a detective story about children in a small town being kidnapped. What a wonderful imagination, I thought.

The teachers—I had worked with them daily. My wife and I saw them frequently in almost every community activity. What was happening to them?

Probably every vehicle hurrying to the school grounds held people with similar thoughts. Many talked openly and freely of their anxiety to find out more, and when they did, they spoke of their feelings of helplessness. Most said unashamed prayers on behalf of the hostages and their families.

As I parked my car at the curb just outside the school grounds, I saw Dr. Allen Lowe, Lincoln County School District Superintendent, step from his vehicle. His face was ashen. Few words could be found. A voice on the radio came through the silence—something about parents searching for their children. . . .

Here, in front of me, I saw it happening.

Children stood dazed, with a look of incredulity at being alive. Quilts and blankets were hastily gathered from nearby homes. They were being wrapped compassionately around shivering youngsters sitting on lawns, many of whom were waiting for a turn at oxygen tanks. There were ambulances everywhere.

Several children with blackened faces and arms were coughing from the effects of smoke inhalation.

It struck us immediately that although this was an unbelievable event, all the chaos was somehow transforming into precision organization. Everyone was functioning in his own field of expertise, and parents and neighbors were filling in the gaps. Teenagers were handing out blankets and cups of water.

Even though the paramedics came from different counties, they were working as if coordinating a drill.

The frantic faces wore the same wide-eyed expression. The horror of the event had not yet been fully realized, nor would it be for some time yet.

We both jumped out of the car and ran toward the center of activity. Looking through the frenzied crowd, I saw Kamron. He had been calling us from the Taylor's home on Main Street. It must have been an extremely lonely feeling for him to get no answer. He knew his mother would be worrying. His face showed no signs of burns. Just the blankness of shock. Feelings and reality had not yet meshed together.

I raised my hand up and called to him. He said I loomed out of the crowd "like a telephone pole." His eyes could see nothing else but his parents. He came running.

He reached his mother first. There were no words. Just an ecstatic embrace.

Later, mother and son looked at a photograph of that memorable reunion. The picture, taken by a television photographer, captured the elation and relief of the moment. It was circulated on network broadcasts and picked up by a wire service. The look on their faces so effectively told the story of this drama taking place that it ran in several newspapers around the country.

One of the papers to print it was the *Arizona Daily Star* in Tucson. Our oldest daughter, Wendi, lived in Safford, 140 miles northeast of Tucson, with her husband, Don, and daughters, Rachel and Evie. It had been two years since she had seen Kamron. A neighbor boy brought the paper to her home. "Is this your mom and little brother?" he asked Wendi, knowing she was from Cokeville. Wendi grabbed the boy and the newspaper all in one big, excited swoop, and gave both of them a hug.

She recognized the jacket her mother was wearing. "It was your camp jacket," she explained later. "I looked at that picture and thought how the jacket would smell of campfire, and all the fun times we've had on our outings came flooding back.

"The photo came alive to me," she said, "and helped me feel a part of the circle. I needed to be in touch with the family during this crisis."

In her excitement, she impulsively called the *Star* to thank them for the picture.

It was later, in the middle of Evie's two-year-old birthday party that the newspaper called Wendi with some more questions. That night the newspaper ran the same photo again with the headline, "Photo eases worry for Safford woman."

"It was the first time I could visualize my family was fine!" she told the paper.

Wendi had originally learned of the disaster from her husband, who heard reports on the radio. He hurried home to be with her before she got the news elsewhere. She said she had a foreboding all afternoon something was wrong. It might have been precipitated by the minor surgery her husband had a few days before, added to his having to drive a long way alone.

"I cried for an hour. Then Don came home and told me what he had heard. We called the home in Cokeville but couldn't find anyone. I finally reached a family friend in Cokeville, Leon Pope. He told me his sister, Jody, was burned, but that he heard Kam was all right."

In the meantime, hearing reports on our car radio about "a bomb exploding in a school classroom in Cokeville, Wyoming," we worried about what other relatives and friends might think. It would be very easy to imagine the worst. Family members in other states soon to get the six o'clock news might think Kam and his friends were killed. Yet we had managed to get only one call through to my mother in Salt Lake City. We were able to spare her concern before she even learned of the crisis, but we could get no further access to an outside line.

Leon had reached us to report Wendi's call. There was still Judene's mother, somewhere in New York on vacation, and our other married daughter, Julie, in Virginia. Two other children, Peggy and Wade, were working for the summer as guides on the Colorado River, away from telephones for a week or more. They must be informed.

Getting through to them seemed impossible. Telephone lines, of course, were jammed by many people trying to reach acquaintances that afternoon. My nephew Mark Pierson reached us from Salt Lake City by continually pushing the telephone redial button "until he got something besides a busy signal." Then he was able to alleviate fears of his own family.

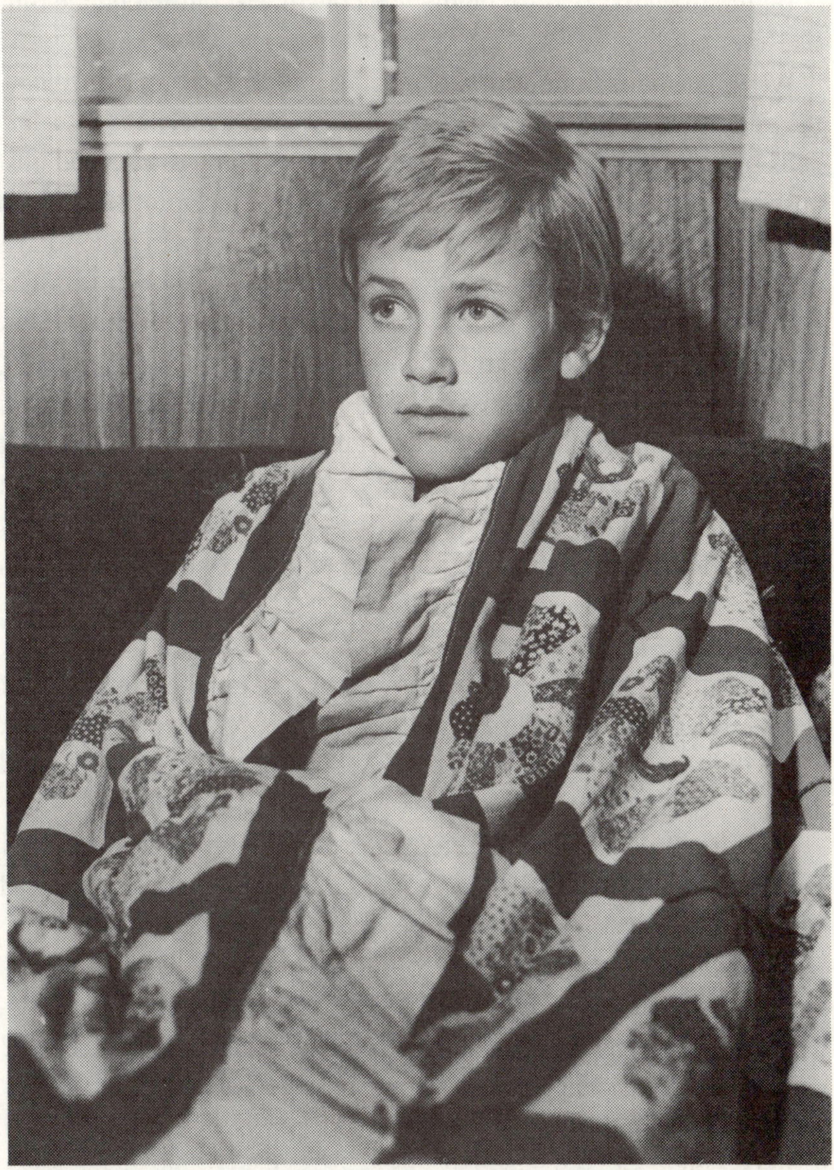

Wearing the dazed look of someone whose young life has been threatened and spared in the course of one afternoon, Kam Wixom discusses events of an incredible day with reporters. (Gerald Silver photo courtesy of Deseret News)

Before the next thirty-six hours had concluded, our telephone bill, like many others in the area, soared to nearly $200.

As we continued our efforts to reach family members and friends, the reality of the day's events weighed on us heavily.

Kamron, now huddled in a quilt in the living room, had just answered extensive questions for many reporters, including some from Salt Lake City's *Deseret News*. The latter interview by Ellen Fagg and photographer Gerald Silver was sensitive and thoughtful. The atmosphere was subdued yet poignant in the reporter's opening lines.

"In a trailer home about six and a half miles from Cokeville, Wyoming, Kamron Wixom sits on a couch, cross-legged, with a patchwork quilt draped around his shoulders," Ellen wrote. "He just finished talking long-distance to a reporter from New York—not an everyday experience for the twelve-year-old Cokeville Elementary sixth grader. But neither is the bombing of a school room a common experience in this sleepy town of 550."

"'I felt kind of mad. Now I feel shaky," Kamron told the reporters.

"I think . . . there may be more mental harm than physical," I interjected to the reporters.

"Will you be scared to return to school next week?" reporters asked Kam.

"Not really," he said, "because I know they're both dead."

But by now, Kamron was beginning to feel the "shakiness" he had earlier mentioned. He grew more quiet.

The phone rang. Peggy was calling from Moab, Utah. "What's going on there?" she asked Kamron.

"Yeah," Kam responded. What was insanity and what was reality?

"I mean, what happened?" Peggy asked.

"It was a bomb."

"Are you OK?"

"Yeah." She could almost hear him shrugging his shoulders. "No big deal," she thought. "The news must be sensationalizing it."

She'd had a stressful day herself. A mix-up with rides earlier in the day had left her stranded 50 miles from civilization. After walking barefoot for six miles along a dirt road, she hitched a ride with an acquaintance who happened to drive by and finally arrived at her destination. Exhausted, she headed directly for her room.

"Hey," her co-workers called. "There's something on the news about Cokeville!"

"No one even knows where Cokeville is," she thought to herself. "How could they have something on national news?"

After talking to Kamron, she still wasn't sure what was happening. It seemed to her there was a gap between the news on television and her eyewitness brother. She put a call in to her older brother, Wade, who was visiting his girlfriend, Amy Shifflet, in Pueblo, Colorado. Peggy figured he had seen the broadcast and would want to know that Kam was safe.

"Bomb kills two, injures 75 in Cokeville, Wyoming elementary school explosion . . . Details later." That was what Wade had heard. The report was factual and true. Yet he was only one of hundreds of family and friends outside of Cokeville who wondered just who the two dead were or how extensive were the injuries. "And not just Kamron," Wade later explained. "That was **my town**. Who of all I knew were numbered among the dead?"

Cindy had a very different experience. As a high school senior, she had been in the prayer circle held that afternoon. She rode with us to town and saw Kamron herself. She knew who was injured and that it was the terrorists who were killed. The incident had a very real impact on her life.

"It became a turning point for me," she was to later say. "I had been troubled for years with things I thought were major. But in comparison to this, they suddenly seemed so small.

"With the help of the psychological counseling made available to us, I gained some coping techniques. I also learned a new perspective about myself and others and quit demanding so much. It gave me space to grow and improve. I also saw for myself how very much people need people, and I became a warmer, more trusting person."

Julie finally got through from Virginia. She had been receiving some intensive military training away from home and returned just in time to catch the news report. "I heard 'Wyoming' mentioned and hurried in to catch the details out of curiosity," she explained. "Then they said 'Cokeville' and 'school kids' and I went cold."

Julie and her husband, Tony, both with extensive medical training in the Navy, heard reporters say something about the hostages having "black on their bodies like hot oil." She was horrified. "I knew the painful and destructive power of such a thing," she said.

Speculation was traumatic for many members of Cokeville families scattered across the United States who were listening and waiting for details. Julie was gratified to finally learn the full story, particularly about her little brother's welfare.

That left only Judene's mother to get in touch with. The hope was that our nephew had managed to reach her somewhere, somehow.

We learned later that she had been watching television at a home of friends in Poughkeepsie, New York. Someone called her attention to the Cokeville story, and she watched incredulously for more details.

Her reaction was just as we had feared. "I couldn't quite grasp the reality of it all," she later said. She tried unsuccessfully for two hours to reach us in Cokeville.

She finally called Salt Lake and learned from Mark that he had spoken to us. Though still reeling from the inconceivable story, she had her fears temporarily alleviated.

The morning newspapers showed a picture of a mother and child emotionally embracing. "That's my daughter . . . and my grandson!" she exclaimed. The feeling was indescribable as she tried to deal with a whirl of facts. An explosion—in a grade school? Why? Hostages—ransom—but they're SAFE!"

Still, until Judene and her mom were able to embrace each other a week later, it was not really over. . . .

Similar emotional-psychological repercussions were occurring with each of the hostage families as the shock waves reverberated across the nation.

A Cokeville native, Barbara Perry, was driving through Donner Pass with her husband. "We had been listening to tapes for about two hours," she said. "I suggested we tune in to catch a little news and heard what had happened in my home town. The broadcast out of California said two people in Cokeville had been killed after teachers and children were taken hostage."

Her husband described her as "frantic." She immediately began figuring the odds of those two dead people possibly being her sister and her sister-in-law, both teachers at the elementary school. When they reached a phone, they tried but failed to get through to Cokeville. It was thirty-six hours before they were finally able to learn the whole story.

Barbara's mother experienced her own alarm right there in town. Lois Dayton was tending grandchildren while daughter-in-law Cindy substituted at the high school. Lois was unaware of any excitement just three blocks away at the school.

"I answered a hurried knock at the door. It was Carlene Nuss, from across the street. 'Take my baby!' she said, and thrust the youngster in my arms. I had no idea what was going on. Minutes later, Cindy came in for her children. She was crying and so shaken that she couldn't speak. There I was, wondering why I had Carlene's baby, seeing Cindy nearly hysterical, and knowing nothing. All I could do was wait until Cindy was calm enough to explain. The anxiety I experienced in all this was horrible!"

Every story added impact to what was unfolding before us. How far-reaching would it be?

It brought to mind something Doris Young had told the children. "Think of this as an adventure . . . something to tell your grandchildren about." It was not quite what Mrs. Young had in mind. But if adventure can be defined as "a hazardous risk or a remarkable experience," at least she was right about that part before she died.

This "adventure" was to touch many outside the immediate community. Columnist Kathy Jones of the *Eastern Arizona Courier* recognized the psychological trauma. Following a conversation with our daughter in Arizona, she wrote: "Wendi's greatest wish was for some way she could help. With a disaster like a flood or tornado there would be work to do in cleaning up, she said. It would help her better deal with the emotions about the incident." But in this situation, there seemed nothing Wendi could do, the column emphasized.

Wendi kept asking her younger brother on the telephone, like many family members living far away asked loved ones, "Are you sure you're OK?"

For Wendi, it would require a hug, real and physical with her hostage brother, before the tensions could be released.

Many families would deal with the trauma in different ways. Some would take the attitude they did when the temperature dipped to fifty below, or when kicked by a cow: "When the going gets tough, the tough get going." In the past, I had inclined toward the "just-grit-your-teeth" types. Over the years, my wife and I had seen many such joys and tragedies.

There was something different here, not only because it struck close to home, but because it was more than physical adversity. There was much emotional sorting out to do, not just for the hostages' personal feelings about themselves, but for others.

Most of the hostage children, in all of their previous lives, had not encountered so many new challenges within a single afternoon. This was not something they could turn off like on TV.

This matter focused on a youngster's faith in himself and mankind. Trust and ability to love responsibly was, in essence, the future ladder to inner personal growth.

How would we respond to help our own son? Tougher or more lenient? With discipline? Just love?

It was mostly the latter. When our family moved to Provo to be closer to my work, we lived in a student housing area. In the warm summer nights, laughing and splashing in the pool next door could be heard until midnight. While it irritated my wife and me as we tried to get to sleep, it was sweet music to Kam's ears. People enjoying themselves meant no tension. He had much more difficulty getting to sleep after we moved from the student housing.

From it we gained a useful clue. He had experienced a lifetime of tension in one afternoon. Now he deserved something different. Harmony was the goal.

Several parents with children held hostage quickly saw that trying to force the memory away didn't solve their children's ills. Here was a matter to be more than reacted to—it had to be understood. For example, a child writing "CRAZY" and "INSANE" over a photograph of David Young's face might be a prosecuting attorney's nightmare, but it seemed excellent therapy to parents. When Kamron did just that, the entire family understood the full meaning behind the picture with the scribbled words on it.

The evening just before bedtime was not a good time for the former hostage son to be watching television. Terror, hostages, bombs, guns in Iran, Nicaragua, or elsewhere, represented former horror brought back to mind. Some teachers held hostage had to leave lights on at night. Parents felt sympathy was now in order for youngsters who had faced the same threat of death.

There was also the wonder of it. Judene reminded me that more people were accidentally killed leaving soccer games around the world than were seriously harmed by an exploding bomb and four guns. Maybe it was worth reflecting on with a degree of sympathy for these young hostages as often as they wanted it.

I also remembered something Janel Dayton told me: "During the actual crisis we had to be careful not to sympathize too much, or the children would take a clue from us that it was worse than they thought it was; but we gave a measure of sympathy, yes."

Concerning the many prayers said, I remember reading something Ralph Waldo Emerson had said about it: "Prayer is the contemplation of the facts of life from the highest possible point of view." Had the prayers of all these humble children on their knees toppled the kingdom of an arrogant philosopher on his tiptoes?

"Who could say it wasn't primarily the childrens' prayers which prevailed in the Cokeville crisis?" my wife asked.

"If not that, what?"

These children were not fatalistic, I-can't-make-a-difference types at any time, it would appear. I thought of the space shuttle Challenger incident. Some people might take the give-up attitude that things happen in a predestined manner, that it makes little difference what people do. Yet the Cokeville children thought they could make a difference in raising funds for the Challenger program—and in their minds they did.

It would appear they also made a difference in their own behalf. Whatever it was they had to do in the "Cokeville Incident," they perservered even if some did act like mere children as the afternoon wore on. They could take pride in being survivors.

As for lingering fears, it became increasingly clear it would do no good to attempt any rapid purge of them. One day Kam went to a movie, but this time there was little recollection about the film's story. A man sitting at the end of the aisle looked like David Young. Other children also "saw him" for months when they closed their eyes. Kam's concerns and the others would fade with time—and patient understanding.

Even after months went by, it required effort for Kam's long-distance sister. As a former school teacher, Wendi had thought school safe, like her home. She had the adult responsibility of coping bravely. Sometimes coping "bravely" could be a gigantic pain in the neck. She just wanted to be a little girl again, to forget logic, vent her feelings, and be rid of them. Tenderly, her father-in-law, Ernie Taylor, invited her to unload them on him. She did and she felt immediately better.

Peggy had the same experience, seven months later, as she placed the pages of this book onto a computer. She had managed to laugh about the day her raft flipped in a Colorado River rapid, leaving her gasping for breath in the stream's roaring white water. There she wondered for a time about her own survival.

Just a week later, May 16, she arrived home exhausted to learn she may have lost her little brother. "I could deal with the river and the rapids and the dangers. I knew what I was up against. Even something unexpected often had an explanation, a logical reason behind it.

"But the little kids, just going to school—they're all good kids just minding their own business. It didn't make sense. How could a person behave rationally and courageously toward something so completely irrational and cowardly?"

Many of her feelings could be multiplied by each of the hostage families at Cokeville.

Part of the therapy for everyone included learning more details of the incident—how the hostages won their trial by terror. With school and community psychologists offering service without cost to the parents or hostages, Judene took advantage of this opportunity to talk things over. It was the positive approach, meeting an obstacle and overcoming it.

Among the greatest rewards were the long hours spent with families absorbing spiritual events. This was not something to be taken lightly by anyone. It confirmed to witnesses that people still believe miracles happen in modern times.

Our family had moved to Cokeville from the city to enjoy the experience of a small rural town. We had grown to love the people and the natural, human enrichment which became such an integral part of our lives. Best of all, Cokeville proved to be an excellent place to raise a family.

Having to move the summer following this town's crisis caused some emotional jarring. Ties were strong, and we have enjoyed the chance to return and visit on occasion. Several other families have moved, pulled away by economic necessity. The healing process continues within family units, wherever they have gone. Folks talk more willingly now of the trials they faced last spring. They continue to recall little details that shock and terror had partly clouded from their minds before.

The process of uncovering and recording facts of this story has been personally helpful in the long term as it forces the peeling away of emotional bandages. We have had to look at it objectively and in detail. It has given us something tangible to work with.

We discovered that the full impact of the crisis was not felt by many families, including ourselves, right at first. Some did not assess what was happening even as it was unfolding. I learned of one woman who had a grandchild in the hostage room, yet still made a trip out of town as planned.

"I just naively thought things would work out," she said. "When I realized later the entire story, I couldn't believe how nonchalant I had been."

I've thought since that her thinking was quite typical of Cokeville. People here are so optimistic and have such a we-can-do-it attitude that if two fell over a cliff, one would crack a joke to the other on the way down. Rub dirt where it hurts and don't let anyone see your frown.

One has to realize the presence of this self-reliant confidence in the town before comprehending the humorous comments made during the hostage ordeal—things like, "You're just going to die when you see that bathroom." It was a little room designed for little children. Of course, when they said that to David Young, they had no idea he was soon to shoot himself in that room.

Such an attitude isn't limited to this place on earth, of course. An American general in World War II made somewhat the same statement when a German officer surrounding the U.S. forces asked him for a quick answer on when he was going to surrender. Trying to think of a way to tell him he wasn't going to surrender at all, the general finally replied, "Nuts."

The Cokeville incident was like a story which had been assigned to my own journalism students. First they received information about a girl losing her dog. Then they learned she was a blind girl. King was her seeing-eye dog. Suddenly, what was happening became much more meaningful when all the facts were in. In the Cokeville situation, the facts kept snowballing until those outside the hostage room began to understand what the people inside had really endured. Then, as it turned out, it was even worse than *they* thought.

Few inside the room wanted to talk of hating the perpetrators. They wanted to forget it. The best way to do that was not talk much about it—for a time. Then no one could keep it inside.

An intriguing facet from the researching on David Young was his search for the strong and the pinnacle of strength. To him it was to bolster himself and his environs with armor, guns, and explosives. In contrast, the hostages armed themselves with spiritual strength. The outcome proves which one was the more effective. It seems the Cokeville story is a classic one for finding such an answer—a modern David and Goliath event in history. True, for a time Young's definition seemed to prevail. Yet when those he used it on admitted their helplessness, they found strength sufficient enough to win.

There were many other educational and adventurous experiences in the writing of this book. Some efforts seemed fruitless, such as my driving hundreds of miles to contact Doyle Mendenhall. He was listed by the police as living near Preston, Idaho, in nearby Franklin, according to the telephone book. His neighbors said Mendenhall hadn't lived in the community since well before May 16. I felt he could shed some light on Young's philosophies. He wasn't found.

With more information, perhaps we could find it easier to forgive and forget. Our son was not injured, but many children were. In his emotionless, mathematical mind, Young could not have considered what he was doing to human beings. If we can become more aware of others who might be heading on such a course, there might be a way society can help prevent the tragedy.

The process of gathering information for this book also brought some painful moments. One afternoon while alone looking over new photographs for this book, Judene felt overwhelmed seeing them, especially of the people who unwillingly took part in the hostage episode. In some pictures from the *Star Valley* (Wyoming) *Independent*, the devastation of the hostage classroom was shown clearly. She recalled the heavy smell of old smoke as she had visited that room following the explosion. Then there was the close-up shot of David Young's shopping cart with little left of its twisted frame.

Somehow, all the objectively gathered facts swept together in a whirlwind of emotion. Tears washed through the day's routine. "My son! He was there in that room, only six feet away from that shopping cart. He could have been taken away. We came that close to losing him, to not having his loving arms and bright spirit in our lives. . . ."

As Judene later told her family, the sobs came. Great heaving sobs that almost left her gagging. She felt strangely out of control, as if emotion from some other source had taken over her body. Yet through it all, she was aware the sobs were also of deep gratitude—an overwhelming gratitude that this thing had not been what it could have been. Then the crying stopped more suddenly even than it had begun.

"I almost felt a little foolish," she confessed. Then she felt relief. What had happened seemed to be necessary, vitally important. Another stage of the healing process had occurred. She was a little more relaxed, a little more grateful, a little more in control.

As for the families now coping, I thought of a pair of barn swallows which built a nest on the eave of our family's Cokeville home in the spring of 1985. It seemed a safe place for the young birds. Yet, a heavy rain pounded away at the roof, then washed through to the nest, dislodging it. The whole nest fell to the ground. Returning parent birds searched frantically for their offspring. Those fledglings perished.

The next spring, during the hostage crisis, the birds grittily returned to build another nest on the same eave. This time, however, they constructed their home in a slightly different spot where less water would wash in. They also used more heavy mud. The rains came, but this time did not destroy the nest.

I watched much of an afternoon as the parents nourished the little ones. In time, the youngsters flew with strength from their home to build nests and raise little ones of their own.

It struck me as symbolic. This is what the families in Cokeville would do following their adversity. Of course, their children did not perish, but their "nests" would be made safer and stronger.

And there would be another spring.

"Press release" Kamron prepared to help answer questions of concerned family and friends.

The Bomb

by Kam Wixom

COKEVILLE— (May 16, 1986) Our sixth grade class was on a bathroom break when a lady came up to us and said, "Go in the First Grade room, and we have a surprise for you." Our teacher, Mr. Mitchell, asked what kind of surprise. She said, "You'll find out."

The teachers told us the man in the room had bombs, and we thought it was an assembly, that he was an expert helping us get through a possible Libyan attack. He said he was the "most wanted man in the culture." That was about all he said. He talked privately with some of the teachers who went up to him, and we learned he and the woman were holding us hostage until they could get $2 million for each of us. There were about 150 students gathered in this one classroom.

The man had three pistols attached to his belt, and they had two .22 rifles and an M1 leaning against the wall by the door. They had a metal shopping cart full of batteries, and an old milk jug filled with gasoline, and we could see metal wires for the trigger, some battteries, and copper coil inside. There were four or five bombs found later elsewhere in the school.

The sixth grade, and some of the younger kids around us agreed we should say a prayer. We were all sitting on the floor. We folded our arms and Allyson Cornia just started saying a prayer for us. She said she wanted everybody to be safe, that we would all survive. We felt we had done our part in asking the Lord to help us. Now it was up to us to cooperate and do all we could.

A lot of kids were crying softly. All of us were scared, but some didn't want to show it because we knew it wouldn't do us any good. I thought "I just don't want to get in trouble and have the bomb go off." None of us ever thought about going out of the room even though we were near the door that had been propped open. We didn't want to do anything they didn't want us to do. We asked the teachers how long we would have to stay there. They said, "Maybe ten days, maybe just a couple more hours."

The teachers were trying to get our minds off it by letting us watch TV and read books, and play games like Leggos. Brenda Hartley and I built a tank out of Leggos, complete with guns. I said to Brenda, "OK, men, we're going to cross the "death line" and blow'em up." The "death line" was the tape on the floor that Mr. Mitchell had placed around the bomb and the man sitting on the desk next to it. He had said, "OK kids, we are going to play a game. This is the magic square, and if you pass it you'll be out." No one tried to get near the square. Brenda had laughed when I said what I did about our tank. Then we got up and went to the table near the door where some magnets were that we could play with.

We had all been in the room together now since about 1:30. It was now a little before 4. The man had called his wife to come and hold the trigger to the bomb, and he went into the bathroom which is connected to the classroom. He had been in there about two minutes. We were all beginning to feel a little more relaxed, then BOOM! I looked up and saw the ball of fire and a cloud of black smoke. The fire stayed low, but the smoke spread quickly through the room. There were pieces of paper in flames floating around the room, and falling in front of me. Everybody started yellling and running. I went out the door and ran north toward the main doors. I was the first one to go through those doors, and ran on toward Main Street saying softly to myself, "I'm alive!"

Our band teacher, Mr. Miller, had run out of the school through the south doors, and was shot in the back by the man who had come out of the rest room when the bomb went off. Mr. Miller collapsed at the corner on main Street near where I was standing.

There were ambulances, crowds of people searching for brothers and sisters with tears in their eyes. It was like I had come back into civilization after being out in the wilds alone. Kids were being hosed off to cool their burns. I went into Steve Taylor's house to call home, but no one was there. I went back out onto the street, looking for someone to leave a message with someone that I was going to go down to city hall with some of the other kids, and get out of the crowd. That's when I saw Dad with his arm raised, and Mom with her arms open. I ran to them. I was sure glad to see them. Mom and I hugged for a long time, then Dad caught up to us and we had a "three-way" hug. I cried. It felt good to cry. I had been too mad to cry before.

Love Pours In

"God bless as you now attempt to recover and to put yesterday in the past. Have a good day and a better tomorrow."

—Lutheran pastor from Elliott, Illinois

It had only been a few days since the elementary school was filled with guns and bombs and fear. Now the community was quickly filled with cards and letters and posters bringing encouragement. Love came pouring in from everywhere.

The community found itself cemented together in a common experience of incredible intensity. Extended family members kept Cokeville's phone lines hot with calls of hope and concern. Encouragement came from old friends, stunned by news which suddenly struck so close to home. Encouragement also came from many new friends who had only been strangers before. People from all over the country felt compassion and empathy, and took time to express it.

Tina Cook, back to work in her office, was kept busy opening mail and posting greetings of every shape and size on the giant wall in the foyer of the school. Some messages were on miniature notepaper. Others carrying signatures of dozens of school children spanned 15 feet. One was shaped like a teddy bear.

One large banner depicted each of the students attending a school across the state, holding hands symbolically reaching across the miles to the Cokeville children.

Another letter included a warm and sensitive poem about courage and a reminder that "what we make of ourselves with the time given in this life is what matters most." The letter was full of love. It was written by a youngster dying of leukemia.

Numerous letters included money, donated to help alleviate the mounting medical costs of those injured in the flames. A fund was set up for "The Cokeville Kids."

An elderly man from New York wrote to share his hope and encouragement, apologizing that he had no money to spare. "But," he added, "I have my skin, and will donate it for skin grafts if you need."

From coast to coast, messages and donations swamped the little post office in this rural town. Over 16,000 dollars was soon collected. As money continued to flow in, it was enough to cover hospital and doctor expenses for every child injured. School health insurance only defrayed part of the expense. Some of the most serious injuries involved children from families without work.

This little town was unknown in the Mountain West prior to May 16th. Now it was in the news in far-off lands, evidenced by calls of love and concern from Brazil, Japan, England, and Egypt.

Support came from professional quarters, too. Calls from dozens of psychologists across the country came in, offering services.

Counseling was available to anyone in town. "It is important that no feelings in the community be held in," psychologists stressed.

Listening was considered a valuable service. The victims of this crisis began listening to each other. It became a noticeable part of the healing process. As neighbors listened to each other, love poured in.

Among the many letters from throughout the nation was one from a retired elementary teacher in a rural South Dakota town. She shared something especially helpful to hostages. "Fear is a counterfeit of faith. When we put faith to work, it will always overcome fear. Love always overcomes hate. The counterfeit of anything is never as powerful as the real thing."

Love did, indeed, prove to be the real thing—a connection among people thousands of miles away. In a heartfelt wish for something better, a Lutheran minister from Illinois said, "We will be praying for all of you in church Sunday. God bless as you now attempt to recover and to put yesterday in the past. Have a good day and a better tomorrow."

Some months later, a fifteen-foot long banner arrived from a Latter-day Saint primary in Bakersfield, California. Covered with hearts, it bore photos of dozens of children aged three to twelve. With the theme "Our hearts reach out to you . . . " messages were included that warmed the hearts of readers. "I'm nine years old. I am glad you are safe." From other nine-year-olds: " . . . glad you are all rite," and "My name is Mike. I am glad you guys didn't die." An eleven-year-old drew a picture of a hand-held bomb. The message at the side read: "I hope you are ok. You are lucky the bomb didn't work. P.S. Come to Bakersfield. You'll like it." Another invitation was even more convincing: "Please come to Bakersfield and see my skateboard." Teachers of the organization summarized the feelings as they enclosed their message: "Our primary loves you all! Best wishes to you!!"

Love just kept pouring in.

It was love people wanted to feel, not fear. Some were motivated by personal experience. The pastor of St. Margaret Mary Church in Algonquin, Illinois wrote: "Our parish community has witnessed the power of prayer . . . part of our parish were members of the pilgrimage group hijacked on TWA's flight 847 last June. Therefore, we are very understanding of what you have just gone through."

From a school principal in Fayetteville, North Carolina: "Our thoughts and prayers are with you . . . as you recover from the tragedy that took place last week at your school. I know these are difficult times for you. . . ."

The traumatic event which unexpectedly seared the minds of this town was not easy to deal with. Just as unexpected was the depth

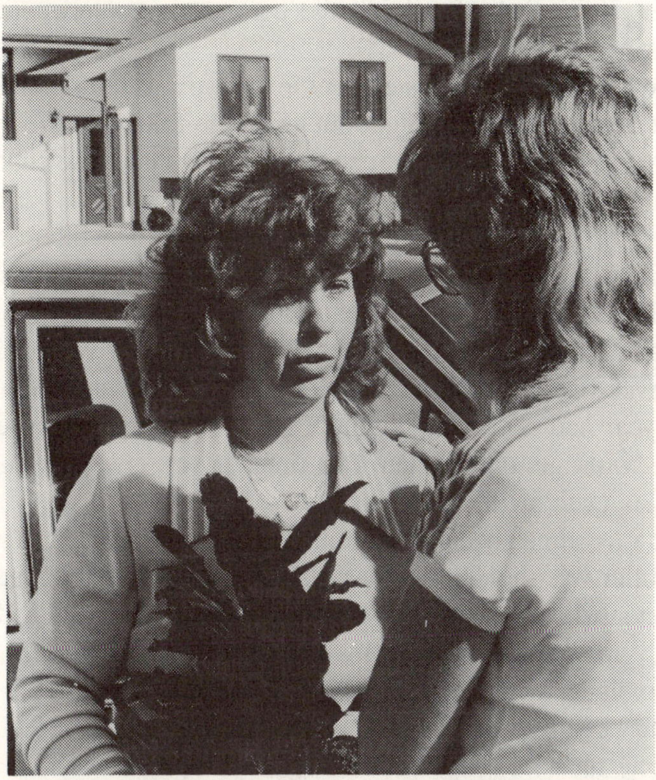

How do you say "Thank You" to a hero? Susan Cory, mother of two girls burned in the explosion, gives a plant to teacher Jean Mitchell as her way of showing gratitude that lives were not lost. (Gerry Avant photo courtesy Deseret News Church News)

of caring coming in from total strangers, from places which had surely never heard of Cokeville, Wyoming before this. It was a healing balm.

One woman expressed her concerns for the circumstances that brought this tragedy about. " . . . What have we pushed out of our lives that allows hate to creep in and take over? Do we as a nation have to declare a moratorium for a week to reassess ourselves?"

Some knew of the loving nature of the Cokeville school. A former resident wrote: "I was glad that my kids were not there last Friday, but had they been, I know they couldn't have been in better hands . . . [since] the Lord and the best teachers anywhere were there taking care of them"

Love overcoming fear was evident in the various church meetings that first Sunday. It was brought out again the following Wednesday at the annual Cokeville High School spring concert. The conductor was John Miller.

One of the youngest teachers at the high school, Miller enjoyed a good rapport with parents of the community. What he could get musically out of the relatively small number of young people in this town was akin to the record of the football team. Everyone sang. Nearly everyone played a musical instrument. The concerts throughout the year had become a highlight for the community to see just what he could get out of them this time. It was always rewarding, sometimes even a little amazing.

There was some speculation that the concert would be cancelled when Miller was shot. Initial fears that the injury might be fatal had been alleviated. It was now known that the .22 caliber shell had coincidentally missed his vital organs and spine and lodged in his left shoulder blade, where it remained.

He had been released from the hospital, but would he feel up to conducting an hour-long concert?

"I'm not in pain, I'm glad to be here," he announced to the packed auditorium. It was a simple statement, but it reached the hearts of everyone there. The crowd erupted into a spontaneous standing ovation for Miller, for the children, and the teachers. It was also for the entire community . . . for victory. The applause continued for some time. People felt they were getting control of their lives again. To cheer, to whistle, to applaud felt good.

As the audience settled in their seats again, it was said, "If Miller's arm gets tired, he'll just switch the baton to his other hand."

Tall and dark, his well-built frame was always sharply attired. He wore a medium-sized moustache and a big smile. Tonight his mischievous dark eyes seemed brighter even than usual. He was obviously very happy to be present as scheduled.

Miller is a quiet, private person who doesn't usually say much publicly. But on this night he wanted to share some stories about his recent experience. Though a bit hesitant about embarrassing his wife who was seated in the audience, he proceeded to explain how hospital attendants had taken all his clothes in Montpelier and left him with little more than his traditional not-so-private hospital gown. Then he was air-lifted to Bannock Memorial Hospital in Pocatello. He said, "When a nurse came in to check the list of valuables in my possession, she started off with my watch, my wallet . . . I could see it was long list. So I told her I could save her some time. 'I have nothing with me but my shorts,' " Miller related.

The audience roared with laughter. He continued, "Thank goodness for those shorts."

"While I was waiting on a stretcher to be taken into the examining room, I opened my eyes to see my Episcopal minister, Rev. Lawrence Perry, and the Rev. Gerald Sullivan of Cokeville's Catholic congregation. They had come all the way to Pocatello to see me."

"We would like to give you a blessing," they said.

"I would very much like you to *give* me a blessing," I told them emphatically.

"You might say," said Father Sullivan, "that we're the SWAT team for God."

The audience's applause transcended all religious boundaries. This time the tears were those of sheer joy.

"It appears that the healing process is well under way if we can laugh like this," Sherrie Cornia commented to those seated nearby.

Before Miller turned back to the program, he explained more of his feelings. "I wondered," he said, "if we could have this concert, But I realized that I really wanted to be here. I guess it was meant to be, because here we are! The reason I had to be with you is because of the words of the song we just sang. . . ."

The words had been snappily presented by the forty-five voice high school choir . . . "Rhythm of life . . . feel the powerful beat . . . Spread your wings and fly up high . . . you can do it if you try . . . Rhythm on the inside, rhythm in the street . . . to feel the tingle of life."

"Now," said Miller, with considerable solemnity, and enough emotion for his voice to crack slightly, "here is my message to *you!*"

He turned to the choir, raised both arms, and gave the downbeat.

"Cry out and shout . . . Praise unto Him, sing . . . Give glory to God . . . Rejoice . . . Praise Him, Hallelujah!"

Expressions of love came in many ways. Sixth grade boys, disappointed in themselves that they "hadn't stayed around to help some of the little ones out of the room," tried to make up for that. They gave special attention to small ones they had previously ignored.

Asked how many of the children involved in the crises were his, Jack Mitchell answered, "All of them!"

When gratitude was expressed to the warm and efficient EMTs, one of them said, "We had our hands full caring for the injured, but there were a lot of children who needed emotional first aid. I saw you parents hugging children you possibly didn't even know. One mother I saw had three in her arms. Only one was hers."

Acts of love came from unexpected sources. After spending several hours sorting out facts and interviewing confused and emotional people, the news media swarming down on this little town were undoubtedly tired and ready to head back home. Yet it seemed many wanted to stay and talk with the younger children.

Jackson and Big Piney, Wyoming school children collected door-to-door from neighbors "for the Cokeville people." One school, saving for a special field trip, voted to forego the long-awaited event. They donated the money for the trip to the hospitalized hostage victims.

One of the television stations, early on the scene to cover events, put together a special party for the hostages. It lasted a full summer day at Lagoon Resort north of Salt Lake City. KUTV, in conjunction with the resort, spent thousands of dollars to bus hostages and their families to enjoy all the rides, in addition to providing them lunch. The children soaked up this type of love—translated into something they could get their hands on . . . from bumper car steering wheels and merry-go-rounds, to punch and hot dogs. It was additional salve for the wounds from the bizarre day back in mid-May.

All three local channels were on hand at the resort to record happy faces. The children acted just like any others at a giant fantasy playground. Except for an occasional bandaged arm or face and an overabundance of hats protecting tender new skin from the sun's rays, they looked like any other kids. "That's the beauty of it," said a parent—"normalcy." Except their laughter sounded a little extra special.

A musical program from volunteer singing groups at the party tuned into the children with understanding words and smiles. The children felt empathy; most of them shunned sympathy. If anyone talked about physical pain, they turned away. But discussion of psychological pain equated to understanding; then they stood and talked.

All this love has had an effect on the healing process in Cokeville. Nine days after the bomb exploded, Gina Taylor participated in a church program where her father spoke. As she sang "I Am a Child of God," she saw the audience with both eyes. The audience saw only a little white patch on her face where she had been burned. There will be only a small scar under the eye that doctors once feared she would lose.

Pretty as ever, she enthusiastically rendered her number. " . . . Lead me, guide me, walk beside me. Help me find the way. . . ." Those words may never had been felt more deeply than now.

In time, doctors said only a few victims would carry permanent scars. "That in itself is something of a miracle," said one parent, "judging from what the doctors first feared."

The emotional impact from the incident has left its mark. Since the Cokeville crisis, there have been others across the country. They are viewed differently now. The pain is shared.

When the postal workers were gunned down in Oklahoma, the town was thrown into deep mourning. Cokeville was fortunate enough to have had no mourning, but the shock they felt in that little suburb of Oklahoma City sent waves to western Wyoming.

Various tragedies in Montana throughout the year following the Cokeville episode brought out a great deal of empathy. In fact, psychologists working with the hostage students in Wyoming were called on for help with the Montana high school students who saw their French teacher killed by a fellow student. Cokeville townspeople, who now understood very well, poured out their love.

Life will not be taken as casually as before. It is too precious. There is more understanding and compassion, which makes a better world. Had David Gary Young felt more of those emotions, this story might never have taken place.

His philosophy, that "knowledge is all we have and knowledge is nothing," overlooked the more important understanding that love for one another can transcend all else. That oversight probably cost the Youngs their revolution and their lives. That love for one another was breathing life back into this entire community.

A poem, written by a hostage's mother, touches on the feelings of people in the community of all religions . . . something more powerful than one man's malice:

"Knowledge," he said, "is all that we have,
And knowledge is nothing—a zero."
But something far greater than knowledge was shown
On that day, which made each one a hero.

The children who bravely withstood the demands:
"You can't cry, don't get sick, or be frightened."
The teachers whose safety came second to theirs
Uttered prayers and were blessed and enlightened.

The law gathered here from all over the land,
Showing courage and patience and training.
Volunteer firemen, medical techs
Gave freely of help life sustaining.

Doctors and nurses who rushed to the scene
Of hospitals suddenly bustling,
Parents and neighbors with comfort to give,
From one to another were hustling.

Counselors volunteered time to help salve
The turbulent turn of emotion.
Cards and donations began flooding in—
Caring people from ocean to ocean.

To listen, to care, to unselfishly give,
To ask of their welfare and mean it.
For God in His Heaven, heard all our pleas
And reached out His hand. We have SEEN it!

Certainly, love has poured in. In turn, it is pouring back out to others. As the pastor said, it just might be "a good day and a better tomorrow."

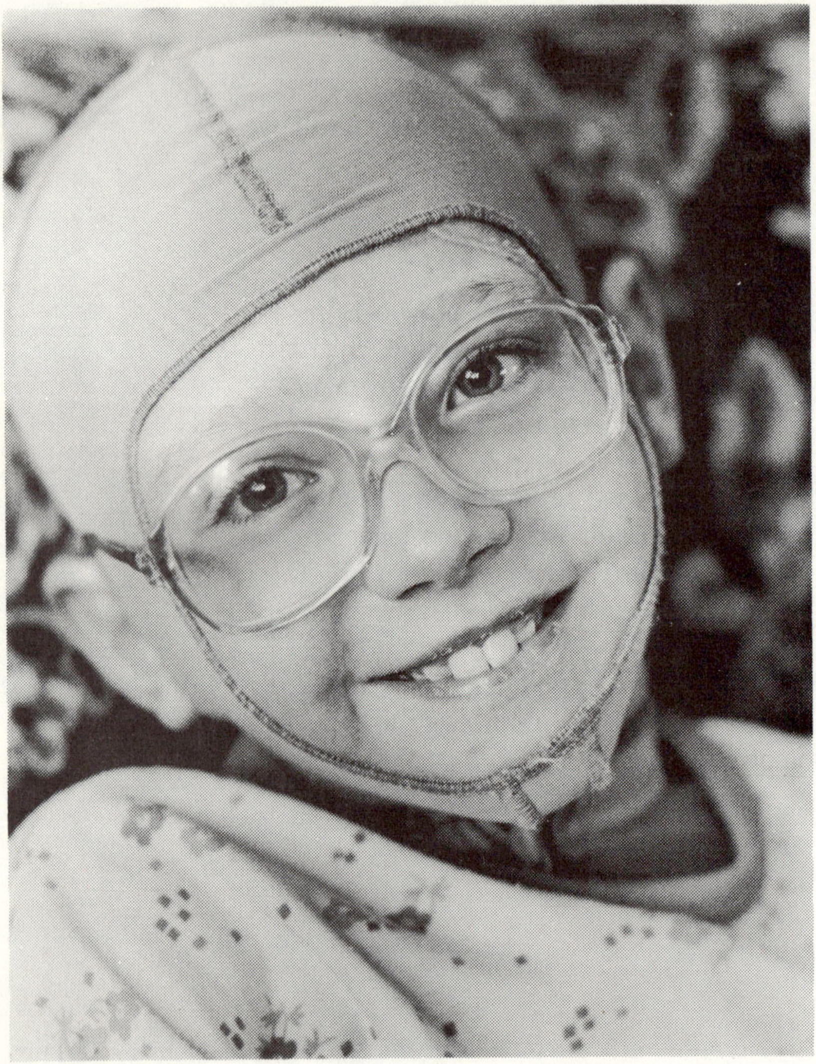

Billie Jo Hutchinson's face says it all. In spite of the Jobst bandage that would cover her more than a year, her smile and bright eyes of faith promise a better tomorrow. (Jack Monson photo courtesy Deseret News)

Index

A

Anderson, Brad—59, 103, 115-16, 133-36, 174.
Anderson, Carrie—229.
Anderson, Jeremy—116.
Anderson, Josh—116.
Anderson, Kaylene—116.
Arduser, Janet—36.

B

Bennion, Pat—22, 130, 169, 179.
Bennion, Sam—179.
Bennion, Verlene—72, 114, 130, 182.
Billingslea, Jim—44.
Birch, Andra—107.
Birch, Glen—23.
Birch, Rusty—28, 182.
Buckley, Cheryl—115.
Bunn, Brent—60.
Burton, Allen—138.
Brown, Charlene—226.

C

Carlisle, Randall—226.
Carroll, Earl—59-60, 132, 136, 192, 197-202.
Cassidy, Butch—15.
Chadwick, Gayle—108.
Chournos, George—181-82.

Clark, Beverly—130.
Clark, Christy—82, 124, 131, 139, 169.
Clark, Eva—26, 76, 130-31, 139.
Clark, Kathy—26, 76, 82, 85, 128.
Clark, Lowell—26, 76, 130-31, 139.
Clark, Paul—26, 76, 85.
Cook, Tina—67-69, 114, 122, 168, 227.
Cornia, Allyson—88, 248.
Cornia, Drew—111.
Cornia, Sherrie—187, 255.
Cotherman, Audrey—185.
Cowden, Cynthia—67, 71, 108, 129, 184.
Cox, Vern—150, 152.
Cummings, Mike—181.

D

Dana, Nadine—57.
Davison, Kathy—58, 60.
Dayton, Bob—61.
Dayton, Cindy—230-31, 239.
Dayton, Clara—23.
Dayton, Ed—25, 118.
Dayton, Janel—69, 71, 77, 80, 86, 104, 123, 127, 170.
Dayton, Jerry—74.
Dayton, Jodi—169.
Dayton, John—36, 174, 196-97, 207.
Dayton, Lois—16, 239.
Deppe, Gerald—46, 51-52, 65.

E

Eastman, Fawna—143, 169.
Elliott, Flossie—157.
Excell, Glenda—81.

Excell, Max—67, 74, 78-79, 88, 98, 103, 105, 107, 113, 132, 138, 145, 148, 169, 179, 182-84, 210, 215, 217, 223-26, 228, 231.
Excell, Rick—164.

F

Fagg, Ellen—236.
Ferguson, Bob—25.
Ferrin, Jenny—169.
Fogarty, William—197.
Fredrickson, Cal—17, 59, 135.
Fredrickson, Colleen—169.

G

Gonzales, Sandy—76, 184.
Goodman, Greg—134.

H

Harrison, Robert—51.
Hart, Ada—164.
Hartley, Brenda—111-12, 127, 148-49.
Hartley, Claudia—157, 169.
Hartley, Nathan—156-57.
Hartley, Ron—49, 59, 139, 145, 156-57, 192, 197-98, 201.
Haskell, Rich—142, 143, 145, 147, 163, 207.
Himmerich, Judy—126.
Hoyt, Arthur—47.
Hutchinson, Billie Jo—28, 124, 139, 143, 161, 183, 217.

J

Jacobsen, Rod—174.
Jones, Joshua—128, 226.
Jones, Kathy—227, 240.

K

Kasper, Kim—138.
Kasper, Kris—117, 129.
King, Colleen—142.
King, Johnny—126.
King, Michelle—226.

L

Lamborn, Dale—61.
Lefevere, Greg—225.
Leonard, Richard—191-92, 203-4, 212.
Looney, Bob—58.
Lowe, Allen—167, 232.

M

Mendenhall, Doyle—46, 51-52, 65, 245.
Metcalfe, Aaron—231.
Metcalfe, Jay—108, 169.
Metcalfe, Joanne—231.
Meyers, Wesley—35.
Mikita, Carol—225.
Miller, John—19, 23, 74, 108-9, 114, 127, 147, 187, 215-16, 254.
Mitchell, Billy—61, 118-19.
Mitchell, Chad—61, 102, 126.
Mitchell, Danny—61, 118-19.
Mitchell, Jack—18, 76-77, 84, 100-3, 106, 110, 114, 118, 123, 126, 132, 161-62, 182, 256.
Mitchell, Jean—71, 73, 84-85, 97, 100, 102-4, 106, 116-18, 121, 123, 126, 158, 161-62, 182.
Moore, Jeremiah—28, 109, 226.
Moore, Rocky—19, 69, 70, 88, 102, 103, 125-29, 161, 167, 182, 187, 226.

N

Nate, Brian—109.
Nate, Greg—109.
Nuss, Carlene—239.

O

Olsen, Larry—40.

P

Peery, Craig—159.
Perez, Julie—234, 238.
Perez, Tony—238.
Perry, Barbara—239.
Petersen, Bernie—37-41, 47-48, 53, 56, 174.
Petersen, Brent—53.
Petersen, Carol—26, 81, 104, 114, 123.
Petersen, Gwen—115, 143, 228.
Petersen, Joanna—200.
Petersen, Richard—200.
Pieper, Richard—61.
Pierson, Mark—234.
Pope, Jody—26.
Pope, Leon—234.
Pope, Shiloh—21, 26.

R

Rand, Ken—60, 106, 130.
Reagan, Ronald—65.
Rentfro, Delbert—74, 78, 105, 107.
Richins, Michael—193.
Robinson, Art—13, 25, 59, 127.

S

Sandahl, Nohl—172.
Shifflet, Amy—237.
Silver, Gerald—255.
Smith, Teyana—174.
Sparks, Kliss—76, 109, 132, 182, 227.
Spurling, Robin—60, 106.
Sorensen, Grant, 58.
Sullivan, Gerald—255.

T

Taylor, Don—233-34.
Taylor, Ernie—242.
Taylor, Evie—233.
Taylor, Gina—28, 143, 147, 169, 184, 257.
Taylor, Rachel—233.
Taylor, Ryan—169.
Taylor, Wendi—233-34, 240, 242.
Teichert, Briant—22, 179.
Teichert, John—19, 58, 171.
Thompson, Betty—225.
Thompson, David—225.
Thornock, Kimberly—28.
Thornock, Shirley Ruth—154.

W

Walker, Glenna—60, 89, 149, 152-56.
Walker, Katie—118, 149-55.
Walker, Kevin—57, 60, 89, 138, 153-54.
Walker, Rachel—118, 150, 153-55.
Walker, Travis—24, 27-28, 60, 117-18, 124, 149, 151-53, 158-59, 181.
Walker, Shane—149.
Wixom, Cindy—61, 151, 237.

Wixom, Jenny—229.
Wixom, Kamron—26, 111-12, 118, 124, 126-27, 158-59, 225.
Wixom, Peggy—232, 236, 241.
Wixom, Wade—234, 237.
White, Randy—137, 192.
Wolfley, Deb—193, 196, 214, 219.

Y

Young, Angela—52.
Young, Princess—52, 55.